# Career Development

*Career Development: A Human Resource Development Perspective* offers a strategic framework that demonstrates the role of career development within the human resource function. It goes beyond conventional interventions and includes key topics such as diversity, work–life balance, and ethics.

Historically, the career development literature has been viewed either from the perspective of the individual (how to build a career) or from an economic perspective (how an organization benefits from developing employees). In this book, McDonald and Hite bring together the strengths of both traditions, offering an integrated framework for career development. The theoretical foundation expands on the counseling literature by incorporating the literature from human resource development and related fields. The application section reflects on the wide range of ages and working options that characterize the current and future workplace. The final section of the book addresses career development issues such as managing a diverse, global workforce; ethics; and work–life balance.

This book will help prepare human resource development students, scholars, and practitioners to develop and maintain successful career development programs, and to foster more innovative research that advances the discourse.

**Kimberly McDonald** is Professor of Organizational Leadership and Supervision at Indiana-Purdue University Fort Wayne, USA. Her research focuses on career development, ethical issues in human resource development, and diversity education. She recently completed her term as editor-in-chief of the journal *Advances in Developing Human Resources*.

**Linda Hite** is Professor of Organizational Leadership and Supervision at Indiana-Purdue University Fort Wayne, USA. Her research focuses on workforce diversity, career development, and diversity education. She is book and media review editor for *New Horizons in Adult Education and Human Resource Development.*

# Career Development
A Human Resource Development Perspective

Kimberly McDonald and
Linda Hite

Routledge
Taylor & Francis Group

NEW YORK AND LONDON

First published 2016
by Routledge
711 Third Avenue, New York, NY 10017

and by Routledge
2 Park Square, Milton Park, Abingdon, Oxon OX14 4RN

*Routledge is an imprint of the Taylor & Francis Group, an informa
business*

*Library of Congress Cataloging in Publication Data*
   McDonald, Kimberly.
   Career development : a human resource development
perspective / Kimberly McDonald & Linda Hite. – 1 Edition.
      pages cm
   1. Career development. 2. Personnel management. I. Hite, Linda.
II. Title.
   HF5549.5.C35M383 2015
   658.3'124–dc23
   2015017694

ISBN: 978-1-138-78612-7 (hbk)
ISBN: 978-1-138-78613-4 (pbk)
ISBN: 978-1-315-76740-6 (ebk)

Typeset in Times New Roman
by Sunrise Setting Ltd, Paignton, UK

To Dave and Rich, our spouses and soulmates. Thanks for your continued patience, support, and love.

# Contents

# 1 An Introduction to Career Development

Think of yourself not as the architect of your career but as the sculptor. Expect to have to do a lot of hard hammering and chiseling and scraping and polishing.

B.C. Forbes, founder of *Forbes* magazine

Your work is to discover your work and then with all your heart to give yourself to it.

Attributed to the Buddha

## What Does It Mean to Have a Career?

This book is about careers and how they develop, but, to understand what it means to have a career, we should begin at a more foundational level, specifically, work and the role it plays in our lives.

The meaningfulness of work in life has global and enduring appeal, as seen in the two quotes that open this chapter. Work and careers are such an integral part of life that the discourse devoted to those interrelated topics spans centuries and extends from social media and popular press to scholarly articles and books. For example, over two decades ago, an article appeared in *Fortune Magazine* titled "Why do we work?" (Dumaine & Sample, 1994). Then, as now, the most obvious answer seemed to be to make money. Yet, the point of the article was that work encompasses more than just financial security. While some work primarily to make ends meet, given the choice, then as now, people tend to seek out occupations that enhance a sense of self. As Warren Bennis, leadership scholar and consultant, observed, "Work really defines who you are. So much of a person's self-esteem is measured by success at work" (Dumaine & Sample, 1994).

More recently, Hall and Las Heras (2012) reinforced the idea that, in some cultures, work and career are closely tied to individual identity and help define one's sense of life purpose. It is a means to fulfill one's potential. Similarly, Duffy and Dik (2013) have noted the prevalence of the idea of a calling in scholarly literature on careers. While definitions vary, three components seem to make up a sense of calling: "an external summons," feeling drawn to do a particular type of work; "meaning/purpose," connecting work to a life purpose; and "prosocial motivation," contributing to the well-being of others (p. 429). While more research is needed regarding this concept, links are evident between seeing one's career as a calling and positive outcomes such as career commitment and job satisfaction (Duffy & Dik, 2013). Not surprisingly then, the loss of a job often means more than just reduction of income. It may bring into question one's sense of worth and purpose. In short, careers matter to us and may have a profound impact on how we see ourselves and how happy we are in our lives.

The idea of meaning and work is also revealed in how employees determine their career goals. Hall and Las Heras (2012) observed that careers can be seen from two different perspectives: the subjective, derived from an individual sense of meaningfulness regarding a career; and the objective, focusing on what others often identify as key indicators of success (e.g., promotions, pay). While traditional career research often honed in on the objective hallmarks, the subjective aspect has gained in prominence as the career environment has changed. Our current view of careers is much more expansive and open to individual interpretation and initiative. As a result, the study of careers and career development has become not only more varied, but also more important to human resource development (HRD). Before we go further, let's define key terms for our continued discussion.

## Defining Careers and Career Development

Moore, Gunz, & Hall (2007) provided a helpful context by observing that, while people have worked for millennia, the word "career" in reference to a path of employment was not used prior to the nineteenth century, and it did not come into common usage until the twentieth century. Herr (2001) was more specific, noting that "the term *career* was rarely used before the 1960s" (p. 196).

While definitions of "career" may be found in any dictionary, in the research literature, those descriptors often reveal the scholar's view of how s/he perceives two key elements, time and space. Time refers to how a career evolves during an interval, while space addresses the scope of what a career entails; is it only work-for-pay positions or all of one's work-related experiences, paid or not? (Baruch & Bozionelos, 2011). Arthur (2008) called upon his previous work and that of Gunz and Peiperl (2007) to define a career as "the evolving sequence of a person's work experiences over time" (p. 166). This description is intended to include unpaid work and it leaves out references to advancement as a prerequisite for success, reflecting a more intrinsic view. Inkson (2007) added that the definition also illustrates the continuity of a career, including the past while suggesting the future. Further, it confirms that "each person has only one career" (p. 3), reinforcing that, although an individual may change jobs or cross into different industries from time to time, all of those experiences contribute to the same career journey. So, a career path unfolds over time in steps that may or may not be linear and it may span across several professional domains as well as different organizations. It is important to clarify at this point that the perspective of careers in the US and many parts of Europe has an individual focus, based on the interests and goals of the person, not on the needs of the family or larger group, as might be expected in more collectivist societies (Inkson, 2007). This viewpoint makes a difference in the sense of individual agency that one has when approaching career decision making and planning.

Just as there are many definitions of "career," "career development" has been defined in varied ways, often depending on the discipline. Those differences highlight one of the interesting aspects of the career development field. Some have approached it from an individual perspective (i.e., focusing on the person's interests, abilities, goals), while others have taken an organizational productivity perspective (i.e., concentrating on the needs of the organization and how individual employees can help fulfill those needs). As we will discuss later, that dichotomy of viewpoints reflects a point of contention in the field that is still playing out. An early definition endeavored to combine these two perspectives:

> Career development is an ongoing process of planning and directed action toward personal work and life goals. Development means growth, continuous acquisition and application of one's skills. Career development is the outcome of the individual's career planning and the organization's provision of support and opportunities, ideally a collaborative process which focuses on both the individual and the organization.
>
> (Simonsen, 1997, pp. 6–7)

A few years later, Gilley, Eggland, & Gilley (2002) offered this variation: "career development is a process requiring individuals and organizations to create a partnership that enhances employees' knowledge, skills, competencies, and attitudes required for their current and future job assignments" (p. 94). In light of current research, we suggest this definition. Career development is the process of acquiring and experiencing planned and unplanned activities that support attainment of life and work goals. Within an organization, this will be a collaborative process that enhances individual skills and employability while fulfilling organizational needs. This definition recognizes that career development will be individually driven, so it accommodates career paths built outside of organizations and acknowledges that, while some activities will be part of a thought-out strategy, spontaneous, unexpected opportunities may be equally valuable in this process.

Before we explore the HRD–career link further, a historical review will provide context for how what we now recognize as "career development" evolved and how we arrived at our current crossroads regarding career development and HRD.

### Historical Context

As noted, our current connotation of "career" is relatively recent, and the phrase "career development" was not used extensively until the 1950s according to Pope (2000) or the late 1960s, as noted by Herr (2001). It is not because the concept was unknown, but because the traditional terminology was more likely to be "vocational guidance" in the earliest years and, later, "career counseling" as that field rose into prominence. The origins of what we now know as career theory represent varied fields and a series of developments over decades.

Moore et al. (2007) suggest that the discourse on careers and career development has a long history, beginning with the ancient philosophers Cicero and Plato, who alluded to careers in their writings on how individuals should approach life and discern a calling. Moving forward by millennia, the foundational roots of what we now know as career development were evident in the vocational education offered through the European trade guilds of the twelfth century. Once accepted into a guild, apprentices worked under the tutelage of a master until they reached journeymen status and could ply their trades (Wollschlager & Guggenheim, 2004).

Coming to the late nineteenth and early twentieth centuries, the industrial revolution in the US and in Europe prompted the need for vocational training to match the needs of the newly emerging manufacturing-based economy (Herr, 2001; Pope, 2000; Savickas & Baker, 2005). In the UK, much of the focus was on helping young people "to make the transition to work" (Watts & Kidd, 2000, p. 485). At the same time in the US, two factors brought eager job seekers into the factories in numbers that necessitated more job training. The first was increasing immigration of those seeking work with higher wages by relocating to the US; and the second was domestic movement from farms to cities as equipment replaced many manual labor jobs (Herr, 2001; Pope, 2000). The move towards a manufacturing society also meant exploration of varied future job options, representing a shift from a more agrarian culture, where work patterns tended to be more regimented, with fewer choices.

While the world faced a shift in how and where work would be accomplished, scholars from varied fields began to contemplate issues that would affect a future workforce. An example is eminent sociologists Emile Durkheim and Max Weber. Although they did not directly address careers and career development in their writings, their work brought to light the ideas of division of labor, the struggle of balancing the security of working within an organizational bureaucracy with maintaining individual freedom, and the differing status of occupations. While their writings first appeared in the late 1800s and early 1900s, the topics remain relevant in the current workplace (Moore et al., 2007).

A key figure in the early establishment of vocational guidance also represented a field not typically associated with career development. Frank Parsons, an engineer and lawyer by background, is credited with originating the phrase "vocational guidance" (Herr, 2001). Although other books at the time and some written earlier addressed occupational selection and success, his 1909 *Choosing a Vocation* (published posthumously) provided an early model for the career counseling of the day (Herr, 2001; Moore et al., 2007; Pope, 2000). Although Parsons based his model on his practical experience rather than on research, his work was well respected. He was an early proponent of matching individual interests and skills with job requirements. With that in mind, he proposed three basic tenets of vocational guidance: understanding oneself, recognizing what different types of work require, and coordinating those two factors to find a suitable job (Parsons, 1909). Parsons's approach was focused on working one-on-one with the individual and, rather surprisingly for his era, he saw vocational guidance as applicable to both men and women (Herr, 2001).

At this early stage, Parsons was not alone in grounding his vocational guidance model on application rather than research. This was largely the case throughout the US and Europe. Researchers on both continents rose to the occasion by beginning to develop instruments that might be used to shore up the practice with theoretical constructs (Herr, 2001).

One mechanism for finding this fit between person and job was centered on testing. The testing movement resulted over time in three types of instruments designed to inform individuals and organizations of potential best matches: "ability or intelligence testing, aptitude or technical competence testing, and interest or personality testing" (Moore et al., 2007, p. 23). Early uses included intelligence and aptitude testing to match people and jobs, fueled by US military interests in World War I and widespread unemployment. In the career context, the 1920s–'30s were characterized by economic depression in Europe and the US, giving rise to federal jobs programs and organized labor movements, one designed to boost employment and the other born out of concern for the potential exploitation of workers so desperate for work that they would endure poor wages and treatment (Pope, 2000). Then, beginning in the late 1920s, but coming to the forefront later, interest testing offered a different approach by seeking to tap into individual preferences rather than divining a "static, inherited ability" (Moore et al., 2007, p. 24).

The 1940s and '50s saw an upswing in career counselor training in colleges and universities, verifying its place as a profession. As often happens, the needs of society influenced careers in this era through the dual impact of more women entering the workforce during World War II and returning veterans seeking new careers through the GI Bill (Pope, 2000).

While the three-step approach advocated by Parsons persisted in some circles, it was challenged in the '50s and '60s by developmental psychologists, advocating the view that career development was not a one-time, rational match, but rather a longitudinal process (Hershenson, 2009). Donald Super, a key scholar in the developmental approach, was particularly noted for proposing a model of career development that was based on life stages and roles. It was built on the idea that different aspects of the career journey became more salient as an individual moved through stages of life and that vocational maturity would be indicative of progress in the career development process (Hershenson, 2009). Although stage-based career models like Super's have come under some criticism over time, they mark significant milestones in the development of career practice and theory. We will explore that further in later chapters.

The late 1960s–'70s, often remembered in the US for John Kennedy's presidency and the Vietnam War (during the latter decade), brought legislation to promote a more diverse workplace and interest among employees in finding meaningful work (Pope, 2000). This era also saw a revival of Parsons's matching idea in John Holland's theory of linking types of people with occupational environments (Hershenson, 2009). His RIASEC (realistic, investigative, artistic, social, enterprising, and conventional) system of categorizing remains the mainstay of key interest inventories.

During the 1980s–'90s, job losses fostered growth of outplacement counseling, declines in labor unions, and more concern about developing career theories that addressed diverse groups (Pope, 2000). The ramifications of job loss during this period had a profound and lingering influence on how work and careers are perceived.

## A Changed Career Landscape

The current career landscape has been characterized as turbulent, unpredictable, and challenging. Several interconnecting factors have contributed to this changed environment, including economic turmoil, technological advances, a more diverse workforce, governmental policies, and societal influences. As noted in the timeline, a less than robust economy and widespread global debt led to unemployment as organizations embarked on extensive downsizings in an effort to regain financial balance (OECD, 2011). Technological advances ushered in the rising knowledge-economy and have influenced not only types of jobs available, but also how work is done (i.e., virtual teams, on-line meetings), where work is done (i.e., telecommuting from home, airports, the beach!), and the scope of work (i.e., global access to potential suppliers and customers) (Arthur, 2008). Changing domestic demographics, global access to workers, and government legislation have created a widely diverse workforce that, not surprisingly, has varied career goals and interests. Combined economic, global, and societal influences have had wide-ranging impact, prompting more dual wage-earner households; the expansion and shrinking of some career fields (i.e., proliferation of health care workers to accommodate an aging society; the decline of labor unions); and the reality of hopscotch careers, as workers transition frequently from one job to another. The result is a less stable and more precarious career environment (Savickas et al., 2009) that presents significant challenges for career development and, by extension, HRD.

This turmoil has fundamentally changed how career development is viewed by individuals and how it is addressed by organizations. Ultimately, by dismissing employees with apparent disregard for work records or skills, companies inadvertently gave up employee loyalty and commitment. Researchers refer to this as breaking the psychological contract that had implicitly existed between employer and employee, upholding a mutual exchange of good work performance for job security (Rousseau, 1995; Turnley & Feldman, 1998). In response to this shift, many individuals no longer were willing to trust their future employment or development to their employers and began taking control of their own career trajectories. This approach was noted and described by Hall (1996) as pursuit of the protean career. Near the same time, the term "boundaryless career" (Arthur, 1994) came to the forefront as a way to describe eschewing ties to any one organization or profession and being ready to move when opportunities appear. Those concepts will be described in more detail in a later chapter, but they are presented briefly here to illustrate the challenges facing HRD as it reviews its current and future role in career development.

### Career Development and HRD

The connection of career development to HRD officially began with Patricia McLagan's 1989 assignment of three sub-areas to HRD. Along with training and development and organization development, career development was identified as an integral component of the field. As the historical timeline suggests, career development in practice and theory had a well-established history by this point. Given the role of HRD in organizations, career development would seem a natural fit. However, over time, career development has receded from the forefront in HRD. One illustration of this is evident in Swanson and Holton's definition of HRD, which notes organization development and training and development as the field's "major realms of practice" (Swanson & Holton, 2009, p. 5). They include career development in a longer list of HRD-related components, but the implication is that career development has been pushed into the background. How did this happen?

Once the bond of the psychological contract was breached, the goal of organization-based, mutually beneficial career development fell by the wayside, and it has yet to be fully recovered within HRD. Systems, scholars, and practitioners entrenched in the traditional career development mindset seemed perplexed for a time about what to do when employees were no longer expected to have long careers climbing higher within a single organization. At the same time, the interdisciplinary character may also have contributed to HRD's lack of decisive progress. Multiple areas of research and practice lay claim to career development as an interest (e.g., sociology, education, economics, psychology). These diverse roots often have led to more confusion than collaboration, creating a field with varied interpretations and little agreement about approaches or sharing of expertise (Gunz & Peiperl, 2007).

One of these subfields, vocational psychology, has had continuing influence on career development scholarship and practice over time. However, Savickas and Baker (2005) have expressed concern that current factions within that field may be weakening psychology's historically strong presence in career development. They described a sharp divide between scholars advocating the dominance of "occupational choice" in the field (a decidedly individual focus held by those in counseling psychology) and their equally adamant peers who value "work adjustment" (an organizational focus supported by industrial/ organizational psychologists) (p. 43). A similar schism exists in HRD that has made the revival of career development as a viable and vibrant aspect of human resources (HR) more challenging. Those who view career development as focused on the individual and his/her needs recognize that workers need to be flexible and strive for employability in their overall careers rather than stability within one organization. This mindset cautions against linking the career development process too closely to any one system, particularly when future careers are expected to be fluid across industries as well as between organizations. Those who perceive career development as primarily a staffing function, building and maintaining a pipeline of qualified workers to ensure organizational productivity, are cautious of expending resources on individuals who may not stay with the organization. This dichotomy in perspectives has resulted in what has been called the "contested terrain" of career development (Inkson & King, 2011). Just as the disparate viewpoints in psychology threaten to derail career studies in that field, this dissention in HRD has slowed the progress of developing a responsive career development approach. This will be addressed in more detail in a later chapter, but it is important to note here briefly in order to provide a context for addressing career development in HRD. Despite the current fractious and somewhat chaotic environment surrounding career development, Herr (2001) has urged career development practitioners and researchers not to give up but to continue to evolve to meet the challenges of the global, technologically advanced future. He noted the value of career development as a way to affirm human dignity to individuals buffeted by harsh economic realities and persistent workplace discrimination, and to help them build the flexibility that they will need to thrive in a constantly changing world of work. Other HRD researchers have called for new approaches to career development that will revive its relevance and reinforce it as a critical function of HRD by responding to the realities of the current and future workplace (Egan, Upton, & Lynham, 2006; McDonald & Hite, 2005). One way to begin that process is to expand our view of career development to embrace research and practice from other fields as a way to build a stronger, more resilient career development within HRD (Cameron, 2009). We will explore more of those options throughout this book.

### *Competencies for the New Era of CD*

A revised career development process will require HR practitioners to have a more extensive skill set to meet the needs of individuals and organizations. Professional career development associations in other fields provide insights into competencies required (e.g., British Columbia Career Development Association; The Canadian Standards & Guidelines for Career Development Practice; Career Industry Council of Australia; National Career Development Association—NCDA). The following list provides representative highlights from the Canadian Standards (2012) and NCDA (2009). In addition to an insightful and open-minded attitude, practitioners should have knowledge and skills in:

- career development models and theories
- career resources (including organizations or other sources of information)
- career counseling for individual and group work
- career assessment
- career development for diverse populations
- ethical career counseling practices
- technology related to career planning
- developing and implementing a career development program

Career practitioners also must be knowledgeable about ways to help individuals continue to develop their careers throughout their lives (Herr, 2001), because the current (and future) uncertain career environment puts individuals in control of setting their own career paths. These competencies reinforce the importance of recognizing career development as a critical part of HRD that requires a depth of knowledge and skills not always addressed in the HRD curriculum. This book provides a starting point to building those competencies. HRD professionals particularly interested in career work may even choose to pursue additional training, such as the National Career Development Association career development facilitator certification (see Chapter 5 for more on this). Recalling the rich and varied history of career development,

HRD career development practitioners can seek out additional resources in those related fields, particularly counseling and psychology. By spanning boundaries and exploring the full complement of multidisciplinary research on career development from other fields of study, HRD can learn from what others have already investigated and implemented (Cameron, 2009). This integration of knowledge can better prepare future career development practitioners for guiding individuals and systems and discovering new ways to bring synergy to career development in HRD. (See Chapter 5 for a more detailed discussion.)

**Overview of the Book**

This book is divided into sections, inviting you to read it all the way through or in segments that best fit your interests. Part one provides the fundamentals, this Introductory chapter and Chapter 2 on key theories and concepts. Part two (Chapters 3–5) addresses career development within HR specifically, including an overview of strategic career development/HR, HR interventions related to career development, and how career counseling fits into the current approach to career development within HRD. Part three (Chapters 6–8) includes critical issues that span across career development and HR: the diverse workforce, work–life balance, and ethics. Each chapter invites you to reflect on the future of career development in HRD and to develop your knowledge and skills to help build that future.

As we start this journey, let's review some key assumptions about careers and career development as context. The first five appeared in an earlier publication (McDonald & Hite, 2005, pp. 422–423). You may find others that you would like to add as you go through this book.

- HRD remains integral to the career development process.
- The return on investment of career development must be considered in order to gain organizational interest in expanding career development efforts.
- Career development should not be restricted to a select few or to those at particular levels within the system.
- Career development can be both formal and informal and may take place within and outside of the organization.
- Individual life and work priorities influence choices about careers and development opportunities.
- Careers are complex and multi-dimensional with diverse challenges and benefits.
- Individuals are responsible for their careers, but organizations have a responsibility to assist in that process.

- Career development can be mutually beneficial to individuals and organizations.
- Career development practitioners need particular competencies.
- Career development programs must continue to evolve to match the changing career environment.

## Summary and Implications for Individuals and Organizations

This new era of career development in HRD will require individuals to be actively involved in their own career development and planning. While organizations once pre-determined career paths within their own systems and designated particular steps to climb the rungs of career advancement, employees now must set their own routes to reach their goals. Some may see this as a daunting task, preferring the relative security of following a well-worn course towards an easily identifiable title or position. Others will be energized by the possibilities of setting their own trajectories, finding security in building their knowledge and skills to increase their employability, preparing to move from one system to another in pursuit of their own definition of career success.

Organizations must adapt as well. Traditional career development programs, designed to ensure a pipeline of qualified replacements for key positions, are being questioned and often replaced by more fluid mechanisms. The old standard that employers held the power in determining career paths is no longer the norm. While some will choose to remain in the same organization for much or all of their career, others will be ready to move on to new endeavors. Employees in charge of their own careers will be most attracted to organizations that offer them growth opportunities and most likely to stay with systems that continue to foster their engagement. This will require organizations to acquire a new mindset: one that invests in employees, without expecting or providing a long-term commitment. Career development will be a vibrant part of this process, but it will need to be re-constructed to respond to this new era of careers. So our exploration begins.

## References

Arthur, M. B. (1994). The boundaryless career: A new perspective for organizational inquiry. *Journal of Organizational Behavior, 15*, 295–306.
Arthur, M. B. (2008). Examining contemporary careers: A call for interdisciplinary inquiry. *Human Relations, 61*(2), 163–186.

Baruch, Y. & Bozionelos, N. (2011). Career issues. In S. Zedeck (Ed.), *APA handbook of industrial and organizational psychology, Vol 2: Selecting and developing members for the organization* (pp. 67–113). Washington, DC: American Psychological Association.

Cameron, R. (2009). Theoretical bridge building: The career development project for the 21st century meets the new era of human resource development. *Australian Journal of Career Development, 18*(3), 9–17.

Canadian Standards and Guidelines for Career Development Practice (2012). Retrieved from http://career-dev-guidelines.org/career_dev/index.php/the-standards-guidelines/core-competencies.

Duffy, R. D. & Dik, B. J. (2013). Research on calling: What have we learned and where are we going? *Journal of Vocational Behavior, 83*, 428–436.

Dumaine, B. & Sample, A. (1994, December 26). Why do we work? *Fortune Magazine, 130*(13). Retrieved from http://money.cnn.com/magazines/fortune/fortune_archieve/1994/12/26/80094.

Egan, T. M., Upton, M. G., & Lynham, S. A. (2006). Career development: Load-bearing wall or window dressing? Exploring definitions, theories, and prospects for HRD-related theory building. *Human Resource Development Review, 5*(4), 442–477.

Gilley, J. W., Eggland, S. A., & Gilley, A. M. (2002). *Principles of human resource development* (2nd edn.). Cambridge, MA: Perseus.

Gunz, H. & Peiperl, M. (2007). Introduction. In H. Gunz & M. Peiperl (Eds.), *Handbook of career studies* (pp. 1–12). Thousand Oaks, CA: Sage.

Hall, D. T. (1996). Protean careers of the 21st century. *The Academy of Management Executive, 10*(4), 8–16.

Hall, D. T. & Las Heras, M. (2012). Personal growth through career work: A positive approach to careers. In K. S. Cameron & G. M. Spreizer, *The Oxford handbook of positive organizational scholarship* (pp. 507–518). Oxford: Oxford University Press.

Herr, E. L. (2001). Career development and its practice: A historical perspective. *Career Development Quarterly, 49*(3), 196–211.

Hershenson, D. B. (2009). Historical perspectives in career development theory. In I. Marini & M. Stebnicki (Eds.), *The professional counselor's desk reference* (pp. 411–420). New York: Springer.

Inkson, K. (2007). *Understanding careers: The metaphors of working lives.* Thousand Oaks, CA: Sage.

Inkson, K. & King, Z. (2011). Contested terrain in careers: A psychological contract model. *Human Relations, 64*(1), 37–57.

McDonald, K. S. & Hite, L. M. (2005). Reviving the relevance of career development in human resource development. *Human Resource Development Review, 4*(4), 418–439.

McLagan, P. A. (1989, September). Models for HRD practice. *Training & Development Journal*, 49–59.

Moore, C., Gunz, H., & Hall, D. T. (2007). Tracing the historical roots of career theory in management and organization studies. In H. Gunz &

14    *An Introduction to Career Development*

M. Peiperl (Eds.), *Handbook of career studies* (pp. 13–38). Thousand Oaks, CA: Sage.

National Career Development Association (NCDA) (2009). *Career counseling competencies*. Retrieved from http://associationdatabase.com/aws/NCDA/pt/sd/news_article/37798/_self/layout_ccmsearch/true.

OECD (2011). *"Economic growth perspective weakening as recovery slows," OECD says.* Retrieved from www.oecd.org/document/25/0,3746, en_21571361_44315115_48633433_1_1_1_1,00.html.

Parsons, F. (1909). *Choosing a vocation.* Boston, MA: Houghton Mifflin.

Pope, M. (2000). A brief history of career counseling in the United States. *Career Development Quarterly, 48*(3), 194–211.

Rousseau, D. M. (1995). *Psychological contracts in organizations: Understanding written and unwritten agreements.* Thousand Oaks, CA: Sage.

Savickas, M. & Baker, D. B. (2005). The history of vocational psychology: Antecedents, origin, and early development. In W. B. Walsh & M. Savickas (Eds.), *Handbook of vocational psychology: Theory, research, and practice* (3rd edn.) (pp. 15–50). Mahwah, NJ: Erlbaum.

Savickas, M., Nota, L., Rossier, J., Dauwalder, J.-P., Duarte, M. E., Guichard, J., Soresi, S., Van Esbroeck, R., & Van Vianen, A. (2009). Life designing: A paradigm for career construction in the 21st century. *Journal of Vocational Behavior, 75*(3), 239–250.

Simonsen, P. (1997). *Promoting a development culture in your organization.* Palo Alto, CA: Davies-Black.

Swanson, R. A. & Holton, E. F., III. (2009). *Foundations of human resource development* (2nd edn.). San Francisco, CA: Berrett-Koehler.

Turnley, W. H. & Feldman, D. C. (1998). Psychological contract violations during corporate restructuring. *Human Resource Management, 37*(1), 71–83.

Watts, A. G. & Kidd, J. M. (2000). Guidance in the United Kingdom: Past, present and future. *British Journal of Guidance & Counseling, 28*(4), 485–502.

Wollschlager, N. & Guggenheim, E. F. (2004). A history of vocational education and training in Europe—from divergence to convergence. *European Journal of Vocational Training, 32*, 1–17.

# 2   Career Theory and Concepts

Regardless of one's enthusiasm for the idea of a radically changing career environment, common wisdom has it that careers nowadays are more erratic and diverse than they were several decades ago.

Strunk, Schiffinger, & Mayrhofer, 2004, p. 496

As we noted in the previous chapter, global economic, technological, and lifestyle changes have had a significant impact on careers. As a result, the past three decades have seen the development of new approaches and concepts related to careers and career development. While several perspectives have been proposed, we will focus on four: the protean career, the boundaryless career, the organizational career, and the kaleidoscope career. These are significant for a variety of reasons. First, they help us to understand how careers are evolving in the twenty-first century. This is valuable for individuals wanting to develop career competencies that will help them experience career success. Additionally, they provide practitioners engaged in career development with varied tools and perspectives that will help them be better equipped to assist others. Second, these approaches provide a framework for more research on careers, which ultimately should broaden our knowledge and practice of career development. This is important because the current and future career environment requires flexibility and innovation that is informed by and grounded in solid research. We will begin this chapter by examining the two perspectives that have received the most attention from both scholars and career practitioners in recent years: the protean and the boundaryless career (Briscoe & Hall, 2006).

## Career Perspectives

### *The Protean Career*

The protean career got its name from the Greek god Proteus, a sea-god who was capable of changing his shape. From a career perspective, this suggests a person who can be flexible and adaptable in a turbulent, ever-changing career landscape. Hall (1976) described the protean career as "a process which the person, not the organization, is managing" (p. 201). In other words, the individual is in charge of his/her own career. For many of you this will not seem particularly novel—of course, one is in control of one's career! However, prior to the 1970s, a career was often conceived of as one's job within an organization. Individuals went to work for an organization, remained there for most of their working lives, and found their chances for advancement were often managed by the organization and guided by the needs of that system.

The protean career is comprised of two dimensions: (a) a values driven dimension, meaning that one's internal values drive how a person views one's career and its development; and (b) self-directed career management, suggesting that an individual is responsible for his/her career choices and development. Self-directed career management can be further broken down into two components: a reflective and a behavioral component. In other words, individuals who take charge of their own careers think about their professional goals and plans, developing insights about their careers (reflective), and they can then choose to act on those thoughts (behavioral) (DeVos & Soens, 2008).

As Briscoe and Hall (2006) pointed out, the notion of a protean career is a mindset about careers more than anything else. It is "an attitude toward the career that reflects freedom, self-direction, and making choices based on one's personal values" (Briscoe & Hall, 2006, p. 6). It is an "internally focused" career orientation (Briscoe, Henagan, Burton, & Murphy, 2012), reinforcing that the individual determines his/her own career path, rather than relying on direction from organizational systems.

The development of the Protean Career Attitude scale (Briscoe, Hall, & DeMuth, 2006) prompted more empirical research on the protean career. For example, studies have found that a protean career attitude is positively related to career satisfaction and perceived employability (DeVos & Soens, 2008) as well as performance, career success, and psychological well-being (Briscoe et al., 2012). Each of these factors is valuable, particularly the idea of employability, which has become increasingly important as organizations reconfigure and individuals strive to keep their skills updated, ready to move on to new opportunities.

While there is evidence of positive career outcomes associated with a protean career orientation, this approach also has been criticized for not reflecting the careers of most individuals. As Kuchinke (2014) wrote:

> While there is little doubt that some individuals in the current era have been able to carve out their own niche and succeeded in remaking their careers in line with their talents, values and desires, there is little evidence to suggest that this model is true for a majority. ... It is hard to envision the protean career as the blueprint for anyone other than an educated elite or a lucky few.
>
> (pp. 212–213)

These dichotomous views pose one of many questions for the future of career development. In this case, can the idea of a protean career be generalized across varied income and education levels? Does it fit for many types of work or will it be seen as available only to those with sufficient financial means and educational capital?

### The Boundaryless Career

The boundaryless career is characterized as "one of independence from, rather than dependence on, traditional career arrangements" (Arthur & Rousseau, 1996, p. 6). In their seminal work, Arthur and Rousseau identified various forms that the boundaryless career might take. One form, for example, would involve "mobility across the boundaries of separate employers," moving readily (and perhaps frequently) from one organization to another to take advantage of new opportunities. Another form would be "constructed around personal and family commitments," allowing individuals to re-configure their work to better accommodate their other life needs and interests (Tams & Arthur, 2010, p. 631).

Boundaryless careers include both physical mobility (e.g., moving across jobs, occupations, countries, etc.) and psychological mobility, which is "the capacity to move as seen through the mind of the career actor" (Sullivan & Arthur, 2006, p. 21). Early studies tended to focus on physical mobility because it was much easier to operationalize (Sullivan & Arthur, 2006). The development of the Boundaryless Career Attitudes scale provided a way to measure psychological mobility (Briscoe et al., 2006). This scale measures both a "boundaryless mindset," which is the "attitude that people hold toward initiating and pursuing work-related relationships across boundaries" (Briscoe et al., 2006, p. 31), as well as "organizational mobility preference," which is the amount of interest one might have regarding actual movement (for example, across multiple employers).

The advent of Briscoe et al.'s scales has prompted a great deal of research examining boundaryless careers. The boundaryless mindset and mobility preference have been found to be related to certain personality characteristics (i.e., proactive personality) (Briscoe et al., 2006), career competencies (Colakoglu, 2011), and motivators (e.g., autonomy, affiliation) (Segers, Inceoglu, Vloeberghs, Bartram, & Henderickx 2008). However, some studies have had conflicting results. For example, Verbruggen (2012) found that having a boundaryless mindset led to tangible indicators of career success (e.g., increased promotions and salaries); however, having an organizational mobility preference tended to result in fewer promotions, and lower job and career satisfaction.

The notion of the boundaryless career has been criticized by some scholars in the field. Some believe the concept to be overly ambiguous, confusing due to the various ways it has been defined, and misleading since the focus actually appears to be on crossing boundaries, rather than not having boundaries, which the term seems to suggest (Inkson, Gunz, Ganesh, & Roper, 2012). Rodrigues and Guest (2010) argued that there is still a need for boundaries in careers. While many boundaries have been re-defined and modified due to the economic environment (as organizations merge and downsize, often on a global scale), they still exist and are still needed. Perhaps the most compelling criticism of the boundaryless career is the lack of empirical support for it (Inkson et al., 2012; Rodrigues & Guest, 2010). These scholars point to labor statistics on job tenure and stability to suggest that most individuals are still employed in traditional organizational careers. Dries, Van Acker, & Verbruggen (2012) also found that many employees still desire traditional careers and that these careers result in more satisfaction than those that fit the "boundaryless" ideal.

So, perhaps when we discuss the boundaryless career, it might be helpful to consider it as a continuum. For example, it might range from being fully bounded (i.e., seeing one's career within the confines of one organization or field), through permeable boundaries (i.e., retaining the mindset of flexibility and opportunity whether one acts on it or not), to boundaryless (i.e., those who readily and perhaps frequently move from one organization and/or profession to another). This perspective might better fit the variety of workplaces and career opportunities that make up our global society.

### The Organizational Career

As indicated above, some evidence suggests that the traditional career, characterized as occurring "within the confines of traditional organizational structures" (Sullivan & Baruch, 2009), is still alive and thriving. A study conducted with managers in an Australian public organization found that many still followed a traditional career path based on tenure and steady advancement through the ranks (McDonald, Brown, & Bradley, 2005). Another study comparing 1970 and 1990 business graduates found marginal changes in the two groups' career patterns. Both cohorts tended to make traditional intra-organizational and upward transitions. Chudzikowski, the author of the study, concluded that the traditional career "appears far from dead" (2012, p. 304).

However, like most social phenomena, the nature of the organizational career has changed. Clarke explained (2012) that "there are indications that over time the organizational career has evolved into a new hybrid form which combines aspects of the old bureaucratic career, while incorporating other dimensions more commonly associated with the 'new careers'" (p. 696).

She elaborated on potential characteristics of the "new organizational career," including:

- continuity in employment, "long-term" rather than "lifetime" employment
- flexibility and adaptability on the part of employees to handle change
- medium-term tenure across different roles
- loyalty to organization and to outside groups
- jointly managed career (both organizational and self)
- development to meet both organization and individual needs
- career focus that is both internal and external to the organization
- career path is a spiral progression
- relational employment contract
- both objective and subjective measures of success (Clarke, 2012, p. 697).

Clarke's view reminds us that we must think expansively when we view the past, present, and potential future of careers. Increasingly, career research and practice suggest the need to build on parts of the past while we adapt to where we are now and envision where we are headed as a global workplace. Similarly, career development is not bounded by phases locked in time, but rather is a fluid, moving entity that must continue.

### The Kaleidoscope Career

Mainiero and Sullivan developed their model using the metaphor of a kaleidoscope to describe careers. Imagine a kaleidoscope which changes patterns as a result of rotating the tube; every movement reveals a new perspective. Similarly, according to their model, careers develop and evolve in patterns as well. The resulting kaleidoscope career model (KCM) "describes how individuals change the pattern of their career by rotating the varied aspects of their lives to arrange their relationships and roles in new ways" (Sullivan & Baruch, 2009, p. 1557).

Mainiero and Sullivan (2005) proposed three parameters as important in influencing career decisions:

- authenticity: making choices that allow one to be true to oneself
- balance: making choices that allow an individual to balance both work and non-work responsibilities
- challenge: making choices that provide interesting and stimulating work, and opportunities to advance in one's career and continually develop.

Mainiero and Sullivan's research clearly suggested that one of these three parameters would be the primary focus at different times during an individual's career, depending on changes occurring in one's life.

In formulating this model, they were particularly interested in understanding women's career patterns. They found that relationism typically dominated women's thinking when making decisions regarding their careers. They also found gender differences in what issues dominate at different times in men's and women's careers. Both men and women appear most concerned with challenge and goal accomplishment in the early years of their careers. The differences between men and women tend to appear during mid- and late career stages. Balance issues seem to be a major influence for women during mid-career, while authenticity becomes increasingly important to men during this time. In late career an emphasis on authenticity often dominates women's careers, whereas balance is more likely the focus for men in late career (Cabrera, 2008; Mainiero & Sullivan, 2005).

Empirical research supporting the KCM is limited. However, Sullivan and Mainiero (2008) offered specific suggestions as to how HRD might support and promote individuals' authenticity, balance, and challenge. For example, they suggest developing short sabbaticals and corporate wellness programs to support authenticity, policies that allow for "stop-out career interruptions" to promote balance, and job rotations and overseas assignments to support the challenge parameter (pp. 38–41).

The four approaches or career perspectives described above are distinct, yet all respond to the complex landscape where careers are enacted in the twenty-first century. They offer new ways of thinking about careers and how individuals evaluate their careers. In addition, they consider the impact and importance of networks, work–life issues, technology, and other environmental influences. Table 2.1 summarizes the four approaches.

### *Implications for Practice*

These four career perspectives suggest a variety of ways by which human resource development (HRD) practitioners might help individuals develop their careers. For example:

- Help individuals develop protean and boundaryless career attitudes. Briscoe et al. (2012) found that these attitudes may facilitate

*Table 2.1* Career Perspectives

| Career Perspective | Description | Focus | Measures |
|---|---|---|---|
| Protean Career | The career is directed and controlled by the individual. It is driven by internal values and the individual self-directs his/her career. | Individual | Protean Career Attitudes scale (Briscoe et al., 2006) |
| Boundaryless Career | The career does not rely on traditional organizational structures; rather, it is independent of these potential constraints. It includes both physical and psychological mobility. | Individual | Boundaryless Career Attitudes (Briscoe et al., 2006) |
| Organizational Career | The career occurs within an organization and is jointly managed by the employee and the organization. | Individual and organization | |
| Kaleidoscope Career Model (KCM) | The career develops and evolves in patterns. Three parameters influence how the career progresses: authenticity, balance, and challenge. One of these parameters is likely to be most influential at different times during one's career. | Individual and organization | 15-item scale that measures authenticity, balance, and challenge (Sullivan, Forret, Carraher, & Mainiero, 2009) |

career skill development, which may be beneficial in navigating insecure employment environments. According to these authors and DeVos and Soens (2008), both protean and boundaryless attitudes can be learned.

- Create opportunities to develop employees' flexibility and adaptability. More information regarding career adaptability is provided in Chapter 3, including a description of a training program designed to increase adaptability.
- Encourage employees to establish both external and internal networks and provide support for the development of various networks (e.g., based on interests, group affinity). More information regarding networks is provided in Chapter 4.
- Provide creative development opportunities that allow employees to do cross-function work and that encourage lateral movement as well as vertical movement within the organization.
- Carefully consider development opportunities that will bring challenge to individuals' careers, promote balance between work and family/other life issues, and build one's sense of authenticity.

## Career Concepts

Additional understanding of careers includes becoming familiar with various concepts that are used in the study of careers. We will focus on four major concepts: career success, career competencies, career transitions, and career identity.

### *Career Success*

The majority of us will at various times in our lives reflect on and assess our careers. We may deem that they are successful or unsuccessful and, like many things we make judgments about, these assessments are likely to change with the passage of time and vary from individual to individual. Career scholars have devoted a lot of attention to the notion of career success in an attempt to understand what it entails and what predicts it. Let's first examine what career success means.

Career success has been defined as a positive outcome of a career experience and as a process of achieving work-related goals (Arthur, Khapova, & Wilderom, 2005; Mirvis & Hall, 1996). Most acknowledge that career success involves two distinct components: subjective career success which is internally focused, meaning it is an individual's unique and personal assessment of his or her career, and objective career success which include those indicators of achieve-ment that are more tangible and externally focused (Arthur et al., 2005; Heslin, 2005). Subjective career success has most commonly been conceived as a sign of career satisfaction (Heslin, 2005), although other judgments like the value of individuals' human capital and self-appraisals of one's efficacy and capabilities would also be considered measures (Stumpf & Tymon, 2012). Common indicators of objective career success include salary, promotions, and occupa-tional status—all of which can be assessed by others (Ng, Eby, Soren-sen, & Feldman, 2005). It is important to recognize that these two types of career success are interdependent; for example, objective indicators of success are likely to influence subjective factors such as career satisfaction.

However career success is a lot more complicated than simply identifying these two components. Heslin (2005) argues that another compelling issue when considering career success is the criteria used to evaluate one's career experiences. Some are more likely to use self-referent criteria, with standards set by the career agent. For example, one of the authors of this text wanted to achieve the rank of professor by the time she was 50 (which was considered a success since it was accomplished!). Another way that career outcomes are assessed is through the use of other-referent criteria (Heslin, 2005). Usually this involves making comparisons to others —for example, an individual might feel as if she failed because her colleague has already made partner in the law firm and she has not. It also could include the idea of living up to others' expectations regarding your career. Some individuals may feel an obligation to enter a certain profession, make a particular salary, or attain promo-tions due to expectations placed on them from family, peers, super-visors, for example. As Heslin points out, individuals will evaluate objective and subjective career success using both self- and other-referent criteria.

Dries (2011) further illustrates the complexity of defining career success by identifying a variety of contextual factors that influence our meanings of career success. Specifically, she explains how histor-ical, cultural (e.g., national culture), and ideological (e.g., societal and organizational) contexts will influence our definitions and our perspec-tives of career success. She pointed out that, while we may understand this influence, as employees and employers we often don't use this knowledge in developing careers. One suggestion she offered is that both employees and employers need to broaden their perspective of what career success means. This broadening will enhance employees' "feelings of authenticity," which will lead to a more diverse and more productive workforce (Dries, 2011, p. 380).

Beyond understanding how career success is defined and perceived, it is important to consider what predicts it. Research has identified various predictors of career success including, but not limited to, the following:

- Human capital such as education, training, and work experience: Ng et al. (2005) in their meta-analysis of predictors of objective and subjective career success found that many of these factors related to success, particularly objective career success (e.g., salary and promotions).
- Social capital such as interpersonal relationships, networks, and mentors: for example, a study conducted by Seibert et al. (2001) found that social capital related to both subjective and objective career success; however, they also found that it is not a simple matter of "schmoozing." Rather, through developing social capital, individuals gained three important networking benefits: access to information, resources, and career sponsorships, which led to higher salaries and more promotions, and career satisfaction.
- Organizational sponsorship such as supervisory support and HRD initiatives (e.g., training and development) (Ng et al., 2005; Wayne, Liden, Kraimer, & Graf, 1999): while we recognize that organizational sponsorship overlaps with both human and social capital factors, we want to highlight it given the HRD focus of this book. These initiatives will be explored in greater detail in Chapter 4.
- Socio-demographic variables such as gender, race, and age: for example, you are likely to have a higher salary if you are White, male, married, and older (Ng et al., 2005). While progress has been made, women, minorities, and individuals raised in poverty are still less likely to experience career success, particularly when considering objective indicators such as salary and promotions. Further discussion of inequalities in career development will be included in later chapters.
- Stable individual characteristics or traits such as the Big Five personality factors, locus of control, and cognitive ability (Ng et al., 2005): while these variables may be relatively fixed, they do impact career success. Measures such as conscientiousness, cognitive ability, and even physical attractiveness have been found to be predictors (Judge, Higgins, Thoresen, & Barrick, 1999; Judge, Hurst, & Simon, 2009).
- Structural or contextual factors: Baruch and Bozionelos (2011) indicate that organizational characteristics (e.g., size, ownership),

environmental factors (e.g., economic conditions), and societal factors (i.e., legislation, education systems) will impact career success. Judge, Cable, Boudreau, & Bretz (1995), for example, found that variables such as type of industry and the perceived success of the organization positively predicted executives' salaries and satisfaction with their careers. Certainly, the recent global economic downturn created havoc for many people's careers.

Clearly the notion of success is an important concept in the study of careers. It is an important way in which we, as career agents, and others evaluate our worth. Additionally, it is a complex phenomenon that continues to be re-defined and re-investigated to more appropriately reflect contemporary society.

### *Career Competencies*

What are the essential elements needed to enact a career? Career competencies develop over time and are important to both individuals working to acquire the necessary capabilities to facilitate their careers and to organizations attempting to attract and develop talent (Francis-Smythe, Haase, Thomas, & Steele, 2012). DeFillippi and Arthur (1994) offered three major career competencies: know why, know how, and know whom. *Know-why* competencies focus on self-awareness; in other words, it is an understanding of one's interests and values. According to DeFillippi and Arthur these competencies "answer the question 'Why?' as it relates to career motivation, personal meaning and identification" (p. 308). *Know-how* competencies are the job-related knowledge and career-relevant skills that career agents possess and that contribute to organizations' and individuals' capabilities (DeFillippi & Arthur, 1994). Training is a common initiative offered to enhance these competencies. Finally, *knowing-whom* competencies are those career-related networks and contacts that benefit organizational communication and individuals' learning and marketability (DeFillippi & Arthur, 1994; Eby, Butts, & Lockwood, 2003).

There is evidence suggesting that developing these competencies can enhance one's career. These three competencies have been found to be predictors of perceived career success and perceived marketability (Eby et al., 2003). In addition, Colakoglu (2011) found that two of the competencies—knowing why and knowing how—increased feelings of autonomy and reduced career insecurity.

Other career competency models have been proposed. Francis-Smythe et al. (2012), for example, argued that a model such as DeFillippi and

Arthur's overlaps with personality traits and that competencies suggest that behaviors should be emphasized. Their alternative model identified seven career competencies:

1    goal setting and career planning
2    self-knowledge (e.g., of interests, values, strengths, weaknesses)
3    job-related performance effectiveness
4    career-related skills (e.g., seeking out development opportunities)
5    knowledge of (office) politics
6    career guidance and networking
7    feedback seeking and self-presentation (Francis-Smythe et al., 2012, p. 236).

This model may more accurately illustrate the complexity of career competencies (Francis-Smythe et al., 2012). In addition, it may be more useful to both organizations and individuals by providing specific behaviors to identify, assess, and develop. Francis-Smythe et al., developed the Career Competencies Indicator (CCI) to assess these competencies. Their initial studies provide support for the reliability and validity of the CCI, however, more work is needed to determine the usefulness of this instrument for both research and practice.

### Career Transitions

Career transition has been defined as "events or non-events in the career development process causing changes in the meaning of the career, one's self assumptions, and view of the world" (O'Neil, Fishman, & Kinsella-Shaw, 1987, p. 66). Most career transitions involve either a change in tasks, position, or occupation (Heppner, Multon, & Johnston, 1994) and will vary considerably based on the controllability, the magnitude, and the ambiguity of the transition (Wanberg & Kammeyer-Mueller, 2008).

Common career transitions experienced by many individuals include initial career choice, entry into the organization, reassessment of career, involuntary job loss, and retirement (Wanberg & Kammeyer-Mueller, 2008). While initial career choice occurs prior to entering an organization, HRD can play an important role in most of the transitions listed above. Initial entry into an organization can be quite stressful as the new employee is filled with ambiguity and anxiety regarding his/her supervisor, colleagues, and the job itself. Well-developed orientation programs, networking opportunities, and coaching are just a few of the initiatives that have the potential to assist employees through this adjustment process. Career counseling and alternative career paths could be beneficial to the individual re-evaluating his/her career. Outplacement services and career counseling can help employees who experience job loss due to downsizing, restructuring, closings, etc. Finally, offering alternative work structures such as bridge employment and phased retirement, as well as educational programs to prepare employees for retirement, are examples of HRD initiatives that can help the employee making the transition to retirement (Callanan & Greenhaus, 2008).

Regardless of the type of transition, individuals experiencing some type of change in their careers are likely to encounter feelings of or a period of instability. According to Ng, Sorensen, Eby, & Feldman (2007) "careers unfold with alternating periods of equilibrium and job mobility transitions" (p. 367). They propose that three important factors will cause this equilibrium to be disrupted:

- structural factors, including: economic conditions, societal characteristics (e.g., war, technology breakthroughs, social movements), industry differences (e.g., male or female dominated, compensation practices, industry growth), and staffing policies within organizations (e.g., internal mobility options);
- individual differences, including: personality traits, career interests, values, and attachment styles;
- decisional perspective, suggesting that intentions to make a transition are determined by subjective norms about the change (e.g., popularity of a particular type of job mobility make it easier to change), desirability of mobility, and readiness for change.

Ng et al. (2007) point out that these factors are not independent and in most situations one factor will influence another, suggesting that decisions to engage in job mobility are complex.

In a study conducted across five countries, individuals reported internal causes for making career transitions, specifically those individuals from the US and from three European countries (Chudzikowski et al., 2009). The participants from the US in particular were motivated to change due to some individual reason, for example the desire to do something different or the desire to change careers to create more balance in one's life. Those study participants from China attributed transitions to external factors such as government policies and organizational re-structuring, similar to the structural factors identified by Ng. et al. (2007).

Two studies on career transitions have important implications for career development practitioners and HRD. A study of Korean post-retirement workers examining the transition from voluntary retirement to post-retirement employment found that the transition process consisted of four stages:

- a period of disequilibrium in a previous career;
- a period of reflection regarding self and situations before making any changes;
- a period developing new professional connections and changes;
- committing to a new career (Kim, 2014, p. 9).

Kim pointed out that these stages are not necessarily linear—instead "each is an iterative process that requires disruptions at each step" (p. 15). In addition, learning (both formal and informal) played a significant role in the career transition process of these post-retirement individuals.

Another study of Chinese MBA graduates found that individuals experience constraints and challenges when undergoing a career transition. The three most common challenges perceived by the respondents all focused on lack of knowledge—lack of knowledge regarding career paths, unfamiliarity with the "environment and the mechanism of career transition," and "lack of industry knowledge and experience" (Sun & Wang, 2009, p. 521). The authors point to the inadequacy of organizations and education in preparing workers to deal with career transitions. Both of these studies illustrate the important role of learning in successfully moving from one career to another. HRD systems and career development practitioners can assist individuals during these transition processes through a wide variety of initiatives such as career coaching and counseling, training, and mentoring.

### Career Identity

Many of us, in attempting to define "who we are," will use our occupation or profession as one means of identifying self. Fugate, Kinicki, & Ashforth (2004) explained and differentiated career identity in the following manner:

> Career identity resembles constructs like role identity, occupational identity, and organizational identity in that they all refer to how people define themselves in a particular work context. Career identity, however, is inherently *longitudinal* because it involves making sense of one's past and present and giving direction to one's future.
>
> (p. 20)

Holland and colleagues identified and defined the construct "vocational identity" as "the possession of a clear and stable picture of one's goals, interests, and talents" (Holland, Gottfredson, & Power, 1980, p. 1191). Vocational identity has been found to relate strongly with tasks associated with crystallizing one's preferences regarding a career (Savickas, 1985). While vocational identity is clearly related to career identity, it usually has been used in career counseling and in research on young adults' career choices (Ashforth, Harrison, & Corley, 2008), thus having limited application to the ongoing construction of identity associated with work and careers. Additional criticisms of Holland et al.'s construct are offered by Vondracek (1992), who argued that it "is too simple and sterile to be of much use" (para. 25).

Identities are constructed and re-constructed during the course of one's career (Turnbull, 2004) and particularly when individuals are experiencing career transitions (Ibarra, 1999). A qualitative study of career transitions being made by junior management consultants and investment bankers found that participants engaged in three adaptive behaviors to construct a professional identity that would be perceived as "credible with important role-set members and congruent with one's self-concept" (Ibarra, 1999, p. 782). These three behaviors included: observing successful role models, experimenting with provisional selves (either by imitating role models or through experimenting to find their authentic style or approach), and evaluating the results through internal standards and feedback from others. These behaviors suggest that mentors, networks, and coaches can play important roles in identity formation and that ultimately the development of a career identity is a complex learning process (Meijers, 1998).

While career identities will evolve over time, some speculate that this form of identity will be increasingly important. Ashforth et al. (2008) explained: "Of the many possible bases of identification in one's work life, occupational and career identification may become more important to individuals as environmental turbulence continues to erode long-term relationships with organizations and the various bases nested within them" (p. 352). Meijers (1998) reinforced the importance of developing a career identity in a climate of insecurity, change, and individual control over one's employment.

These four concepts, success, competencies, transitions, and identity, have significance to any individual interested in careers. HRD practitioners, in particular, need an understanding of these concepts and recognize how they can enhance individuals' careers through this knowledge. Table 2.2 provides a listing of some of the ways in which these concepts are operationalized, measured, and assessed in the literature. Some of these measures could be useful to both individuals and practitioners working to develop their own and others' careers.

*Table 2.2* Career Concepts

| Career Concepts | Measures, Assessment Tools |
|---|---|
| Career Success | Objective success: common measures include salaries, promotions, occupational status<br>Subjective success: one of the most commonly used scales is the Career Satisfaction Scale (CSS) (Greenhaus et al., 1990), a five-item, self-reported scale |
| Career Competencies | Career Competencies Indicator (CCI), 43-item scale that measures seven competencies:<br>• goal setting and career planning<br>• self-knowledge<br>• job-related performance effectiveness<br>• career-related skills<br>• knowledge of office politics<br>• career guidance and networking<br>• feedback seeking and self-presentation (Francis-Smythe, et al., 2012) |
| Career Transitions | Career Transitions Inventory (CTI), a 40-item measure of five factors facilitating a successful career transition:<br>• readiness: motivation to make a transition<br>• confidence: to do the necessary tasks to complete a transition<br>• control that one feels in handling the transition<br>• social support<br>• decision independence (or are the considerations of others important in making a career transition decision?) (Heppner et al., 1994) |
| Career Identity | Vocational Identity Subscale (VI) of the My Vocational Situation (MVS) is an 18-item true–false scale (Holland, Gottfredson & Power, 1980).<br>    Narratives are considered an important way to understand how individuals construct their career identities (Ashforth et al., 2008; Fugate et al., 2004) |

## Implications for Practice

There are a variety of ways that HRD practitioners might help individuals develop their careers through knowledge of these concepts. For example:

• understand the varying ways in which individuals define and perceive career success and act as an advocate in the adoption of a variety of practices that will support individuals' pursuits of success;

- using a career competency model such as the one proposed by Francis-Smythe et al. (2012), design initiatives that will assist individuals in developing their career competencies. A wide variety of activities could help, such as training, performance improvement strategies, coaching, mentoring, and networking. Francis-Smythe et al. concluded that organizations will benefit as well as individual employees, citing lower turnover rates and increased commitment to the organization as potential results from developing workers' career competencies;
- recognize that voluntary and involuntary career transitions are inextricably tied to learning. As a result, there are numerous ways (many of which were mentioned earlier) in which HRD can assist individuals through these transitions with the goal of restoring equilibrium and achieving success (however they define it) in their new career;
- acknowledge the important role that careers play in identity construction and re-construction. HRD can facilitate the process of locating role models for individuals to observe and learn from and provide support for the external feedback process that is necessary during identity formation.

## Summary

This chapter provides an overview of four career perspectives: the protean, boundaryless, organizational, and kaleidoscope career. Three of these approaches (protean, boundaryless, and kaleidoscope) were conceived and developed to address the "radically changing career environment" that Strunk et al. (2004) were describing in this chapter's opening quote. While the organizational career has a long history, scholars and practitioners are focusing on new ways to configure it to reflect changing times. In addition, four career concepts—career success, career competencies, career transitions, and career identity—are introduced and explained. Human resource practitioners play an important role in developing employees' careers through an understanding of these career perspectives and concepts.

## References

Arthur, M. B., Khapova, S. N., & Wilderom, C. P. M. (2005). Career success in a boundaryless career world. *Journal of Organizational Behavior, 26*, 177–202.

Arthur, M. B. & Rousseau, D. M. (1996). *The boundaryless career: A new employment principle for a new organizational era.* New York: Oxford University Press.

Ashforth, B. E., Harrison, S. H., & Corley, K. G. (2008). Identification in organizations: An examination of four fundamental questions. *Journal of Management, 34,* 325–374.

Baruch, Y. & Bozionelos, N. (2011). Career issues. In S. Zedeck (Ed.), *The APA handbook of industrial and organizational psychology* (pp. 67–113). Washington, DC: American Psychological Association.

Briscoe, J. P. & Hall, D. T. (2006). The interplay of boundaryless and protean careers: Combinations and implications. *Journal of Vocational Behavior, 69,* 4–18.

Briscoe, J. P., Hall, D. T., & DeMuth, R. L. F. (2006). Protean and boundaryless careers: An empirical exploration. *Journal of Vocational Behavior, 69,* 30–47.

Briscoe, J. P., Henagan, S. C., Burton, J. P., & Murphy, W. M. (2012). Coping with an insecure employment environment: The differing roles of protean and boundaryless career orientations. *Journal of Vocational Behavior, 80,* 308–316.

Cabrera, E. F. (2008). Protean organizations: Reshaping work and careers to retain female talent. *Career Development International, 14,* 186–201.

Callanan, G. A. & Greenhaus, J. H. (2008). The baby boom generation and career management: A call to action. *Advances in Developing Human Resources, 10,* 70–85.

Chudzikowski, K. (2012). Career transitions and career success in the "new" career era. *Journal of Vocational Behavior, 81,* 298–306.

Chudzikowski, K., Demel, B., Mayrhofer, W., Briscoe, J. P., Unite, J., Milikic, B. B., Hall, D. T., Las Heras, M., Shen, Y., & Zikic, J. (2009). Career transitions and their causes: A country-comparative perspective. *Journal of Occupational and Organizational Psychology, 82,* 825–849.

Clarke, M. (2012). The organizational career: Not dead but in need of redefinition. *The International Journal of Human Resource Management, 24,* 684–703.

Colakoglu, S. N. (2011). The impact of career boundarylessness on subjective career success: The role of career competencies, career autonomy, and career insecurity. *Journal of Vocational Behavior, 79,* 47–59.

DeFillippi, R. J. & Arthur, M. B. (1994). The boundaryless career: A competency-based perspective. *Journal of Organizational Behavior, 15,* 307–324.

DeVos, A. & Soens, N. (2008). Protean attitude and career success: The mediating role of self-management. *Journal of Vocational Behavior, 73,* 449–456.

Dries, N. (2011). The meaning of career success. *Career Development International, 16,* 364–384.

Dries, N., Van Acker, F., & Verbruggen, M. (2012). How "boundaryless" are the careers of high potentials, key experts and average performers? *Journal of Vocational Behavior, 81,* 271–279.

Eby, L. T., Butts, M., & Lockwood, A. (2003). Predictors of success in the era of the boundaryless career. *Journal of Organizational Behavior, 24*, 689–708.

Francis-Smythe, J., Haase, S., Thomas, E., & Steele, C. (2012). Development and validation of the Career Competencies Indicator (CCI). *Journal of Career Assessment, 21*, 227–248.

Fugate, M., Kinicki, A. J., & Ashforth, B. E. (2004). Employability: A psychosocial construct, its dimensions, and applications. *Journal of Vocational Behavior, 65*, 14–38.

Greenhaus, J. H., Parasuraman, S., & Wormley, W. M. (1990). Effects of race on organizational experiences, job performance evaluations, and career outcomes. *Academy of Management Journal, 33*, 64–86.

Hall, D. T. (1976). *Careers in organizations.* Glenview, IL: Scott Foresman & Co.

Heppner, M. J., Multon, K. D., & Johnston, J. A. (1994). Assessing psychological resources during career change: Development of the Career Transitions Inventory. *Journal of Vocational Behavior, 44*, 55–74.

Heslin, P. A. (2005). Conceptualizing and evaluating career success. *Journal of Organizational Behavior, 26*, 113–136.

Holland, J. L., Gottfredson, D. C., & Power, P. G. (1980). Some diagnostic scales for research in decision making and personality: Identity, information, and barriers. *Journal of Personality and Social Psychology, 39*, 1191–1200.

Ibarra, H. (1999). Provisional selves: Experimenting with image and identity in professional adaptation. *Administrative Quarterly Science, 44*, 764–791.

Inkson, K., Gunz, H., Ganesh, S., & Roper, J. (2012). Boundaryless careers: Bringing back boundaries. *Organization Studies, 33*, 323–340.

Judge, T. A., Cable, D. M., Boudreau, J. W., & Bretz, R. D., Jr. (1995). An empirical investigation of the predictors of executive career success. *Personnel Psychology, 48*, 485–519.

Judge, T. A., Higgins, C. A., Thoresen, C. J., & Barrick, M. R. (1999). The big five personality traits, general mental ability, and career success across the life span. *Personnel Psychology, 52*, 621–652.

Judge, T. A., Hurst, C., & Simon, L. S. (2009). Does it pay to be smart, attractive or confident (or all three)? Relationships among general mental ability, physical attractiveness, core self-evaluations, and income. *Journal of Applied Psychology, 94*, 742–755.

Kim, S. (2014). The career transition process: A qualitative exploration of Korean middle-aged workers in postretirement employment. *Adult Education Quarterly, 64*, 3–19.

Kuchinke, K. P. (2014). Boundaryless and protean careers in a knowledge economy. In J. Walton & C. Valentin (Eds.), *Human resource development: Practices and orthodoxies* (pp. 202–222). London: Palgrave MacMillan.

McDonald, P., Brown, K., & Bradley, L. (2005). Have traditional career paths given way to protean ones? *Career Development International, 10*, 109–129.

Mainiero, L. A. & Sullivan, S. E. (2005). Kaleidoscope careers: An alternate explanation for the "opt-out" revolution. *Academy of Management Executive, 19*, 106–123.

Meijers, F. (1998). The development of a career identity. *International Journal for the Advancement of Counseling, 20*, 191–207.

Mirvis, P. H. & Hall, D. T. (1996). Psychological success and the boundaryless career. In M. B. Arthur & D. M. Rousseau (Eds.), *The boundaryless career* (pp. 237–255). New York: Oxford University Press.

Ng, T. W. H., Eby, L. T., Sorensen, K. L., & Feldman, D. C. (2005). Predictors of objective and subjective career success: A meta-analysis. *Personnel Psychology, 58*, 367–408.

Ng, T. W. H., Sorensen, K. L., Eby, L. T., & Feldman, D. C. (2007). Determinants of job mobility: A theoretical integration and extension. *Journal of Occupational and Organizational Psychology, 80*, 363–386.

O'Neil, J. M., Fishman, D. M., & Kinsella-Shaw, M. (1987). Dual-career couples' career transitions and normative dilemmas: A preliminary assessment model. *Counseling Psychologist, 15*, 50–96.

Rodrigues, R. A. & Guest, D. (2010). Have careers become boundaryless? *Human Relations, 63*, 1157–1175.

Savickas, M. L. (1985). Identity in vocational development. *Journal of Vocational Behavior, 27*, 329–337.

Segers, J., Inceoglu, I., Vloeberghs, D., Bartram, D., & Henderickx, E. (2008). Protean and boundaryless careers: A study of potential motivators. *Journal of Vocational Behavior, 73*, 212–230.

Seibert, S. E., Kraimer, M. L., & Liden, R. C. (2001). A social capital theory of career success. *Academy of Management Journal, 44*, 219–237.

Strunk, G., Schiffinger, M., & Mayrhofer, W. (2004). Lost in translation? Complexity in organizational behavior—the contributions of systems theories. *Management Revue, 15*, 481–509.

Stumpf, S. A. & Tymon, Jr., W. G. (2012). The effects of objective success on subsequent subjective success. *Journal of Vocational Behavior, 81*, 345–353.

Sullivan, S. E. & Arthur, M. B. (2006). The evolution of the boundaryless career concept: Examining physical and psychological mobility. *Journal of Vocational Behavior, 69*, 19–29.

Sullivan, S. E. & Baruch, Y. (2009). Advances in career theory and research: A critical review and agenda for future exploration. *Journal of Management, 35*, 1542–1571.

Sullivan, S. E., Forret, M. L., Carraher, S. M., & Mainiero, L. A. (2009). Using the kaleidoscope career model to examine generational differences in work attitudes. *Career Development International, 14*, 284–302.

Sullivan, S. E. & Mainiero, L. (2008). Using the kaleidoscope career model to understand the changing patterns of women's careers: Designing HRD programs that attract and retain women. *Advances in Developing Human Resources, 10*, 32–49.

Sun, J. Y. & Wang, G. G. (2009). Career transition in the Chinese context: A case study. *Human Resource Development International, 12*, 511–528.

Tams, S. & Arthur, M. B. (2010). New directions for boundaryless careers: Agency and interdependence in a changing world. *Journal of Organizational Behavior, 31*, 629–646.

Turnbull, S. (2004). Perceptions and experience of time-space compression and acceleration. *Journal of Managerial Psychology, 19*, 809–824.

Verbruggen, M. (2012). Psychological mobility and career success in the "new" career climate. *Journal of Vocational Behavior, 81*, 289–297.

Vondracek, F. W. (1992). The construct of identity and its use in career theory and research. *Career Development Quarterly, 41*.

Wanberg, C. R. & Kammeyer-Mueller, J. (2008). A self-regulatory perspective on navigating career transitions. In R. Kanfer, G. Chen, & R. D. Pritchard (Eds.), *Work motivation: Past, present, and future* (pp. 433–469). New York: Routledge.

Wayne, S. J., Liden, R. C., Kraimer, M. L., & Graf, I. K. (1999). The role of human capital, motivation and supervisor sponsorship in predicting career success. *Journal of Organizational Behavior, 20*, 577–595.

# 3   Strategic Career Development

Change in career systems does not mean that organizations need to abandon their role in managing careers. Instead, the organization has a new significant role—being supportive, enabler, developer of its human assets. Organizations need to move away from the traditional "command and control" approach, and become "supportive and developmental."

Baruch, 2006, p. 130

The past two to three decades have been characterized as turbulent for careers. Economic fluctuations, amazing advances in technology, globalization, and demographic shifts have led to new and different conceptualizations of the meaning of career and the role that individuals and organizations play in the shaping, growth, and development of careers. Some have concluded that career development must be individually driven, rather than relying on organization structure and support. While there is some merit to this argument, it is important to remember that, for the most part, individuals experience their careers through organizations. As Inkson and King (2011) pointed out, "Careers ... result from deals negotiated between individual career actors and the organization in which they work over their working lives" (p. 37). This suggests that organizations still play a vital role in career development but, as Baruch (2003) noted, a "new paradigm" is needed. Gilley, Eggland, & Gilley (2002) described the career development relationship between the organization and the individual as a "marriage." This marriage involves:

organizations engage in developmental planning, the process of assessing appropriate goals and objectives, and the proper allocation of physical, financial, and human resources. Concurrently, employees engage in career/life planning, which includes analysis of personal goals, competencies, and a realistic evaluation of future opportunities.

(p. 65)

## Contested Terrain

Yet like most marriages, tension between partners is likely to occur. Often there will be conflict between the individual's career needs and desires, and the interests of the organization. Inkson and King (2011) suggested that this can often result in careers becoming "contested terrain" between the two parties. This term was introduced by economist Richard Edwards (1979) in his book entitled *Contested Terrain*. To describe this tension, Edwards wrote:

> Conflict exists because the interests of workers and those of employers collide, and what is good for one is frequently costly for the other. Control is rendered problematic because, unlike the other commodities involved in production, labor power is always embodied in people, who have their own interests and needs and who retain their power to resist being treated like a commodity.
>
> (p. 12)

While Edwards focused on the workplace in general, Inkson and King (2011) provided a psychological contract model of careers which outlined both individual and organization inputs and objectives to explain how the notion of contested terrain applies to careers. They emphasized the significance of careers becoming contested terrain:

> Career-related issues create particular tensions for the contract because career goals are often long-term and tentative, because the timing and size of the payback is uncertain, and because violation of the contract may not be apparent until long after the investments have been committed.
>
> (p. 46)

While it is important to recognize these often competing interests, career systems can be developed that will promote the goals of both the organization and the employees. Communicating expectations and needs is critical, as is listening and understanding each party's interests regarding career development (Inkson & King, 2011). HRD practitioners can play an important role in facilitating negotiations between employees and employers regarding these issues (McDonald & Hite, 2015). We will further discuss this later in this chapter.

So how can career systems be created that satisfy the needs and interests of both organizations and employees? What would be the essential elements? What needs to be considered before implementing career development within an organization? How will the effectiveness of career development be determined? In this chapter we will attempt to answer these questions by providing a framework which will outline the processes necessary to achieve an effective career development system. Baruch (2003) argued that career management systems have become antiquated and need to become much more "integrative." He wrote: "An adequate model should reflect the complexity and multi-dimensional nature of career systems, as well as examining the need to adjust them to the contemporary dynamic business environment" (p. 232). We hope that the framework presented here will address these concerns.

## Strategic Career Development

Effective career development requires integrating career issues with the strategic direction of the organization (Baruch, 2003; Gilley et al., 2002; Greenhaus, Callanan, & Godshalk, 2010). To be strategic, career development must be an integral part of all human resource management (HRM) functions. This is essential if organizations wish to recruit and retain talent (Kaye & Smith, 2012). As Baruch (2003) pointed out:

> It has long been established that an essential part of HRM is the strategic aspect. Integrating HRM into a strategic management of the organization, rather than holding a minor supportive role of an administrative function is a distinctive sign of the role of HRM, and this should be reflected in the career management systems.
>
> (p. 238)

Current, as well as future, career needs should be considered when strategic decisions regarding the organization are made. Likewise, career development initiatives must address the business needs of the organization and adapt as the strategic direction of the organization changes. This fluidity is explained by Brousseau, Driver, Eneroth, & Larsson (1996):

> Firms should view organizational career culture as dynamic, requiring periodic readjustments as strategic considerations demand

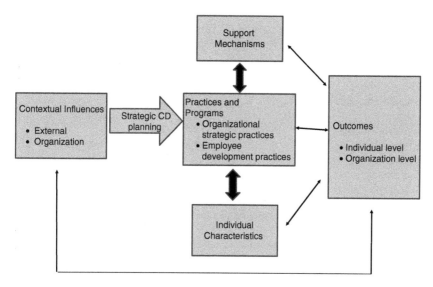

*Figure 3.1* A Framework for Organizational Career Development

and as the changing mix of employees' career motives and competencies shift, either as employees turn over, or as individual employees change career motives and competencies over time.

(p. 63)

With these thoughts in mind, we offer a framework that can be used as a way to develop strategic career development within an organization. This framework attempts to capture the importance of integrating career development with other HR systems and recognizes that a career development system must be nimble—able to adapt to changes in the environment, organization, and the individual employee (Figure 3.1).

## Contextual Influences

Career development does not occur in a vacuum. Yet, often, career development efforts in organizations are criticized for not recognizing the various factors that should influence how career development is enacted in an organizational system. At some level, this is understandable—the accelerated rate of change in society results in many systems in organizations scrambling to keep up. So, traditional career management systems are likely to be outdated (Baruch, 2003; Doyle, 2000). However, these contextual factors are critical to consider because they

*Table 3.1* Careers

| Extinct or nearly extinct careers | Emerging careers |
|---|---|
| Bowling alley pinsetter | Mobile app developer |
| Ice cutters | Web content strategist |
| Lamp lighters | Elder care specialist |
| Switchboard operator | Emergency management specialist |
| Lector | Computer game designer |
| Elevator operator | Biomedical engineer |
| River driver | Physical therapist assistant |
| Milkman | Logistic analyst |
| Typesetter | Event management |
| Telegraph operator | Biostatistician |

Source: https://latestcareersopportunities.wordpress.com/2014/02/17/emerging-careers-for-young-professionals-in-2014.
www.boredpanda.com/extinct-jobs.
www.schoolanduniversity.com/featured-jobs/7-emerging-jobs.
www.simplyhired.com/blog/jobsearch/job-search-tips/top-10-emerging-careers/.
www.npr.org/templates/story/story.php?storyId=124251060.

affect careers at both the individual and the organizational level. Careers and organizations may become extinct or emerge due to these contextual influences. See Table 3.1 for some examples.

So what are these contextual influences? The *environment external to the organization* and *characteristics of the organization* will both significantly affect how career development is planned and implemented within an institution. Let's examine both of these influences more closely.

*External environment*: specific outside forces impacting career development include the following:

• *Technology* has influenced and will continue to influence careers and career development in a multitude of ways. Clearly, from the list offered in Table 3.1, one can see how careers often expire and emerge due to technological changes. Advances in technology can change how we work, when we work, and the speed at which we work. An article entitled "How Technology is Destroying Jobs" (Rotman, 2013) presented varying views from economists regarding the impact that technology has on jobs. While many believe that technological advances are eliminating jobs, others contend that technology simply allows for the creation of other employment opportunities. Among the issues discussed in this article is the contention "that technology is widening the income gap between the tech-savvy and everyone else" (para. 33). Clearly, decision makers within organizations must consider these issues and the implications for development of employees' careers. Lack of consideration of the impact of technology is likely to result in organization obsolescence.

- *Workforce demographics* have shifted dramatically in the last 30 years. Women constitute almost half of the labor force in many countries. For example in Australia, Canada, Israel, South Africa, and the US the percentage of women in the workplace ranges from 45.8 percent in Australia to 47.3 percent in Canada (Catalyst, 2014). Increasingly, immigrants are becoming a larger percentage of the workforce in developed countries (Guest & Rodrigues, 2012; Lyons, Ng, & Schweitzer, 2014). For example, in the US it is estimated that immigrants currently constitute approximately 16.4 percent of the labor force as compared to approximately 5 percent of the labor force in 1970 (Singer, 2012). Additionally, the workforce is becoming more diverse in terms of age. Many Western countries (e.g., the US, Canada, and Europe) are faced with an aging labor force (Lyons et al., 2014; Toossi, 2012).

  These are just three important demographic trends that will significantly impact career development efforts within an organization. These changes in demographics (as well as others not highlighted here) suggest that the workforce will have greater diversity in terms of career expectations and experiences, which will need to be addressed if organizations want to remain competitive and relevant (Lyons et al., 2014).

- The *economy* greatly influences career development efforts. Both Chapters 1 and 2 outline some of the ways in which economic trends have impacted careers. New career approaches (e.g., protean, boundaryless) have emerged due partly to economic changes, and the consequences of economic turmoil have resulted in many organizations abandoning their career development efforts (McDonald & Hite, 2005). The development of a knowledge-based economy and the move to greater globalization have significantly changed jobs, the knowledge and skills required for these jobs, and competition within firms to attract and retain talent (Guest & Rodrigues, 2012).

- *Industry trends* play an important role in how careers evolve. Whether one is in advertising, health care, banking, or farming, new regulations, new technology, and new knowledge will impact career development. DeFillippi, Arthur, & Lindsay (2006) pointed out that some industries are conducting most of their business virtually, citing the call-center, web-trading, and travel industry as examples. The transportation industry is likely to change as ride-sharing companies like Lyft and Sidecar become popular.

Career development efforts in organizations in those industries and others facing change will need to be tailored to meet employees' career needs and to remain competitive.

Competition within an industry can also influence career development. To survive in this type of climate, organizations will need to design career development initiatives that will enhance employees' skills and that will assist in retaining them.

- There are numerous *social and political issues* that impact careers and career development. The women's movement and the civil rights movement in the US are just two examples of social revolutions that resulted in massive change and continue to have an impact in the workplace, communities, and our homes. International conflicts, legislation, and political systems have affected work and careers for centuries. For example, World War II resulted in an influx of women into the workforce for a period of time; civil rights legislation has resulted in more career opportunities and access to career development for under-represented groups; and careers and career development in communist countries are very different than in democratic nations. For example, Skorikov and Vondracek (1993) described career development in the former Soviet Union as focused on "the attainment of collective goals" with no thought of "individual self-fulfillment." Inkson (2007), emphasizing the importance of examining career contexts, wrote:

  > In many countries, poverty and lack of economic opportunity might mean that contextual concepts that provide the backdrop assumed for career studies—for example, freedom of choice, free enterprise, open labor market, peace, occupation, profession, occupational choice, hierarchy, progress, personal development, full employment, and work ethic—might make Western concepts of career quite alien.
  >
  > (pp. 5–6)

*Organization* factors also need to be considered when planning and implementing career development. A number of characteristics can be influential: the size of the organization, the type of organization (e.g., non-profit/profit; industry type), and whether the organization is international are three that readily come to mind. We will focus on four organization influences:

- The *customs*, *culture*, and *core values* of the organization are important considerations. Organizational cultures can greatly influence employees' careers. Higgins (2005), in her analysis of the health care firm Baxter, characterized its culture as having a "sense of collective identity" and an "extreme pressure to perform." She concluded that

> this particular kind of strong culture, this "up-or-out" culture and the kinds of responsibilities that people at Baxter were given, fed into the kinds of capabilities that were developed— entrepreneurial capabilities that would prove useful later on in their careers.
>
> (p. 66)

- According to Brousseau et al. (1996), the *strategic direction* of the organization needs to be supported by the career culture and should shape the career culture. They identified four different organizational career cultures—linear, expert, spiral, and transitory—that might support various strategic directions. For example, they suggested that a transitory career culture (described as one involving frequent movement from one field or job to another) might work best when an organization is focused on new market creation. Career paths and the types of development opportunities provided to employees are likely to change based on the organization's strategy (Higgins, 2005).

- The *current employee base* will influence career development. Analysis of existing employees' competencies, knowledge, skills, and career goals is needed, as well as an assessment of future labor needs (Gilley et al., 2002; Gottfredson, 2005). For example, is the organization's labor force aging? If so, this will significantly impact a variety of career development initiatives and help determine future ones (e.g., succession planning, training and development offerings). While this factor may seem rather basic, Gottfredson (2005) pointed out that, often, systematic assessment of an organization's workforce has not been done, making it very difficult to establish effective career development practices.

- Finally, the *organization's history of career development* should be considered. How has career development been perceived in the past? Has it been viewed as a nice thing to do or as a core function of human resources (HR)? Has career development kept up with organizational and societal change? Is it perceived as a value-added system or a waste of time and resources? This historical perspective can be informative—particularly in assessing whether a career management system needs to be transformed or simply tweaked.

It also can provide a career development practitioner with a better understanding of resistance to efforts to transform a system.

This is not an exhaustive list of contextual influences on career development. And, while all of these factors potentially will affect career development efforts in an organization, some will have a greater impact than others. But consideration of the contextual elements that shape careers is essential in creating a practical and vibrant career development system.

## Developing a Career Development Strategy

Establishing an effective career development process must begin with the assessment of the contextual factors mentioned above. This assessment, as well as an analysis of resources available, is critical in determining the career development goals for the organization. While these goals will vary from organization to organization, some common career development objectives include:

- assisting employees in managing their careers;
- planning for leadership succession;
- identifying, matching, and assessing the talent within the organization;
- developing employees' competencies and knowledge;
- establishing plans for organizational disruptions that will impact careers (e.g., mergers, downsizing);
- retaining key personnel;
- recruiting and retaining a diverse workforce (Gottfredson, 2005; Kaye & Smith, 2012).

While HR is likely to lead this effort, it is important to have input from a variety of individuals who have a stake in career development:

- Top management, whose support for career development is needed for the process to thrive. These individuals are likely to be focused on the strategic direction of the organization, which can be beneficial in ensuring alignment between strategy and career development.
- Managers, who play a critical role by providing support and guidance to employees in developing their careers. Insightful managers are likely to understand their employees' career needs and trends within the industry that should be considered in developing a career development strategy.

- Employees who are charged with managing their careers. As Kaye, Cohen, & Crowell (2011) pointed out: "No longer can employees wait for career development to happen to them or for them. ... They pave the way by *taking charge of their careers*" (p. 164).

Also important in planning the direction of career development is to establish the evaluation processes that will be employed to determine the effectiveness of the initiatives developed (Gottfredson, 2005; Schutt, 2012). The specific measure to be assessed will be determined, based on the career development goals that have been established. It is reasonable to expect career development efforts to be evaluated at the organizational level as well as the individual level, since both the organization and the employees should benefit from career development and assume responsibility for career development (McDonald & Hite, 2005; Rothwell, Jackson, Knight, & Lindholm, 2005).

Evaluation should be done strategically as well—for example, it may be beneficial to evaluate a new initiative early in its existence to determine what is working and what is not going well. It may be beneficial to re-evaluate after improvements are made and again when it has been in operation long enough to assess its effectiveness. In other words, there will be considerable overlap among planning, implementing, and evaluating. All three processes should continually inform the others.

Most organizations will find it beneficial to assess the benefits that both the organization and individuals derive from career development systems (McDonald & Hite, 2005). While differing career development goals will result in varied evaluation criteria and measurements, organizations will benefit from involving all stakeholders and using both qualitative and quantitative approaches (Rothwell et al., 2005; Young & Valach, 1994). Additionally, organizational support mechanisms, which are critical to an effective career development system, need to be evaluated as well. These support systems will be explored in detail later in this chapter.

## Career Development System Components

When considering a career management system within an organization, often the programs and practices associated with the system become the focus. We believe this should be viewed as *one* element of a complex system. While a lot of emphasis is placed here, programs without consideration of two other elements simply will not be effective. Rather, practices and programs, as well as support mechanisms and individual employee characteristics, must be considered when developing a career development

*Table 3.2* Organizational Career Development Practices

| *Organizational career development practices:* |
| --- |
| Job postings |
| Career counseling |
| Tuition reimbursement/formal education |
| Career paths |
| Career ladders |
| Job rotations |
| Succession planning |
| Mentoring |
| Coaching |
| Career workshops |
| Pre-retirement planning/workshops |
| Assessment centers |
| Training |
| Performance appraisals |
| Orientation programs |
| Expatriation/repatriation |
| Action learning |
| Project-based learning |
| Special assignments |
| Networking |
| Written materials/websites on career issues |

Sources: Baruch & Peiperl (2000); Eby, Allen, et al. (2005).

system. Let's begin by discussing the most popular element, the practices and programs that are relevant to the career development of employees.

### Career Development Practices and Programs

There are a number of career practices frequently used by organizations to accomplish career development goals. Common ones are included in Table 3.2.

Some scholars have created taxonomies or categories of practices as a means of examining how connected HR practices correlate with certain organizational outcomes (Baruch & Peiperl, 2000; Eby, Allen, & Brinley, 2005). These taxonomies can also serve as a best practice, as Baruch and Peiperl described:

> HR managers and others charged with managing careers in organizations should develop career systems as actual *systems*: that is, as sets of practices which naturally fit together and are appropriate to the organization's stage of development, form, and/or industry.
>
> (p. 360)

Eby, Allen, et al. (2005) explained that organizations have a tendency to arrange HR practices into "integrated packages that reinforce the organization's culture and strategy" (p. 568).

Baruch and Peiperl (2000) surveyed managers in the UK to determine what career development practices were commonly employed in their organizations. Through factor analysis, they developed five major factors or clusters of organizational career management practices. The five groups included:

- *Basic*: those most frequently used practices such as job postings, pre-retirement programs, and lateral moves.
- *Active planning*: practices that require active organizational involvement and plans to develop employees. These practices include performance appraisals, career counseling, and succession planning.
- *Active management*: practices that have an "informational element" such as assessment centers, formal mentoring, and career workshops.
- *Formal*: practices in which the organization offers formalized information (usually downward) to assist in career development. These practices include written personal career plans, dual career ladder, and written materials designed to inform employees about career opportunities.
- *Multi-directional*: practices designed to provide employees with feedback to assist in their development. Peer appraisals and upward appraisals are included in this cluster (Baruch & Peiperl, 2000).

In another study examining career management practices and career attitudes, practices were "bundled" in the following manner:

- *Career planning and exploration*: included the practices of career planning workshops and formal mentoring programs.
- *Future strategic planning*: succession planning and outplacement were the practices that comprised this factor.
- *Internal labor market information*: this bundle consisted of individual career counseling, career ladders/paths, and job postings.
- *Formal external training*: this included external training programs and tuition reimbursement.
- *Informal internal training*: in-house training and pre-retirement workshops were the practices comprising this factor (Eby et al., 2005).

*Table 3.3* Individual Development Practices

| Practice | Formal | Informal | External | Internal |
|---|---|---|---|---|
| Mentoring | X | X | X | X |
| Coaching | X | X | X | X |
| Networking | X | X | X | X |
| Education/Tuition Reimbursement | X | | X | |
| Training | X | X | X | X |
| Job assignments/rotations | X | X | X | X |
| Volunteering | X | X | X | |
| Career Counseling | X | X | X | X |

While both of these taxonomies are useful in considering broad categories of practices to consider, they may be too limiting, particularly since the nature of careers has changed significantly. Most of the practices included in these two studies are traditional practices that have been employed in organizations for a number of years. To remain relevant, organizations may need to adopt more innovative practices to support and achieve career development goals. As a result, we suggest two broad categories of practices: organizational strategic career development practices and individual development practices. Individual development practices can be further categorized as being internal or external to the organization and informal or formal. The category "organizational strategic practices" would include, for example: succession planning, career ladders and paths, job posting systems, and outplacement services. Individual development practices would consist of activities such as mentoring, coaching, and training (see Table 3.3 for a more complete listing).

Most of these practices could potentially be both informal and formal and be delivered external to the organization or internally. For example, a lot of training practices are formal—meaning that they have been carefully prepared, offered with a particular set of goals in mind to a specific group, delivered face to face or on-line, and may include specific follow-up and evaluative processes. However, a great deal of training is also done on the job in a just-in-time manner; in other words, it is much more informal in terms of development and delivery. Additionally, many organizations provide a lot of formal and informal training internally, but encourage external training opportunities as well.

When considering who benefits or the outcome of these practices, a Venn diagram may be useful (Figure 3.2). While some practices may

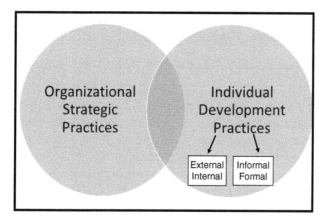

*Figure 3.2* Career Development Practices and Programs

help the organization or the individual more, both parties are likely to profit from many of the activities. Also, there is quite a bit of overlap in terms of the activities themselves. For example, a successful succession plan usually involves several of the individual development practices as ways to ensure that individuals have the capabilities needed to assume leadership positions.

There are a variety of factors to weigh in determining which of these potential practices to employ. The contextual factors discussed earlier in this chapter must be considered. For example, Baruch and Peiperl (2000) found that active planning activities (e.g., career counseling and succession planning) correlated with organizations having dynamic, open, and proactive climates. So organizational culture and climate will influence the practices employed. Information regarding employees might be utilized to determine practices. Baruch and Sullivan (2008) discussed the importance of considering the various career needs of a diverse workforce and suggested different practices for individuals with certain career orientations. Baruch (2003) offered a normative model that practitioners might use to analyze career systems. His six dimensions could be used as criteria to determine practices to employ and to evaluate continued use. The dimensions are:

1. organizational involvement to enact a specific career practice
2. sophistication and complexity of a career practice
3. strategic orientation of the practice

4. developmental focus of the practice
5. the relevance of the practice to organizational decision-making
6. the innovativeness of the practice (p. 239).

It is up to the organization to determine the criteria/contextual factors that will be most critical in determining the career development practices. It is essential that some assessment is conducted that goes beyond "let's do this latest fad." As Baruch pointed out: "practices should not be applied in a vacuum, as individual, stand-alone activities, but rather comprise an integrative career system" (p. 232).

A well planned and effectively developed set of practices can result in a positive impact on employees and organizations. Career development initiatives have been found to contribute to individual career success (Maurer & Chapman, 2013), career attitudes (Eby, Allen, et al., 2005), employee commitment, and career advancement (De Vos, Dewettinck, & Buyens, 2009). More detailed information regarding these practices is provided in Chapters 4 and 5.

### Support Mechanisms

Organizations need to provide a variety of support mechanisms to assist employees' career development efforts. To determine what support mechanisms are needed, it may be useful to first consider the challenges that individuals encounter in developing their careers. These challenges or barriers can significantly affect an individual's perception of his/her career progress, development, and satisfaction (Ng & Feldman, 2014; Van der Sluis & Poell, 2003). A lot of the research on career barriers has emerged from studies examining women's career development (Lent, Brown, & Hackett, 2000), particularly in professions such as medicine, law, management, academia, and engineering. London (1998) identified a number of organizational/environmental barriers (e.g., poor supervision, organizational change, multi-role conflict, limited opportunities) as well as individual barriers (e.g., traits, motivation, skill level, age, gender, race). Some challenges are not easily addressed through organizational initiatives. For example, low motivation or experiencing physical decline in certain professions are challenges that are less likely to receive attention when determining how the organization can support employees' career development. And some (e.g., lack of skill) can be addressed through the practices and programs discussed in the previous section. From that perspective, career development practices are a form of support. However, we wish to focus on those sources of support that will increase the likelihood that employees will engage in career development practices and programs. Specifically, five organizational support mechanisms will be highlighted: policies and reward structures, work–life initiatives, inclusive work environment, supervisory support, and a continuous organizational learning culture.

- *Policies and reward structures*: these structures need to serve both to encourage employees to be active participants in career development efforts and to minimize barriers to participation. Baruch and Sullivan (2008) argued for getting rid of "outdated evaluation and reward systems" and replacing them with innovative policies and reward structures that offer a variety of choices that meet the diverse needs of today's workforce. They also pointed out that many benefits— such as creative work arrangements, flexible work practices or arrangements (FWPs/FWAs), leave, etc.—have become a necessity for organizations to recruit and retain highly performing workers.
- *Work–life initiatives*: work–family issues have a profound influence on employees' careers. Numerous studies have found that women's career choices, aspirations, patterns, satisfaction, and success are affected by family conflicts and/or the desire for balance between family and work (see for example, Eby, Casper, Lockwood, Bordeaux, & Brinley, 2005; Hite & McDonald, 2003; Martins, Eddleston, & Veiga, 2002). However, women and men alike are affected by work–family issues and desire support to minimize the conflicts that they encounter. Increasingly organizations are responding by implementing flexible work practices or arrangements and offering dependent care and other benefits to help employees negotiate career and family obligations. Given the importance of work–life concerns on career development, a more complete discussion of work–life issues is provided in Chapter 7.
- *Inclusive work environment*: employees from under-represented groups (e.g., individuals with disabilities, people of color, GLBT —gay, lesbian, bisexual, transgender people) often experience barriers in the development of their careers (Niles & Harris-Bowlsbey, 2013). A host of societal, cultural, and organizational norms, biases and stereotypes, and practices often result in under-represented employees being denied access to opportunities that may be necessary to experience career success. There are a number of ways in which organizations can create a more inclusive work environment which will be discussed in Chapter 6.
- *Supervisory support*: There is evidence suggesting that supervisors play a critical role in employees' career development (van der Heijden,

2003; van der Heijden, 2002; van der Rijt, Van den Bossche, van de Wiel, Segers, & Gijselaers, 2012; Van der Sluis & Poell, 2003; Wayne, Liden, Kraimer, & Graf, 1999). Lack of supervisory support has been found to negatively affect employees' subjective feelings of career success (Ng & Feldman, 2014). Supervisors are important, particularly since they are likely to observe, provide feedback on, evaluate, and reward employees' performance. There are a number of ways that supervisors can assist in their employees' career development. Some examples are provided in the box below.

## Ways Supervisors Can Support and Develop Employees' Careers

1. Provide high quality feedback.
2. Be knowledgeable about development opportunities, inform employees of these opportunities, and provide access to these career development programs, practices, and resources.
3. Encourage employees to participate in internal and external networks.
4. Work with individual employees, help identify their development needs.
5. Consider both individuals' present career needs as well as their future.
6. Offer opportunities for employees to apply new skills and knowledge.
7. Create an environment where employees are allowed to take risks and make mistakes.
8. Look beyond formal programs to develop employees. Create stretch assignments, job rotations, shadowing opportunities, and special projects to help employees grow and develop in their careers.
9. Be aware of the barriers that employees may encounter in developing their careers (e.g., work–family conflicts, lack of resources, organizational change) and consider ways of assisting employees in overcoming these obstacles.
10. Provide rewards and recognition for career-related activities such as developing new skills, achieving goals, or taking on a challenge at work.

Sources: Brown (2010); London (1998); van der Heijden (2002); van der Rijt et al. (2012)

Managers will not necessarily know how to perform the roles of coach, counselor, and consultant for employees' career development. So opportunities need to be provided to assist supervisors so that they can better serve their employees. HRD initiatives such as training, coaching, and mentoring managers will help them develop the coaching, counseling, and communication skills necessary to be effective developers (Tansky & Cohen, 2001; Wayne et al., 1999).

Additionally, managers need to be evaluated on their abilities to develop employees and be rewarded for their efforts (London, 1998). Without these support mechanisms in place, supervisor support for career development will be less likely to occur and will be potentially ineffective where it does exist.

- *Continuous learning culture*: Organizations that offer a variety of career development practices and the support mechanisms listed above are likely to be perceived as having a culture that promotes continuous learning. Scholars have advocated for a continuous learning culture, suggesting that this type of environment can help in the transfer of learning (Egan, Yang, & Bartlett, 2004; Tracey, Tannenbaum, & Kavanagh, 1995), assist in fostering self-directed career strategies by employees (Park & Rothwell, 2009), and stimulate informal feedback-seeking behaviors, which can be important to employees, particularly in the early stages of their careers (van der Rijt et al., 2012).

There is a great deal of overlap between these support mechanisms. For example, many policies supportive of career development center around work–life issues. Supervisors can play an important role in helping with work–family conflicts that might interfere with one's career. In addition, all four rely on communication to be effective support mechanisms. Employees and managers must be aware of policies, reward structures, and work–life initiatives offered by the organization that may assist in their career development (Kraimer, Seibert, Wayne, Liden, & Bravo, 2011). Supervisory support relies heavily on managers' communication skills and the relationships that they have built with their employees. Finally, communication is an essential ingredient of a continuous learning culture. Marsick and Watkins's (1999) dimensions of a learning organization—1. create continuous learning opportunities; 2. promote inquiry and dialogue; 3. encourage collaboration and team learning; 4. establish systems to capture and share learning; 5. empower people toward a collective vision; 6. connect the organization to its environment; and 7. provide strategic leadership for learning—clearly suggest that communication is an important foundation in all these dimensions.

It is also important that fairness issues be considered regarding these support mechanisms (Guest & Rodrigues, 2012). Wooten and Cobb (1999) wrote:

By its very nature, CD involves basic issues of fairness over the allocation of CD resources, the policies and procedures used to decide who receives them, and the interactions between those who provide and those who not only receive CD rewards but also experience its losses.

(p. 173)

The literature on women and under-represented groups clearly indicates that fairness needs to be addressed in developing career development systems. For example, lack of access to opportunities such as mentors and networks is often cited as a reason for the glass ceiling (Elacqua, Beehr, Hansen, & Webster, 2009). Many organizations choose to concentrate their career development efforts on their professional and technical staffs, as well as their managerial employees, often leaving their hourly and less skilled workers to fend for themselves (Gutteridge, Leibowitz, & Shore, 1993). See Chapter 6 for more information on the disparate treatment of women's and under-represented groups' career development.

Managing perceptions of fairness does not mean that employees have to necessarily be treated the same. As Rousseau (2005) pointed out, "workers as individuals don't always want the same things. Moreover, it is often impractical for employers to offer the same things to everyone" (p. x). Rewards, for example, can be distributed based on different "rules"—one might apply an "equality" rule, where everyone receives the same outcome; an "equity" rule, which allows for differing amounts based on differences, such as performance; or an "individual need" rule, which distributes outcomes based on particular need such as flexible working hours to handle childcare issues (Bowen & Ostroff, 2004, p. 213). All of these practices could be perceived as fair if the rules are clearly explained and understood, and employees understand how decisions are made (Bowen & Ostroff, 2004). Allowing and using input regarding policies, rewards, work–life initiatives, etc. is another way to increase employees' perceptions that organization-sponsored career development is fair and just (Bowen & Ostroff, 2004; Rousseau, 2005). A specific way of providing voice regarding career development efforts is through idiosyncratic deals (see box for additional information).

### I-DEALS: Idiosyncratic Deals

According to Denise Rousseau, most formal employment arrangements are not complete; it is virtually impossible for supervisors, employees, and HR to anticipate all of the roles, responsibilities, needs, and demands that may arise during an employee's tenure with an organization. As a result, employees may seek out and negotiate special employment arrangements, which Rousseau has labeled "i-deals." She defines them as "voluntary, personalized agreements of a nonstandard nature that individual employees negotiate with their employers regarding terms that benefit them both" (Rousseau, 2005, p. 8).

While i-deals can vary both in scope and content, the two most common forms are flexible scheduling arrangements of work hours and special opportunities to develop skills and/or careers (Hornung, Rousseau, & Glaser, 2008).

While i-deals can create a mutually beneficial situation for employees and their employers, they can be controversial. Often they are viewed as a way to reward performance and to help an employee in need. However, third parties (usually co-workers) may view the arrangement as unjust and a demonstration of favoritism. These concerns should be carefully considered when i-deals are negotiated. According to Rousseau (2005):

> Despite the potential within-group friction, idiosyncratic arrangements can be seen as fair by their parties, *if* steps are taken to appropriately differentiate i-deals from other arrangements that are patently unjust and self-serving. Differentiating i-deals from favoritism and illicit arrangements is important to protect coworkers, the employer, and the i-dealer from the potentially negative consequences that poorly implemented i-deals can have.
>
> (p. 12)

### *Individual Characteristics*

This chapter is about organizational career development. However, organization-sponsored programs, practices, and support will not be effective unless individuals are motivated and active participants in the process. Because effective career development is a collaborative process, it is critical to include characteristics of the individual employee in this framework.

Traits such as conscientiousness, extroversion, and proactivity have been found to be predictors of career success (Maurer & Chapman, 2013; Ng, Eby, Sorensen, & Feldman, 2005), whereas traits such as neuroticism and low core self-evaluation have been found to be negatively related to career success (Ng et al., 2005; Ng & Feldman, 2014). While it is important to recognize the important role that traits play in individuals' career success, other characteristics may be more susceptible to change. In other words, organizational practices and support mechanisms may influence the development of these individual characteristics, which will then influence individual career success. We will focus on four of these characteristics.

One of these characteristics is *career self-management* which involves the individual taking control of his/her career and being self-reliant and in control of decisions and plans regarding one's career (De Vos et al., 2009; Sturges, Guest, Conway, & Davey, 2002). King (2004) proposed three important behaviors associated with career self-management:

- Positioning behavior, which involves having the contacts, skills, and the experience to accomplish career goals.
- Influence behavior, which is focused on influencing the decisions of "key gatekeepers" (e.g., immediate supervisors, mentors, senior managers) who affect careers.
- Boundary management, which is concerned with handling the boundaries between home and work.

Self-management has been positively linked with perceptions of career success, but studies have determined that it should not be considered as a substitute for organizational career development (De Vos et al., 2009; Sturges et al. 2002). Employees demonstrating high levels of career self-management expect the organization to provide career development practices (De Vos et al. 2009). Additionally, these self-management skills may enhance their ability to access sources of career support within the organization (Sturges et al., 2002). Both career self-management skills and organizational support for career development is likely to result in successful outcomes for both employees and the organization.

The turbulent career landscape has resulted in literature advocating that individuals develop resiliency, adaptability, and employability skills related to their careers. *Career resiliency* is "the ability to adapt to change, even when the circumstances are discouraging or disruptive" (London, 1997, p. 34). The presence of barriers such as age, family demands, low self-confidence, inflexibility on the part of the organization, and financial issues suggest that one needs to demonstrate resiliency to overcome them (Bimrose & Hearne, 2012). There are certain traits associated with resiliency. For example, individuals who are tenacious and determined, goal oriented, and have an internal locus of control are likely to be resilient (Bimrose & Hearne, 2012; Rickwood, Roberts, Batten, Marshall, & Massie, 2004). They also are likely be characterized as doing the following:

> People who are high in resilience need to achieve, believe in their ability to make positive things happen, feel they are able to control events, are willing to take reasonable risks, need to establish why

things happen to them, and are willing to search for negative feedback about themselves and the (sic) their interpretations of events.

(London, 1998, p. xx)

Individuals can develop career resiliency. Many career development practices listed earlier in this chapter can foster career resiliency. For example, career counselors can assist clients in learning coping skills, developing self-awareness, and creating a career action plan (Rickwood et al., 2004). Waterman, Waterman, & Collard (1994) offered a number of ways to create a "career-resilient workforce," recommending that organizations create a system where employees assess their competencies and interests, benchmark their skills consistently, and ensure that they have the skills necessary to remain competitive. More information on resiliency is provided in Chapter 7.

Related to career resiliency is the concept *career adaptability*, which is "the readiness to cope with the predictable tasks of preparing for and participating in the work role and with the unpredictable adjustments prompted by changes in work and working conditions" (Savickas, 1997, p. 254). While both resiliency and adaptability focus on handling change, adaptability is often considered a more "proactive" approach to handling career change (Bimrose & Hearne, 2012). There are four resources and strategies (4Cs) used by individuals to handle "tasks, transitions, and traumas as they construct their careers" (Savickas, 2013, p. 158). These are:

- *Concern* about the future and how to prepare and plan for it. Competence in career planning may be demonstrated.
- *Control*, which allows individuals to take responsibility for their future. Decisive decision making will be evident.
- *Curiosity*, which stimulates individuals to explore future roles and situations. This will prompt a thorough, realistic view of themselves and their career options.
- *Confidence* to pursue their career goals and aspirations. This may be demonstrated through engaging in problem solving when faced with a career obstacle (Koen, Klehe, & Van Vianen, 2012; Savickas, 2013; Savickas & Porfeli, 2012).

The Career Adapt-Abilities Scale (CAAS) has been created to measure these four dimensions (Porfeli & Savickas, 2012; Savickas & Porfeli, 2012). International forms of this scale have been constructed and researchers from various countries have both validated and used it to investigate the relationship between career adaptability and a variety of other variables (Savickas & Porfeli, 2012).

There is evidence suggesting that career adaptability is malleable and that training can enhance individuals' adaptability. Training designed to address the 4Cs enhanced university graduates' career adaptability. The training participants also reported higher employment quality than those who had not attended the training (Koen et al., 2012). More information regarding how the training was designed can be found in the box below.

---

### Training Career Adaptability

Koen et al. (2012) were interested in determining whether training could increase university graduates' career adaptability and if training could assist participants in finding suitable employment. Recent graduates with bachelor's or master's degrees from a large university in the Netherlands were the participants in this study. A control group was employed as well.

The training involved a one-day (8.5 hours) workshop, structured in the following way:

- Introduction: explained the relevance of the training and asked participant to reflect on their career preparation.
- Section 1, Knowing the self: focused on understanding participants' values. Two activities were employed. The first was a card-sort exercise, where participants chose cards with career-relevant values to get them to hone in on what is important to them. The second activity was a job interview in which the participants, working in pairs, interviewed each other regarding their knowledge, skills, and abilities.
- Section 2, Knowing the environment: focused on an activity that asked trainees to "visualize an ideal working day in order to explore career interests and decide upon career options" (p. 400). Another exercise involved a discussion of information-seeking strategies employed to meet career goals.
- Section 3, Implementation (general): participants were asked to create a general plan, using information gained from the exercise completed above.
- Section 4, Implementation (concrete): trainees developed specific and concrete actions and goals to help them accomplish their plan.

The first two sections focused on enhancing participants' curiosity—one of the 4Cs identified by Savickas (1997) as a career adaptability strategy. The last two sections aimed at facilitating concern (planning for the future) and control (taking responsibility for the future). Throughout the training reflection, individualized feedback, role modeling, and written exercises were employed to reinforce learning.

Findings: the training group increased their career adaptability (specifically career concern, curiosity, and control) following training and six months after the training. More difference between the control group and the training group was found at six months on curiosity and control. Additionally, at the six-month follow-up, training participants who had found employment reported higher quality employment than those in the control group (e.g., job satisfaction, lower turnover intentions, career success).

Source: Koen et al. (2012)

The final individual characteristic we want to highlight is *employability* which "refers to an employee's capacity and willingness to remain attractive in the labour market" (Carbery & Garavan, 2005, p. 493). According to Fugate, Kinicki, & Ashforth (2004) it is a "psycho-social construct" consisting of three dimensions:

- career identity, which can serve as a "compass"—providing direction and motivation in pursuing career goals.
- personal adaptability, which suggests flexibility and an openness to change and to learning.
- social and human capital investments such as networking (social), work experience, and education (human capital) that enhance one's career opportunities (Fugate et al., 2004).

Fugate et al. (2004) acknowledged that, while each of these dimensions are distinct and often studied and considered as independent constructs, it is the three of them "in concert" that create "employability" (p. 18).

Many of the career development practices discussed in this chapter can increase employees' employability. Clarke and Patrickson (2008) recommended that organizations help employees develop skills that are needed in most jobs—such as communication skills, problem solving, and decision-making capabilities. There is a risk that organizations that promote employability may lose members of their workforce. However, the perception of an "employability culture" characterized as an organization that encourages experimentation, job changes, and skill broadening was found to be negatively related to turnover intention (Nauta, van Vianen, van der Heijden, van Dam, & Willemsen, 2009). Paradoxically, Nauta et al.'s "results suggest that organizations can retain their employees just by creating opportunities that facilitate leaving" (p. 247).

### Career Development Outcomes

Finally, strategic career development must involve a consideration of the outcomes that can be achieved through a strong system. Since an effective system requires both employee and organization involvement and commitment, it seems logical that the intended outcomes benefit both parties. Therefore, individual-level outcomes include both *objective and subjective career success*. In Chapter 2 it was noted that objective indicators of positive career outcomes would include salary, promotions, and occupational status. While these indicators are important to many individuals, some employees are more interested in how their capabilities and careers help others, or experiencing balance in terms of work and family responsibilities, or having a career that allows for flexibility and autonomy. These would be considered subjective indicators of career success. Many individuals are interested in and desire both forms of these positive career outcomes, and often objective success will impact subjective career success and vice versa.

Several of the factors included in this strategic career development framework have been found to influence career success. For example, supervisory support can influence employees' subjective career success (Ng & Feldman, 2014; Wayne et al., 1999) as well as objective career success indicators such as salary progression (Wayne et al., 1999). Career practices, such as providing training opportunities, can have a long-term impact on career success, particularly if the support is offered early in employees' careers and continues over time (Maurer & Chapman, 2013). Individual characteristics such as career self-management and career adaptability positively influence subjective career success (De Vos et al., 2009; Zacher, 2014). Career success is an important goal and outcome of career development. As a result, a lot of research has been done examining predictors and variables that impact it. More information regarding career success is included in other chapters of this book.

There has been less research done looking at the impact that career development has had on organizational outcomes. The focus of many career researchers and practitioners has been on the individual rather than the organization (Egan, Upton, & Lynham, 2006). The vocational perspective (e.g., career counseling) has traditionally concentrated on individual outcomes (Inkson & King, 2011), and the current emphasis on employees managing their own careers has resulted in less attention on benefits to the organization.

We propose two categories of organizational outcomes resulting from a strategic career development system: *talent retention* and *competitive advantage*. These are very broad categories—most organizations will want to be more specific as to what they want to achieve in terms of outcomes. More precise outcomes will facilitate clearer ways to assess results and determine the effectiveness of the system.

However, most specific outcomes are likely to fall within these two broad-based groupings.

Organizations are likely to experience positive results for their career development efforts if they are done well. There is evidence linking employees' perceptions of organizational support for their development to their affective commitment to the organization (De Vos et al., 2009; Lee & Bruvold, 2003), higher job performance (Kraimer et al., 2011), job satisfaction (Lee & Bruvold, 2003), and employee engagement (Shuck, Twyford, Reio, Jr., & Shuck, 2014). Research also provides support for the notion that career development efforts can impact retention efforts (e.g., Kraimer et al., 2011; Lee & Bruvold, 2003; Peterson, 2009; Shuck et al., 2014). Retaining talent has been identified as a major concern for many companies. A well integrated career development system can be very valuable in helping to address this issue (Kaye & Smith, 2012).

According to Kraimer et al. (2011), employees need to perceive high levels of both organizational support for development and career opportunities for the organization to reap the benefits of higher job performance and lower turnover rates. And Shuck et al. (2014) advised that organizations must go beyond simply promoting their development efforts. They wrote: "It is not about having a robust

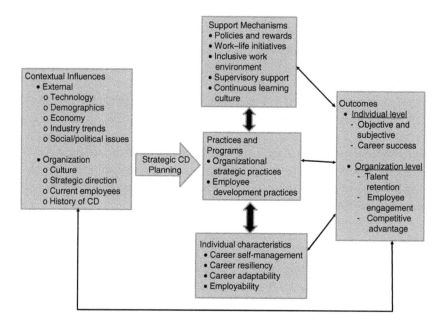

*Figure 3.3* Framework for Organizational Career Development Expanded

offering of programs and colorful catalogues within a corporate learning and development function—it is equally about employees' (sic) perceiving equal access to and support for their involvement in those activities" (p. 263).

A career development system that includes consideration of contextual factors, as well as practices that develop individuals and enhance important HR strategies, and that offers additional mechanisms to promote and support career development will result in organizational success. Many employees will want to remain, and their commitment, productivity, and engagement will result in a highly performing firm. As Lee & Bruvold (2003) concluded:

> If sustained competitive advantage is what most organizations are looking for, then one way to achieve it is through sustained employee development. Not only do such programmes enhance the well-being of individual employees by providing benefits such as skill acquisition and career development, they may also enhance the organization's productivity. In fact, investing in employee development may create a dynamic relationship where employees may work harder because they have a greater sense of job satisfaction and commitment to the organization.
>
> (p. 994)

## Summary

This chapter has provided a framework to employ when creating, modifying, and implementing a career development system within an organization. A more complete listing of the various factors needing consideration is provided in Figure 3.3. Career development is a process that will be influenced by a number of factors, hence a stable, linear process is unlikely. Rather, all of the elements included in this framework have the potential to impact each other. This dynamic process requires adept, knowledgeable career development practitioners working collaboratively with employees and management to ensure that the system meets the needs of everyone involved.

## References

Baruch, Y. (2003). Career systems in transition: A normative model for organizational career practices. *Personnel Review, 32*(2), 231–251.

Baruch, Y. (2006). Career development in organizations and beyond: Balancing traditional and contemporary viewpoints. *Human Resource Management Review, 16*, 125–138.

Strategic Career Development     63

Baruch, Y. & Peiperl, M. (2000). Career management practices: An empirical survey and implications. *Human Resource Management, 39*(4), 347–366.

Baruch, Y. & Sullivan, S. E. (2008). Career development processes in organizations. In R. J. Burke & C. L. Cooper (Eds.), *Building more effective organizations: HR management and performance in practice* (pp. 183–206). Cambridge: Cambridge University Press.

Bimrose, J. & Hearne, L. (2012). Resilience and career adaptability: Qualitative studies of adult career counseling. *Journal of Vocational Behavior, 81*, 338–344.

Bowen, D. E. & Ostroff, C. (2004). Understanding HRM–firm performance linkages: The role of the "strength" of the HRM system. *Academy of Management Review, 29*(2), 203–221.

Brousseau, K. R., Driver, M. J., Eneroth, K., & Larsson, R. (1996). Career pandemonium: Realigning organizations and individuals. *Academy of Management Executive, 10*(4), 52–66.

Brown, P. T. (2010, April). Having their backs: Improving managers' skills in developing others. *T+D*, 60–64.

Carbery, R. & Garavan, T. N. (2005). Organisational restructuring and downsizing: Issues related to learning, training and employability of survivors. *Journal of European Industrial Training, 29*(6), 488–508.

Catalyst (2014). % Knowledge Center: women in labor force in Australia, Canada, Israel, South Africa, and United States. Retrieved from www.catalyst.org/knowledge/women-labor-force-australia-canada-israel-south-africa-and-united-states.

Clarke, M. & Patrickson, M. (2008). The new covenant of employability. *Employee Relations, 30*(2), 121–141.

DeFillippi, R. J., Arthur, M. B., & Lindsay, V. J. (2006). *Knowledge at work: Creative collaboration in the global economy.* Malden, MA: Blackwell Publishing.

De Vos, A., Dewettinck, K., & Buyens, D. (2009). The professional career on the right track: A study on the interaction between career self-management and organizational career management in explaining employee outcomes. *European Journal of Work and Organizational Psychology, 18*(1), 55–80.

Doyle, M. (2000). Managing careers in organisations. In A. Collin & R. A. Young (Eds.), *The future of careers* (pp. 228–242). Cambridge: Cambridge University Press.

Eby, L. T., Allen, T. D., & Brinley, A. (2005). A cross-level investigation of the relationship between career management practices and career-related attitudes. *Group & Organization Management, 30*(6), 565–596.

Eby, L. T., Casper, W. J., Lockwood, A., Bordeaux, C., & Brinley, A. (2005). Work and family research in IO/OB: Content analysis and review of the literature (1980–2002). *Journal of Vocational Behavior, 66*, 124–187.

Edwards, R. (1979) *Contested terrain.* New York: Basic Books, Inc.

Egan, T. M., Upton, M. G., & Lynham, S. A. (2006). Career development: Load-bearing wall or window dressing? Exploring definitions, theories, and prospects for HRD-related theory building. *Human Resource Development Review*, *5*(4), 442–477.

Egan, T. M., Yang, B., & Bartlett, K. R. (2004). The effects of organizational learning culture and job satisfaction on motivation to transfer learning and turnover intention. *Human Resource Development Quarterly*, *15*, 279–301.

Elacqua, T. C., Beehr, T. A., Hansen, C. P., & Webster, J. (2009). Managers' beliefs about the glass ceiling: Interpersonal and organizational factors. *Psychology of Women Quarterly*, *33*, 285–294.

Fugate, M., Kinicki, A. J., & Ashforth, B. E. (2004). Employability: A psycho-social construct, its dimensions, and applications. *Journal of Vocational Behavior*, *65*, 14–38.

Gilley, J. W., Eggland, S. A., & Gilley, A. M. (2002). *Principles of human resource development*. Cambridge: Perseus Books.

Gottfredson, G. D. (2005). Career development in organizations. In W. B. Walsh & M. L. Savickas (Eds.), *Handbook of vocational psychology: Theory, research, and practice* (pp. 297–318). Mahwah, NJ: Lawrence Erlbaum Associates.

Greenhaus, J. H., Callanan, G. A., & Godshalk, V. M. (2010), *Career management*. Los Angeles, CA: Sage.

Guest, D. E. & Rodrigues, R. (2012). Can the organizational career survive? An evaluation within a social exchange perspective. In L. M. Shore, J. A-M. Coyle-Shapiro, & L. E. Tetrick (Eds.), *The employee–organization relationship: Applications for the 21st century* (pp. 193–222). New York: Routledge, Taylor & Francis Group.

Gutteridge, T. G., Leibowitz, Z. B., & Shore, J. E. (1993). *Organizational career development*. San Francisco, CA: Jossey-Bass.

Higgins, M. (2005). *Career Imprints: Creating leaders across an industry.* San Francisco, CA: Jossey-Bass.

Hite, L. M. & McDonald, K. S. (2003). Career aspirations of non-managerial women: Adjustment and adaptation. *Journal of Career Development*, *29*(4), 221–235.

Hornung, S., Rousseau, D. M., & Glaser, J. (2008). Creating flexible work arrangements through idiosyncratic deals. *Journal of Applied Psychology*, *93*, 655–664.

Inkson, K. (2007). *Understanding careers: The metaphors of working life.* Thousand Oaks, CA: Sage.

Inkson, K. & King, Z. (2011). Contested terrain in careers: A psychological contract model. *Human Relations*, *64*, 37–57.

Kaye, B., Cohen, J., & Crowell, B. (2011). Career development: Encompassing all employees. In L. A. Berger & D. R. Berger (Eds.), *The talent management handbook* (2nd edn.) (pp. 159–168). New York: McGraw-Hill Companies.

Kaye, B. & Smith, C. P. (2012, January). Career development: Shifting from nicety to necessity. *T+D*, 52–55.

King, Z. (2004). Career self-management: Its nature, causes and consequences. *Journal of Vocational Behavior, 65*, 112–133.

Koen, J., Klehe, U. C., & Van Vianen, A. E. M. (2012). Training career adaptability to facilitate a successful school-to-work transition. *Journal of Vocational Behavior, 81*, 395–408.

Kraimer, M. L., Seibert, S. E., Wayne, S. J., Liden, R. C., & Bravo, J. (2011). Antecedents and outcomes of organizational support for development: The critical role of career opportunities. *Journal of Applied Psychology, 96*(3), 485–500.

Lee, C. H. & Bruvold, N. T. (2003). Creating value for employees: Investment in employee development. *The International Journal of Human Resource Management, 14*(6), 981–1000.

Lent, R. W., Brown, S. D., & Hackett, G. (2000). Contextual supports and barriers to career choice: A social cognitive analysis. *Journal of Counseling Psychology, 47*, 36–49.

London, M. (1997). Overcoming career barriers: A model of cognitive and emotional processes for realistic appraisal and constructive coping. *Journal of Career Development, 24*, 25–38.

London, M. (1998). *Career barriers: How people experience, overcome, and avoid failure*. Mahwah, NJ: Lawrence Erlbaum Associates, Inc.

Lyons, S. T., Ng, E. S., & Schweitzer, L. (2014). Changing demographics and shifting nature of careers: Implications for research and human resource development. *Human Resource Development Review, 13*(2), 181–206.

McDonald, K. S. & Hite, L. M. (2005). Reviving the relevance of career development in human resource development. *Human Resource Development Review, 4*(4), 418–439. doi: 10.1177/1534484305281006.

McDonald, K. S. & Hite, L. M. (2015). Career development in the context of HRD: Challenges and considerations. In R. F. Poell, T. S. Rocco, & G. L. Roth (Eds.), *The Routledge companion to human resource development* (pp. 67–77). London: Routledge.

Marsick, V. J. & Watkins, K. E. (1999). *Facilitating learning organizations: Making learning count*. Brookfield, VT: Gower.

Martins, L. L., Eddleston, K. A., & Veiga, J. F. (2002). Moderators of the relationship between work–family conflict and career satisfaction. *Academy of Management Journal, 45*(2), 399–409.

Maurer, T. J. & Chapman, E. F. (2013). Ten years of career success in relation to individual and situational variables from the employee development literature. *Journal of Vocational Behavior, 83*, 450–465.

Nauta, A., van Vianen, A., van der Heijden, B., van Dam, K., & Willemsen, M. (2009). Understanding the factors that promote employability orientation: The impact of employability culture, career satisfaction, and role breadth self-efficacy. *Journal of Occupational and Organizational Psychology, 82*, 233–251.

Niles, S. G. & Harris-Bowlsbey, J. E. (2013). *Career development interventions in the 21st century* (4th edn.). Boston, MA: Pearson.

Ng, T. W. H., Eby, L. T., Sorensen, K. L., & Feldman, D. C. (2005). Predictors of objective and subjective career success: A meta-analysis. *Personnel Psychology, 58*(2), 367–408.

Ng, T. W. H. & Feldman, D. C. (2014). Subjective career success: A meta-analytic review. *Journal of Vocational Behavior, 85*, 169–179.

Park, Y. & Rothwell, W. J. (2009). The effects of organizational learning climate, career-enhancing strategy, and work orientation on the protean career. *Human Resource Development International, 12*(4), 387–405. doi: 10.1080/13678860903135771.

Peterson, S. (2009). Career decision-making self-efficacy, integration, and the likelihood of managerial retention in governmental agencies. *Human Resource Development Quarterly, 20*(4), 451–475. doi: 10:1002/hrdq.20024.

Porfeli, E. J. & Savickas, M. L. (2012). Career Adapt-Abilities Scale-USA form: Psychometric properties and relation to vocational identity. *Journal of Vocational Behavior, 80*, 748–753.

Rickwood, R. R., Roberts, J., Batten, S., Marshall, A., & Massie, K. (2004). Empowering high-risk clients to attain a better quality of life: A career resiliency framework. *Journal of Employment Counseling, 41*, 98–104.

Rothwell, W. J., Jackson, R. D., Knight, S. C., & Lindholm, J. E. (2005). *Career planning and succession management: Developing your organization's talent—for today and tomorrow.* Westport, CT: Greenwood Publishing Group.

Rotman, D. (2013). How technology is destroying jobs. *MIT Technology Review.* Retrieved from www.technologyreview.com/featuredstory/515926/how-technology-is-destroying-jobs.

Rousseau, D. M. (2005). *I-DEALS: Idiosyncratic deals employees bargain for themselves.* Armonk, NY: ME Sharpe.

Savickas, M. L. (1997). Career adaptability: An integrative construct for life-span, life-space theory. *The Career Development Quarterly, 45*, 247–259.

Savickas, M. L. (2013). Career construction theory and practice. In S. D. Brown & R. W. Lent (Eds.), *Career development and counseling: Putting theory and research to work* (2nd ed.) (pp. 147–183). Hoboken, NJ: John Wiley & Sons.

Savickas, M. L. & Porfeli, E. J. (2012). Career Adapt-Abilities Scale: Construction, reliability, and measurement equivalence across 13 countries. *Journal of Vocational Behavior, 80*, 661–673.

Schutt, D. A., Jr. (2012). Establishing a thriving career development program. In D. Capuzzi & M. D. Stauffer (Eds.), *Career counseling: Foundations, perspectives, and applications* (pp. 253–277). New York: Taylor & Francis.

Shuck, B., Twyford, D., Reio, T. G., Jr., & Shuck, A. (2014). Human resource development practices and employee engagement: Examining the connection with employee turnover intentions. *Human Resource Development Quarterly, 25*(2), 239–270.

Singer, A. (2012). *Immigrant workers in the US labor force.* Retrieved from www.brookings.edu/research/papers/2012/03/15-immigrant-workers-singer.

Skorikov, V. & F. W. Vonracek. (1993). Career development in the Commonwealth of Independent States. *Career Development Quarterly, 41*(4), 314–330.

Sturges, J., Guest, D., Conway, N., & Davey, K. M. (2002). A longitudinal study of the relationship between career management and organizational commitment among graduates in the first ten years at work. *Journal of Organizational Behavior, 23*, 731–748.

Tansky, J. W. & Cohen, D. J. (2001). The relationship between organizational support, employee development, and organizational commitment: An empirical study. *Human Resource Development Quarterly, 14*, 285–300.

Toossi, M. (2012). Labor force projections to 2020: a more slowly growing workforce. Retrieved from www.bls.gov/opub/mlr/2012/01/art3full.pdf.

Tracey, J. B., Tannenbaum, S. I., & Kavanagh, M. J. (1995). Applying trained skills on the job: The importance of the work environment. *Journal of Applied Psychology, 80*(2), 239–252.

van der Heijden, B. I. J. M. (2002). Individual career initiatives and their influence upon professional expertise development throughout the career. *International Journal of Training and Development, 6*(2), 54–79.

van der Heijden, B. I. J. M. (2003). Organisational influences upon the development of occupational expertise throughout the career. *International Journal of Training and Development, 7*(3), 142–165.

van der Rijt, J., Van den Bossche, P., van de Wiel, M. W. J., Segers, M. S. R., & Gijselaers, W. H. (2012). The role of organizational characteristics in feedback seeking behavior in the initial career stage. *Human Resource Development International, 15*(3), 283–301. doi: org/10.1080/13678868. 2012.689216.

Van der Sluis, L. & Poell, R. (2003). The impact on career development of learning opportunities and learning behavior at work. *Human Resource Development Quarterly, 14*(2), 159–180.

Waterman, R. H., Waterman, J. A., & Collard, B. A. (1994, July–August). Toward a career-resilient workforce. *Harvard Business Review, 72*, 87–95.

Wayne, S. J., Liden, R. C., Kraimer, M. L., & Graf, I. K. (1999). The role of human capital, motivation and supervisor sponsorship in predicting career success. *Journal of Organizational Behavior, 20*, 577–595.

Wooten, K. C. & Cobb, A. T. (1999). Career development and organizational justice: Practice and research implications. *Human Resource Development Quarterly, 10*(2), 173–179.

Young, R. A. & Valach, L. (1994). Evaluation of career development programs. *Canadian Journal of Counselling, 28*(4), 299–307.

Zacher, H. (2014, February). Career adaptability predicts subjective career success above and beyond personality traits and core self-evaluations. *Journal of Vocational Behavior, 84*(1), 21–30.

# 4   Career Development Interventions

Society is very short-sighted as yet in its attitude towards the development of its human resources. It trains its horses, as a rule, better than its men (sic). It spends unlimited money to perfect the inanimate machinery of production, but pays very little attention to the business of perfecting the human machinery, though it is by far the most important in production.

Parsons, 1909, p. 160

As we have noted previously, career development is an interactive endeavor, including both organizations and employees. Although, increasingly, individual employees are taking more responsibility to seek out opportunities to learn and develop the skills and knowledge that they will need for future career initiatives. This is actually good news, because it gives the career seeker more control over those choices.

That was not always the case. At one time, career development planning and implementation was controlled by the organization, designed to build and maintain the skill sets required to keep the system operating efficiently (Forret & Sullivan, 2002). Similarly, employees viewed as having high potential were often singled out to participate in specific learning activities intended to prepare them for promotion. If you did not distinguish yourself early in your tenure with the company, or if you did not fit their image of the ideal high potential candidate (often expected to mirror the existing upper management), your chances of being in that select group were limited; and so, consequently, was your career (Forret & Sullivan, 2002). HRD often coordinated these programs and was integral in their implementation, but typically had little input into who could participate.

Not all career development was focused on promotion to top positions; some was designed to build job-related knowledge and skills, to make people better at their work. However, most of the initiatives sponsored by the organization were created to fill system-specific needs. It was not their goal to train employees to go elsewhere; and often the employees did not see the need to move, staying with the same company throughout their working lives. One co-author experienced this first hand. In the early 1990s, my job in a large manufacturing company included coordinating the tuition reimbursement program. The vice president of human resources (HR) made it clear that employees seeking funding approval for college courses needed to be in majors that fit the company's mission. In his mind, there was no benefit in educating individuals for any purpose than to serve that organization. His rationale was reinforced by the number of people who, at that time, stayed in that system for decades. That kind of system longevity is much less common in the twenty-first century.

The era of the organization-driven career development plan mainly came to an end during the economic downturn that prompted systems to downsize and reduce what they considered to be extraneous programming and people (Brown, 2012). Not surprisingly, employees who lost jobs or saw others released to save money generally lost trust in organizations to care for their careers.

Currently, organizations are striving to boost effectiveness by attracting and retaining skilled and knowledgeable workers, and they are recognizing that one way to do that is to offer employees career development-related services (Brown, 2012). Since individuals realize that they are ultimately responsible for setting and implementing their career development plans, HRD's role in career development is evolving. It now includes bringing the needs of the system and the interests of the individual employees together to create initiatives that will respond to both. In this chapter, we will explore some of these interventions, including both individual development and organizational strategic practices (also see Chapter 3). Within those categories, we will informally group key individual development initiatives that often are addressed in the literature together, for example connecting activities (mentoring, coaching, and networking) and those that we consider experience-building initiatives (training, job assignments, and informal learning). Then we will explore organizational-level strategic practices (career paths, succession planning, and performance appraisals). In our exploration, we will discuss the advantages and drawbacks to each; how individuals can best access these opportunities; and how organizations can develop them to build effective strategic career development processes.

## Individual Development Initiatives: Connecting Activities

Scholars currently writing about developmental relationships may use the phrase "high-quality connections" (HQCs) to describe those that are viewed as energizing, rather than draining (Higgins, 2007). In the workplace, individuals may have multiple types of HQCs that they draw upon for different reasons (Higgins, 2007). We begin by describing three of the most commonly discussed connecting activities: mentoring, networking, and coaching. While coaching and networking seem to appear in the popular press often recently and are gaining a presence in scholarly research, mentoring literature has had a following among scholars and practitioners in HRD and related fields for some time. It is not feasible in this book to fully cover all aspects of mentoring, but we will begin this section by highlighting some of the key points that make it a valuable career development activity.

### *Mentoring*

Mentoring has had a long history, but as a career development intervention, it moved into the spotlight with the publication of Kathy Kram's 1985 *Mentoring at Work: Developmental Relationships in Organizational Life*. In that volume, Kram characterized mentoring as a developmental relationship between a senior professional (someone with more experience) and an individual with less experience that offers the junior member career and psychosocial assistance (Kram, 1985). The career function includes help with career decisions and strategies (i.e., gaining visibility, taking on difficult assignments to prove abilities), while the psychosocial function encompasses helping the junior member build confidence and a sense of professional identity (i.e., providing a sounding board or being a role model; Ragins & Kram, 2007). Research over time has indicated that some mentoring relationships do provide both, but others may vary in how much of each of those functions are fulfilled. Higgins (2007) suggested that, since those variations do not fit the definition of mentoring, they might better be characterized as sponsors (giving only high career support), friends (giving only high psychosocial support), or allies (providing low levels of each). These variations help build the case for diversifying development relationships, a concept that we will discuss later in this chapter.

As the mentoring literature has grown, so has the view of what mentoring can be. For example, Ragins and Verbos (2007) advocated for relational mentoring, as a relationship that is less one-sided, focusing less on just the protégé's career, and more oriented towards mutual learning and development for mentor and protégé. Haggard, Dougherty, Turban, & Wilbanks (2011) reinforced that idea when they suggested that the "three core attributes" that "distinguish mentoring from other kinds of work-related relationships" (p. 292) are:

- reciprocity, meaning that mentoring is a two-way street with all members part of the mutual exchange;
- developmental benefits, connected with the protégé's career (and not limited to a particular organization);
- consistent interaction, over an expanse of time.

Incidentally, while the term "mentor" has become readily accepted to describe the senior member in this relationship, a definitive term for the junior person remains somewhat unsettled, with both "mentee" and "protégé" being used. It may be a helpful reminder also to note that, while one might be considered "senior" due to experience in a particular system or profession, that status is not necessarily age-related; so a mentor may be chronologically younger than the mentee. Similarly, a mentor may or may not share the protégé's profession, company (Ragins & Kram, 2007), or even geographic location. This adaptability makes mentoring flexible as individuals change organizations or span industries during their career journeys.

Much of the mentoring research has concluded that there is a "positive relationship between the presence of a mentor and career outcomes" (Ragins & Kram, 2007, p. 7), supporting mentoring as valuable for the protégé's career development. However, some researchers have questioned if the benefits really are due to the act of mentoring, if they can be accounted for by the type of employee who seeks out mentoring (or who is sought out by influential mentors), or if positive results are a combination of the two (Ragins & Kram, 2007). While this remains to be fully substantiated, most mentoring scholars support the role of mentoring in career success for protégés (e.g., Bozionelos et al., 2011) and for mentors (e.g., Bozionelos, Bozionelos, Kostopoulos, & Polylchroniou, 2011; Ghosh & Reio, 2013). This leads to one of the key issues regarding mentoring: accessibility.

Left to chance, not every aspiring young professional gets a mentor. Initially, mentors typically choose protégés who might carry on their "values and perspectives on the world" and protégés often pursue mentors whom they admire (Kram, 1983, p. 615). Mentoring based on this type of mutual identification and selection is known as informal mentoring (Lankau & Scandura, 2007). While typically successful for those mentoring pairs, this selection process leaves out some individuals who do not find informal mentors. As the potential career benefits of mentoring became better known by research, and a more diverse workforce became an obvious reality, organizations began to explore formal mentoring.

Basically, "formal mentoring refers to organizationally initiated efforts to match mentors and protégés" (Eby & Lockwood, 2005). While some have questioned if formal mentoring can yield the full benefits of informal mentoring, the rationale has often been that some mentoring is better than none at all (Allen, Eby, & Lentz, 2006). Although research indicates that, while formal mentoring can help fulfill career-related functions, the psychosocial support factor is often lacking, suggesting, despite the "mentoring" title, that these may be more like sponsorships (Higgins, 2007).

Research on formal mentoring programs has been limited compared to that devoted to the informal variety (Baugh & Fagenson-Eland, 2007; Parise & Forret, 2008) but it does provide helpful insights. For example, Baugh and Fagenson-Eland (2007) suggested that the differences between the two types of mentoring center around "the initiation and the duration of the relationship" (p. 251). Unlike the serendipitous mutual choice of the informal process, formal mentoring requires some type of matching process to link mentors and protégés. Decisions around this process include if program participants volunteer or are required to take part and if they have input into the matching process. Research suggests that the volunteer aspect makes little difference, but participant involvement in the matching activity contributes to effectiveness of the program (Allen et al., 2006). Similarly, while informally formed relationships are free to run their course, formal matches typically include an expiration date when mentor and protégé are no longer obligated to remain in the relationship. Another distinction is the introduction of participant training into the process in most formal programs to clarify expectations among participants and to reinforce the organization's goals for the program (Baugh & Fagenson-Eland, 2007). HRD often takes a lead in coordinating and structuring these formal mentoring programs.

While research has confirmed many benefits to mentoring, not all mentoring relationships are good. Sometimes it is just a poor fit and the mentor and protégé part ways amicably, with mutual acknowledgment that it is time to move on. Other times, more disconcerting issues arise. Chapter 8 will address ethical issues in career development in more detail, but some issues are particularly related to the mentoring relationship and the power that mentors hold relative to their protégés. While it is not an exhaustive list, Hurst and Eby (2012, pp. 84–86) have identified five concerns regarding mentoring behaviors, based on the Ethical Principles of the American Psychological Association, which address some of the most common difficulties.

- Beneficence and nonmaleficence: mentors demonstrating low investment in the mentoring relationship or not recognizing their competence limitations. This also includes mentors mistreating protégés or hindering their careers.
- Fidelity and responsibility: mentors failing to develop the professional relationship or to uphold standards as role models.
- Integrity: mentors betraying the trust of their protégés; not acting in the protégés' best interests.
- Justice: mentors indulging in favoritism or unfair treatment regarding their professional relationships.
- Respect for rights and dignity: mentors abusing the power of their positions, not respecting protégés' rights of confidentiality, taking a paternalistic approach to the relationship, or not letting go when it is time for the protégé to move on.

We will address how to minimize the risk of these occurring later in the chapter.

Traditionally, mentoring has been interpreted to mean a dyad with one mentor and one protégé, although, even in 1985, Kram referred to the value of individuals seeking out more than one person to assist with their professional growth. In a later collaboration, Higgins and Kram (2001) described what they called a "developmental network" that essentially expanded the mentoring relationship, fitting into changes in the way individuals approach their own careers (e.g., boundaryless and protean), technological advances that foster greater reliance on knowledge work, changing organizational structures (e.g., international expansion), and a more diverse workforce. The focus remained on career and psychological support, but it may come from varied sources, including lateral (i.e., peers) as well as hierarchical relationships. This leads us to networks as another connecting initiative.

*Networking*

The term "networking" is used widely in popular culture as well as in career development literature. Cell phone providers advertise their expansive networking capabilities, campuses sponsor networking events to encourage business connections, and social networking is a global phenomenon. A quick check of Amazon books for the word "networking" showed over 56,000 titles (including of course, *Networking for Dummies*). Clearly, "networking" has become a familiar (if not over-used) word, giving the impression that everyone knows what it means, but do we really? To paraphrase a popular credit card ad:

> *"Who's in your network?"*
> How you respond will depend on how you define "network."

Career development scholars face a similar dilemma in defining networking as a career development initiative. Gibson, Hardy, & Buckley (2014) and Kim (2013) observed that, while career networking may often be grouped with similar types of connecting constructs (i.e., mentoring, social networking) it differs from each. For example, while Gibson et al. (2014) concede that there may be some overlap between behaviors often attributed to mentoring and networking, they saw mentoring as focusing more on the strength of the mentor(s)–protégé relationship and networking, rather than fixing on the protégé and his/her professional development.

Gibson et al. (2014) also noted that one of the weaknesses in the literature "is the lack of a consensus definition" (p. 147). After reviewing some of the definitions that appear in the literature, they devised their own as a way to integrate some of the key concepts addressed by other researchers: "Networking is a form of goal-directed behavior, both inside and outside of an organization, focused on creating, cultivating, and utilizing interpersonal relationships" (p. 150). This definition illustrates three factors that Gibson et al. (2014) and Kim (2013) asserted separate networking from other linking interactions. First is the instrumental motive of a network, meaning that members are deliberately selected for their potential to offer career support. The specific career development goal of a network will vary depending on the individual, but the goal-related aspect separates networking from other types of more open-ended interactions (like groups of friends or Twitter followers). In an effort to clarify this difference, Chandler, Hall, & Kram (2010) revived the adjective "developmental" to distinguish career development networks from other types of networks. Ibarra and Hunter (2007) suggest that these networks are distinct and valuable because they offer referral opportunities. Second is permeability of networking boundaries, including members inside and outside of one's current organization. Strong networks are not confined to any particular system, to make them more flexible when individuals change jobs or career direction. Third, network relationships are scattered across a continuum, with some being more useful than others at different times; so they are constantly in flux, and maintaining a network is a continuous process. Similarly, there is a reciprocity involved in networking (based on social exchange theory) that suggests mutual gain from the relationship over time. It may be helpful to reinforce here that the explicit trading of favors in networking differs from the mutual benefit perspective of relational mentoring, that advocates sharing and helping because one can, not because one is seeking a favor down the road. So, while these may seem like similar ideas, they are based on differing philosophical perspectives.

Given those parameters, establishing a viable career development network does not just happen. While some encounters may occur naturally through work assignments or spontaneous social encounters, networking typically requires planning and effort. Results of Kim's (2013) multinational, mixed gender study identified two key ways to build contacts. Perhaps, not surprisingly, the first was socializing, intentionally engaging others, either in casual conversations or through formal meetings, then building on those initial interactions. However, this contradicted an earlier study by Forret and Dougherty (2004) that found that socializing had little utility in obtaining either subjective or objective measures of career success, but increasing one's visibility in the organization had a significant impact on both. That connects to the second factor identified by Kim (2013), involvement in career-related activities (e.g., professional organizations, company projects or committees) that lets others see one's potential. The potential success of these activities to actually build a network, and not just expand one's list of acquaintances, depends on the individual's initiative and strategic approach (Kim, 2013). Similarly, the next step, maintaining contacts, also requires intentional action. Kim's (2013) study indicated that this requires a mix of self-prioritization (e.g., showing what you can do and communicating your successes) and other-prioritization (e.g., successfully addressing the needs of others in your network). Key at this stage is finding "compatible interests" with network members (Kim, 2013, p. 128) so that there is some investment in staying in contact. In that way, this type of network building is similar to maintaining any relationship, virtual or face to face; if there is not an essential connection, the relationship will be short-lived. So, while this is an iterative process, with building, revising, and maintaining going on simultaneously over time; ultimately, networks are intended to grow and remain viable throughout the career, so longevity matters. This plays into the reciprocity part of the network concept. The idea is not just to seek out favors when you need them, but to develop a cadre of people with whom you have mutual give and take over the years.

**Networking Notes**

There is no one best way to network, but some guidelines can be helpful reminders. The following represent some of the ideas that others have tried. Feel free to add some of your own.

- Look for opportunities to network.
  - Choose events you find interesting to meet like-minded people.
- Bring your best self, ready to engage.
  - It does no good to attend if you hide in a corner.
- Think of some questions ahead of time.
  - It helps to get people talking about their work and interests.
- Ask ... then listen.
  - Being an active listener is a valuable skill in networking.
- Be genuine.
  - Trust that you can make that good impression being your unique self.
- Follow up with new contacts.
  - Exchanging business cards makes this easier, but don't just file them away.
- Remember the mutuality of the relationship.
  - Don't just call when you have a favor to ask.
- Be the kind of networking member you would like to have.

Sources: Dickison (2011, Jan); Navarro (2011, Jan–Feb); Rosato (2009, Apr); Tips for Successful Networking (2013, Sept).

Career networking requires a sustained investment of both time and energy, so what are the career benefits associated with those potential costs? Research supports the value of networking for increased compensation (Forret & Dougherty, 2004; Wolff & Moser, 2009), gaining promotional opportunities (Forret & Dougherty, 2004; Wolff & Moser, 2010), and "perceived career success" (Forret & Dougherty, 2004, p. 431; Wolff & Moser, 2009). Wolff and Moser (2010) added a variation that is not particularly surprising as you think about it. They concluded that internal networks were beneficial for promotions, while external networks had greater potential when one is planning to change employers. However, since openings that lead to career opportunities elsewhere may happen at any time, they advised keeping a viable network of external contacts so you can be ready (Wolff & Moser, 2010). Forret and Dougherty (2004) also included a caveat to their findings. Their research found that networking offered more utility for men than for women. In particular, regarding objective measures of career success (e.g., promotions, salary), men appeared to benefit more than their female counterparts from networking initiatives like increasing their visibility in the organization or participating in professional activities. This is an important consideration for HRD, as they guide career development initiatives. An early step may be exploring the organizational culture and potential inequities in how these constructs (visibility, professional service) are perceived across gender lines.

So, what kinds of networks do you maintain? Which capture your attention and time most often? How do you feel about using your networking relationships to further your career? Since networking is a two-way street, what can you offer to your network participants?

### *Coaching*

Similar to networking, the term "coaching" is so familiar in our current discourse that it is easy to assume that we all know what it means. Athletes and sports observers often have a singular idea of what it means to be a coach. This view frequently popularizes the idea of a coach as a cross between a parent and a military drill sergeant. Outside of sports, the options expand to include executive coaches, workplace coaches, and life coaches (Ellinger & Kim, 2014), each with a different focus. Segers et al. (2011) observed that there are also variations in the source of coaching, professional coaches inside or outside the organization, managers who take on coaching responsibilities, and self-coaching.

Our vague familiarity about coaching gives us some sense of what it is, but it can be confusing at times to identify how it differs from other connecting relationships, like mentoring or even counseling (Ellinger & Kim, 2014). Ellinger and Kim (2014) suggested that the coaching versus counseling distinction may be based on the focus of the interaction (immediate career-related goals versus more extensive planning and exploration) or practitioner credentials (licenses or particular degrees are required to counsel but not to coach). A description of the arc of the career coaching relationship, from contracting to disengagement, provided by Hazen and Steckler (2014) illustrates the clearly defined intent of that relationship.

Garvey, Stokes, & Megginson, (2009) reflected that both coaching and mentoring claim origins in ancient Greece, often (although not always) are enacted in pairs, and share some common competencies (e.g., communication, facilitation). They indicated, however, that the research traditions appear to differ between the two. For example, they found mentoring research tends toward the academic with an emphasis

on theoretically grounded research methods and models for data interpretation. The intent often is to gauge how mentoring impacts career
development and opportunities. In contrast, their analysis of coaching
research suggests a pragmatic, more subjective approach often based on
anecdotal data. The measure of success is "business relevance" focused
on performance improvement and return on investment (Garvey et al.,
2009). The latter description fits with Ellinger and Kim's (2014)
note that coaching has at times been criticized for being atheoretical,
lacking a solid research-based foundation. However, Bachkirova, Cox, &
Clutterbuck, (2014) countered that the multidisciplinary nature of coaching lets it draw on various theoretical backgrounds; so, rather than being
theoretically adrift, coaching is based on a wealth of theories from multiple fields. Overall, this discourse suggests that the lines separating these
approaches to career development are often blurred, and that they are
more likely to converge than to become more distinct over time.

Given the identity dilemma described above, how is coaching
defined? Segers, Vloeberghs, Henderickx, & Inceoglu, (2011) offered
this definition of coaching:

> an intensive and systematic facilitation of individuals or groups by
> using a wide variety of behavioral techniques and methods to help
> them attain self-congruent goals or conscious self-change and self-
> development in order to improve their professional performance,
> personal well-being and, consequently, to improve the effectiveness
> of their organization.
>
> (p. 204)

As you may have noted, this expansive definition seems to reinforce
how much like mentoring and counseling coaching is, rather than to set
it apart. However, since each coaching specialty has its own definition,
let's explore this further.

Stokes and Jolly (2014) suggested that some definitions of executive coaching are so broad that almost any type of development work
with a coach would qualify. They offered the following as a more
defined way to describe this specialty: "work with senior level executives that focuses on the executive becoming more self-aware in
order to carry out their leadership role more effectively" (p. 244).
Although there is limited empirical research to support the utility of
executive coaching (Maltbia, Marsick, & Ghosh, 2014), top leaders
may be particularly inclined to seek out this type of coaching if
they are newly promoted and struggling with adjusting their behaviors
to match the role requirements of that lonely and visible position

(Stokes & Jolly, 2014). The allure must be strong, because, although coaching has had a long history, executive coaching as a professional focus has recently come to the forefront.

It is difficult to determine which came first to prompt the rise of interest in coaching: the demand for coaching or the number of professionals offering their services as coaches. In any event, an increase in professional coaches has led to a proliferation of professional associations, the largest being the International Coach Federation (ICF), which, as its name implies, encompasses multiple types of coaching (Maltbia et al., 2014). The relatively rapid growth has come with some growing pains, particularly in determining issues like credentialing, identification of key competencies, and setting of ethical standards. Maltbia et al. (2014) acknowledged that one current challenge is that the professional associations setting up the credentialing standards are the same entities that accredit the education and training programs to prepare individuals for certification.

Other aspects of coaching key to HRD are managerial, peer, and team coaching, focused on helping employees below the executive level improve their "skills, competence, and performance" (Beattie et al., 2014, p. 186). While some researchers see each of these as a separate type of coaching practice, Beattie et al. (2014) grouped these three with a fourth variation, cross-organizational coaching, under the umbrella of "managerial coaching." They differentiated among them depending on who was acting as coach and the configuration of the relationship. For example, the hierarchical version finds the line manager in the coaching role, representing the more traditional managerial coaching focus. Considered to be an effective method to share learning and foster development, research also suggests that, while managers are well positioned to perform on the coaching role, not all have the facilitation skills and knowledge to take on this key responsibility (Beattie et al., 2014). In contrast, peer coaching relies on colleagues for shared coaching. Ladyshewsky (2014) noted that coaching peers typically have common backgrounds, fostering the sense of "mutual support" (p. 285). Parker, Hall, & Kram (2008) determined that "the effective peer coach adopts the role of 'critical friend,' providing a balance of support and challenge" (p. 499). Beattie et al. (2014) described team coaching being closest to the sports model that we mentioned earlier, with one manager/coach heading up a team of employees who are aligned in goals and provided with regular feedback. As a variation, Clutterbuck (2014) identified four types of team coaching, depending on the role that the coach takes (involved in the action; simply observing and providing feedback for guidance;

observing, but limited to strategic thinking with the team; and getting data from the team, but not involved with them). As the term cross-*organizational* coaching indicates, the key difference in this interaction is that the coaching spans different types of organizational systems. When the "crossing" also involves international borders (e.g., expatriate assignments, multicultural teams, cross-country mergers) the complexities of cultural differences also must be factored into crafting and maintaining the coaching relationship (Abbott, 2014). Recognizing that individual careers increasingly may move across organizational, and possibly international, boundaries, this type of coaching will likely rise in prominence.

### The On-Line Option

E-mentoring and e-coaching are increasingly being considered as ways to expand support outside of the confines of a single organization. Notable for saving money and time, overcoming geographical distance, and optimizing flexibility regarding meeting times and matching opportunities (Hunt & Fielden, 2013), on-line mentoring and coaching options appear to be logistically beneficial. Some suggest that these relationships also foster more egalitarian interactions because the relative anonymity of virtual communication makes status or physical differences (i.e., race, gender) less obtrusive (Hunt & Fielden, 2013). The view of electronic options is not unilaterally positive, though. Empirical data on the benefits of on-line delivery of coaching and mentoring is limited. There are also potential concerns that generational differences in comfort with electronic communication might deter some more experienced professionals from being virtual mentors or coaches (Beattie, et al., 2014).

### Individual and Organizational Actions to Foster Connecting Initiatives

As we have noted, while mentoring, networking, and coaching vary in focus and implementation, they share enough similarities that we can group them together when discussing individual and organizational initiatives to foster these HQCs.

For individuals:

- Be "developmentally proactive" (Blickle, Witzki, & Schneider, 2009; Chandler et al., 2010, p. 49):
  - Actively seek out assistance from others.
  - Follow up on new contacts.
  - Maintain those connections.

- Seek and be open to feedback (Higgins & Kram, 2001):

  ○ Look for opportunities to learn from others.

- Show your skills and reliability (Chandler et al., 2010):

  ○ Prepare well.
  ○ Take on tasks and follow through.
  ○ Build a portfolio of your work that tracks what you are learning and how you are using your skills and knowledge (Forret & Sullivan, 2002).

- Practice strong interaction skills (Chandler et al., 2010):

  ○ Be an active listener and an engaged speaker.

- Access multiple means of connecting (Singh, Ragins, & Tharenou, 2009):

  ○ Expand your types of relationships to add strength.
  ○ Consider alternative support systems, like peers and professional organizations (Allen & Finkelstein, 2003).

This means not only taking responsibility to build HQCs but also making the commitment to maintain them over time. Granted, this will come more naturally to some than to others, but it is rapidly becoming a career skill that one must learn.

For organizations seeking to help foster HQCs:

- Consider a formal mentoring program to maximize equal access:

  ○ Design the program to match the goals of the organization (Baugh & Fagenson-Eland, 2007).
  ○ Let potential participants have input into the matching process.
  ○ Clearly communicate expectations including ethical behavior, responsibilities of each role, meeting frequency.
  ○ Offer guidance on interpersonal skills, gender and race issues.
  ○ Provide alternatives to traditional mentoring pairs such as peer mentoring, mentoring circles or e-mentoring.
  ○ Provide equal access to these opportunities.

- Expand HQC opportunities:

  ○ Include system support for networking and coaching.
  ○ Encourage e-mentoring and e-coaching to augment options outside of the organization.

- Provide training on networking-, mentoring-, coaching-related skills:
  - Include guidance about the benefits and limitations of each.
  - Incorporate practice opportunities (de Janasz and Forret, 2008).
  - Ensure that managers are trained in facilitation and coaching skills.
- Recognize the role of organizational culture on HQC development:
  - Set policies and reward systems that encourage employees to engage with others (Gibson et al., 2014).

HRD is likely to lead the organizational response to developing individuals with skills in HQCs. Part of the task of HRD will be to help balance the needs of the system with those of the employees in the process of developing these initiatives. While it may appear as if the benefits are skewed towards individuals, the system can gain directly from potential improved job performance (Gibson et al., 2014) and well prepared candidates for succession planning, as well as from less tangible benefits that arise from fostering a culture that values learning and development. Additionally, while these connecting developmental activities help prepare individuals for opportunities elsewhere, some employees will choose to stay in an environment that has fostered their professional growth so well.

## Individual Development Initiatives: Experience-building

As noted previously, our exploration of experience-building initiatives will focus on training, job assignments, and informal learning. While each of these has a long history within the work context, compared to the connecting activities that we discussed, relatively little has been researched about how these interventions specifically contribute to long-term career development.

### *Training*

Since training has traditionally been part of HRD, we will begin there. While this may sound contradictory, given the previous statement about research, there is no lack of training and development-related literature. However, often it is focused on topics like training transfer or evaluation, rather than on training as a career development activity. Traditionally, HRD literature has made a distinction, indicating that the "training" part of this function was related to knowledge and skill building for one's current job, while the "development" aspect generally referred to learning that would influence future career opportunities as well as augmenting abilities to perform well in the present (Werner & DeSimone, 2012). The former might include getting oriented to the organization, gaining technical skills (e.g., data entry), enhancing managerial capabilities (e.g., delegation), or even changing behaviors to comply with legal requirements (e.g., preventing sexual harassment; Werner & DeSimone, 2012). Development covers more varied options, such as taking on stretch assignments or working with more experienced employees to learn a process. So, we might think of training as constructing a foundation for developmental initiatives to build upon. However, it might be more accurate to visualize a continuum with training on the left, development on the right, and a range of activities between them, some closer to one side or the other, and many in the middle. From a career development perspective, the dividing line between training and development often is blurred, making the distinction between them rather inconsequential. However, for clarity, we will address some training issues first.

Using a career development lens, when training is done well, it helps individuals gain job confidence and competence. For example, a study by Laud and Johnson (2012) determined that training and education were among the key tactics used by those seeking career advancement. That prompts strong work performance that can foster a greater sense of employability and optimism about future opportunities. The organization providing the training can gain not only the immediate reward of skilled employees doing their jobs well, but also the potential that current employees will choose to stay with a system that invests in their learning, and potential employees will be impressed with their learning commitment. However, reaping the benefits of training depends on several factors, individual and systemic. We will explore those briefly.

Research indicates that motivation to participate in and apply work-related training is an early indicator of individual career development, because it builds that foundation for the future. Feldman and Ng (2008) suggested individual motivational antecedents for training include having the cognitive and physical ability to access and acquire new knowledge, seeing the career mobility potential of the training, and possessing the personality traits most attracted to learning endeavors (e.g., self-efficacy). Other researchers also have identified particular personality or demographic traits as influencing training motivation. For example, Major, Turner, & Fletcher (2006) found that a proactive personality and willingness to take initiative and persist in working for change was positively linked to training motivation. However, Bertolino, Truxillo, & Fraccaroli (2011) determined that age moderates a proactive personality, such that, over time, even a proactively inclined individual may lose motivation for training. They recommended more research to explain why. Not surprisingly, research indicates that Big Five personality traits, such as openness to experience, also affect training motivation (Feldman & Ng, 2008; Major et al., 2006).

Organizational factors are critical in fostering successful training initiatives. Feldman and Ng (2008) identified several that can reinforce or discourage training motivation. They considered individual job empowerment, stress level, and position level as motivational influencers (i.e., more empowerment, less negative stress, and a higher position yield more motivation). Similarly, the organizational culture's support of training (i.e., supervisor encouragement to attend and apply training) helps determine motivation to put time and energy into training (Feldman & Ng, 2008). Gorman, Thibodeaux, Eisinger, & Overstreet (2012) added another key aspect, specifically how potential trainees are selected and how that impacts career options, as illustrated in this statement:

> Selection for training is a critical employment decision because employees who complete certain training programs may improve their knowledge and skills which can lead to an increase in available opportunities for promotions, skill-based pay increases, bonuses, and other career advancement outcomes.
>
> (p. 97)

While these objective measures represent only one type of career success, their point is clear that HRD can assist organizations in reviewing and revising their policies and practices for determining training decisions and building a culture of learning. Ethical and equitable access to training and other growth opportunities is critical in creating and sustaining a successful career development process, as well as for gaining employee trust, which is an essential aspect of a learning culture.

The turbulence of the current career environment has prompted discussions about another potential role of training: teaching career resilience. On our continuum of interventions, this one would likely be placed somewhere between traditional training and more open-ended career development interventions, because it can be taught, but it also becomes a mindset and a practice. Resilience has been described as "a multifaceted construct that includes a person's determination and ability to endure, to be adaptable and to recover from adversity" (Taormina & Taormina, 2014, p. 347). While much of the research to date combining careers and resilience has gravitated toward jobs often susceptible to burn-out (e.g., nursing, emergency services), maintaining employability in a changing career landscape will increasingly require an ability to endure and adapt. Factors often linked to resilience include (Borgen, Amundson, & Reuter, 2004, p. 52; Taormina & Taormina, 2014, p. 347):

- internal locus of control
- adaptability
- sense of purpose
- optimism
- determination
- problem-solving skills
- endurance
- recuperability.

Some of these factors may seem to be personality-driven rather than skills to learn. However, research suggests that training can enhance skills that contribute to a sense of optimism and self-efficacy, and also foster a mindset that encourages a greater sense of purpose and control over one's future (Borgen et al., 2004; Taormina & Taormina, 2014). Empirical research remains scarce on how to build resilience, but it is a concept to watch for in the future of career development.

### Job Assignments

Moving more towards the developmental part of the continuum, we will explore job assignments and informal learning. To begin our discussion, it is helpful to recognize that research supports a positive link between challenging assignments and career advancement (De Pater, Van Vianen, Fisher, & Van Ginkel, 2009). These opportunities are also called stretch assignments, because they require individuals to gain new skills and knowledge, diversify their interactions, and address unfamiliar circumstances (Dragoni, Tesluk, Russell, & Oh, 2009; McCall, 2004), prompting individuals to push on the perceived limits of their capabilities. These assignments may be seen as the double-edged sword of career development: do well and you gain recognition and additional chances to shine; do poorly and you risk a career setback. An example of the latter is the person promoted too far, too fast, suddenly elevated to a position without proper preparation, knowledge, or skills to succeed.

Dragoni et al. (2009) indicated three key factors that influence the potential success of stretch assignments to contribute to career development. One is that the job includes tasks that really are developmental, not an accumulation of the same responsibilities. Another is access to and availability of these assignments. If such opportunities are rare and not well distributed, neither organization nor individuals will benefit fully. The third is the individual learning orientation. They noted, "individuals holding a learning goal orientation perceive challenging tasks as opportunities to learn ... they exhibit an *adaptive* response pattern in which they actively choose more difficult tasks" (p. 734). These ideas reinforce earlier observations by McCall (2004) who stated:

> The challenge of using experience for development lies in giving the right experiences to the people who will learn the most from them (often described as "open to learning" or "learning agile") then providing the kind of support that will let them learn what the experiences offer.
>
> (p. 128)

McCall (2004) also addressed the aspect of access, suggesting that organizations often use a "short-term performance" mindset about challenging assignments, giving them to the people who already are doing that kind of work, rather than taking a "long-term development" view and offering these tasks to talented, but untried, individuals who might learn the most from the experience (p. 128).

An interesting caveat applies when considering stretch tasks. We often think of this initiative as being most applicable to those in the early years of their careers as a way to prove themselves and perhaps speed their professional advancement. An empirical study by Belgian researchers Careete, Anseel, & Lievens (2013) added support to that perception. They studied early- and mid-career employees in the same organization. Their results showed that the performance boost attributed to taking on challenging tasks was in effect for younger careerists, but not for their mid-career counterparts, whose performance declined as the challenge increased. The data prompted them to suggest that organizations consider a measured approach to these types of assignments for mid-career employees, adjusting the demands of the tasks more carefully to match current abilities so that the stretch required is less strenuous. However, their study did not explore how this might play out for a mid-career individual moving into a new organization or making a career change to a different type of work. Might that significant change in direction prompt someone to re-create an "early" career perspective, eager to rise to bigger challenges in their new environment?

So, what can individuals do to be considered for and to succeed in stretch assignments? Sometimes you need to ask for the opportunity. Systems may fall into the risk-avoidance perspective, noted above by McCall (2004), choosing to give tough assignments to the already proven performers. HRD can help to moderate that view, but individuals also need prepare themselves by developing skills, knowledge, and the sense of self-efficacy that comes from believing in your own competence, so that they are ready when the opportunities arise. Additionally, given our current, more mobile career environment, offering individuals the chance to reinvent their professional personas periodically, maintaining an agile learner mindset, might be the most valuable skill that one can practice, not only to obtain challenging assignments but also to retain employability.

Organizational support also can help to maximize the potential for successful challenge assignments by providing mentoring or coaching assistance (McCall, 2004) and advocating a learning culture that acknowledges mistakes and missteps as part of development. Dragoni et al. (2009) suggested that HRD can assist in this process by helping build career development plans that use job assignments and rotations to "systematically increase exposure to more developmental dimensions and thereby enhance managers' overall opportunity to augment competencies" (p. 741), letting individuals build confidence and skills incrementally, instead of in one big leap. This approach also can help minimize the perceived risk of handing a big assignment to a less experienced employee, making it easier for organizations to adhere to their developmental intentions. Stretch assignments may include chances for informal learning, but they are not the only way to engage in these opportunities.

### *Informal Learning*

The phrase "informal workplace learning" covers such a wide range of possibilities that it may be more easily defined by what it is not. In contrast to formal learning, which typically refers to structured, class-focused, organizationally arranged and controlled learning events (e.g., system-wide training sessions), informal learning is initiated and directed by the individual. "Unlike formal learning, informal learning can be planned or unplanned and structured or unstructured" (Lohman, 2005, p. 501). It encompasses multiple means of enhancing workplace wisdom, such as "reading a book or article, asking each other for help and feedback, and sharing knowledge with each other" (van Rijn, Yang, & Sanders, 2013, p. 611). It also may include on-line searches, trying out new techniques to learn by trial and error, and observing others (Lohman, 2005).

By its nature, informal learning is flexible, responsive to the needs of the learner, and readily accessible to individuals. This makes it a valuable career development tool for individuals as well as organizations, which can benefit from this cost-effective, personally directed and driven approach to learning. "Voluntary participation in informal learning activities may enhance individual performance through knowledge acquisition and practice, ultimately leading to increased organizational performance" (Bednall et al., 2014, p. 56).

### Actions to Foster Experience-building Individual Development Initiatives

For individuals: recognize this as an opportunity to take control of your own learning and development:

- Cultivate a proactive, learning mindset.
- Be creative and persistent in seeking out learning opportunities.
- Develop strong self-efficacy.
- Make a commitment to excellence.
- Be supportive of others (Lohman, 2005).

For organizations: recognize that some of what you can offer is less tangible than structured training or workshops, but still critically important:

- Create a supportive environment that encourages knowledge-sharing and collaborative work:
  ○ Foster a learning culture.
  ○ Reward collaboration over competition.
  ○ Develop chat spaces throughout the facility.
  ○ Build in unstructured workplace time for individuals to meet and discuss ideas (Lohman, 2005).

For example, a company in the co-authors' community deliberately designed areas throughout their new corporate building with small groups of tables and comfortable chairs to encourage informal dialogue among employees from different functional areas. These non-meeting-room gathering spots not only offer space and place for conversation, but also serve as a reminder of the company's interest in collaborative innovation.

## Organizationally Based Development Initiatives

While we have already acknowledged that the responsibility for career development has shifted from being wholly organizationally controlled to being more individually driven, some career development initiatives still are systemically based and guided. We will explore three of those in this section: career paths, performance appraisals, and succession planning.

### *Career Paths*

Carter, Cook, & Dorsey (2009) define a basic career path as a layout of sequential jobs that an individual would hold while advancing in his/her career over time. For each position on the list, the path includes the qualifications required at that point (e.g., licensure, education level), developmental experiences linked to moving from that job to the next (e.g., managing a challenging project), competencies that would be learned or enhanced at each step (e.g., managing a complex budget), and critical career success factors to ensure smooth progress within the system (e.g., taking an expatriate position; Carter et al., 2009). At first glance, career paths might appear to be simply a new term for an organizationally controlled career but, if done properly, there is greater transparency about what it takes to continue to advance and a more strategic focus to the process. For the individual, the start-to-finish clarity of the outline can help alleviate anxiety about what criteria will be used to judge performance and what the future may hold. The organization gains a better grasp of their talent management prospects and hopefully can use the system to make wise hiring and promotion decisions. It may also help to reinforce retention when talented individuals can see a clear road to advancement and recognize that the organization has made an investment in their future.

As described by Carter et al. (2009), career paths may seem restrictive and system-bound in an era of boundaryless and protean careers. However, some individuals still prefer the sense of stability that building a career within a particular system can offer, and some organizations use their career paths as a way to let new employees know that they invest in their people and want them to stay. See the box overleaf on Chipotle as an example of the latter.

**Chipotle Career Paths**

Chipotle Mexican Grill is noted for seeking talent within for promotions. The career path is clearly laid out on the company website, complete with expected salary and benefits listed for each step. The journey extends from crew member through apprentice to restauranteur (in charge of a restaurant) and potentially beyond. A LinkedIn review in 2014 (Petrone https://www.linkedin.com/today/post/article/20140922174927-283620963-chipotle-s-brilliant-hiring-process) noted that the company emphasizes career development in tangible as well as intangible ways. For example, an employee aspiring to move up the path is required to train his or her replacement, reinforcing the importance of helping others to move up. Employees also receive financial compensation if someone they hire progresses into management, so that encourages looking for the best potential new hires. The company website offers multiple examples of employees who started at the entry level and followed the career path to the top, a reinforcing reminder for prospective new hires.

Those more inclined to move on could use the career path model to build employability for changing from one system to another. A potential limitation is that the path typically is geared towards one organization within a specific industry, so following it over time may complicate transition to an entirely different type of work. Organizations could alleviate this dilemma by designing career paths that allow for flexibility and help employees develop adaptability (Clutterbuck, 2012). In our changing work environment, individuals who can retain a flexible, adaptable career approach have potential to increase their own employability and to contribute to organizations that need a dynamic workforce.

### Performance Appraisals

Progression through a system leads us to another systemically focused initiative that influences career development, the performance appraisal (PA) process. What do you think of when you hear the phrase "performance appraisal"? Does it bring up anxiety or apprehension, eagerness or anticipation, or maybe opportunity or learning? Your first thoughts are likely the result of your personal experience with performance appraisals to date; or, if you lack personal experience, what you have heard from others. Interestingly, the idea of career development may not be your first thought when you consider PAs, but if used properly, performance appraisals can be a valuable part of career development. Performance appraisals are chances for feedback, and, good news or bad, feedback is important for career progress (as we noted earlier, it can even be considered a type of informal learning).

Grote (2011) defined performance appraisal as "a formal record of a supervisor's opinion of the quality of an employee's performance" (p. 45). While the "opinion" aspect can appear more subjective than one might like, a solid performance appraisal should evaluate behavior (demonstrating the competencies required by the organization) and results (achieving the goals and responsibilities of the job) (Grote, 2011). Unfortunately, in some systems, the established performance appraisal system is "biased against people who do not fit the ideal profile," misrepresenting the potential talents of individuals who vary from the status quo (Clutterbuck, 2012, p. 13). This leads to mistrust of the system and limits developing a diverse workforce, which is an increasing need for organizations operating in our global economy.

From an organizational perspective, a well designed and appropriately implemented PA process can help ensure that employees are contributing to the system's strategic priorities, identify talented individuals for advancement opportunities, inform decisions about pay or other rewards, and develop a skilled and dedicated workforce (Insler & Becom, 2011). Perhaps a key phrase here is "well designed and implemented." Research indicates that an effective performance appraisal system that employees trust and buy into can positively influence their organization commitment and intention to stay (Abdulkadir, Isiaka, & Adedoyin, 2012; Mustapha & Daud, 2012). Additionally, "high-quality performance appraisal (i.e., with high clarity, regularity, and openness) appears to promote increases in reflection, knowledge sharing, and innovative behavior over time" (Bednall et al., 2014, p. 54). Building that "high quality" appraisal format and process is where HRD can make a strong contribution. Performance appraisals should not just be something supervisors check off their "to do" lists, but should be designed to provide quality data for both individuals and organizations. The risk to both individuals and the organization is that a poorly designed or haphazardly implemented PA system will yield inaccurate data that wastes the time and energy of all involved and can lead to mistrust in the process as well as in the organization as a whole.

If done well, however, the potential benefit to individuals may extend beyond just the value of obtaining good feedback. Bednall et al. (2014) observed that "by receiving accurate information about their performance, employees may feel more confident in making informed choices about suitable informal learning activities and, therefore, may feel encouraged to increase their participation" (p. 54). Further, the process can also lead to better goals development and links to other activities that can enhance career progress (Bednall et al., 2014). So individuals can gain insight, guidance for future planning, and ideas for additional career developmental opportunities. Organizations also gain by developing the workforce that they need and laying the foundation for succession plans, our next organizationally based initiative.

### Succession Planning

From an organizational perspective, succession planning often has been seen as a way "to identify, develop, and properly place qualified individuals into key positions to meet present and future strategic needs" (Rothwell, Jackson, Knight, & Lindholm, 2005). Sometimes implemented by way of a list of "haves and have nots" that periodically plucks someone from the ranks to move to the executive office, succession planning often has been perceived as an unknown quantity except for those closest to the top. However, if done well, it can have an impact beyond just filling open slots in upper management. Clutterbuck (2012) suggested conceptualizing this process with a dual focus that includes individuals as well as organizations. He defines succession planning as:

> A dynamic process of aligning employee aspirations and talents with the constantly evolving needs of the organization and of providing employees with the resources and support they need to grow into new roles.
>
> (p. 11)

This perspective makes succession planning less about controlling access and outcome and more about developing talent, which is a much better fit for HRD (Clutterbuck, 2012).

Organizations still benefit because it offers an opportunity to plan strategically for turnover in leadership by determining what competencies are needed to take on those responsibilities (McCall, 2004). The rapidly changing global work environment presents a good reason to regularly review what knowledge and skills future leaders will need. Clearly identifying competencies can help a system minimize the potential for developing an insular upper management that replicates itself when choosing successors. A competencies profile can also help managers begin to identify and develop individuals within the organization to build those competencies, preparing a pipeline of qualified people ready to lead when a vacancy occurs, whether planned or unexpected (McCall, 2004). From an individual perspective, when linked with career paths and performance appraisals, succession planning can become part of the career development process, providing more clarity about potential opportunities.

HRD's role is to be an advocate for integrating succession planning with career development as a strategic initiative and as another way to show employees that the organization is interested in investing in their professional growth. As part of repositioning succession planning as a developmental initiative, HRD can encourage a comprehensive competencies review that may expand how the organization defines leadership qualities and open doors for individuals from under-represented groups who often do not fit a more prescriptive view of leadership potential.

## Maximizing Organizational Initiatives

For organizational-level initiatives, individuals may have limited influence about what is implemented, but they can be prepared to take advantage of opportunities when they arise by:

- learning about career paths and using them to their advantage;
- being an active participant in the performance appraisal process, using it as a way to set challenging goals and gain feedback on their performance;
- seeking out information about their organization's succession plan.

Since organizations have the responsibility for creating and maintaining these initiatives, their responsibilities should include:

- putting as much energy into developing employees as they put into attracting new talent (Clutterbuck, 2012);
- setting up multiple flexible career paths to accommodate different types of work in the system (i.e., technical advancement, administrative advancement) and to foster employability;
- constructing a performance appraisal system that is unbiased and clearly linked to organization goals and strategy;
- training employees on the purpose and use of performance appraisals for goal accomplishment and career development;
- regularly reviewing and revising competencies profiles for upper-level positions;
- integrating career paths, performance appraisals, and succession planning into the career development process (Clutterbuck, 2012);
- setting up evaluation feedback loops and metrics to review the success of career paths, performance appraisals, and succession planning (Clutterbuck, 2012).

**Summary**

The development initiatives described in this chapter represent activities that are not new to HRD nor to career development, but that need to be considered in a more consolidated, comprehensive way for what they can offer to both individuals and organizations. In isolation, each one provides some benefits and each has some drawbacks, yielding a hit-or-miss approach to career development. In combination, they can yield an effective career development program that can be guided by HRD while still fulfilling the needs of the organization and letting individuals take responsibility for accessing the options that fit best for them.

**References**

Abbott, G. (2014). Cross-cultural coaching: A paradoxical perspective. In E. Cox, T. Bachkirova, & D. Clutterbuck (Eds.), *The complete handbook of coaching* (2nd edn.) (pp. 342–360). London, CA: Sage.

Abdulkadir, D. S., Isiaka, S. B., & Adedoyin, S. I. (2012). Effects of strategic performance appraisal, career planning and employee participation on organizational commitment: An empirical study. *International Business Research, 5*, 124–133.

Allen, T. D., Eby, L. T., & Lentz, E. (2006). Mentorship behaviors and mentorship quality associated with formal mentoring programs: Closing the gap between research and practice. *Journal of Applied Psychology, 91*(3), 567–578.

Allen, T. D. & Finkelstein, L. M. (2003). Beyond mentoring: Alternative sources and functions of developmental support, *The Career Development Quarterly, 51*(4), 346–355.

Bachkirova, T., Cox, E., & Clutterbuck, D. (2014). Introduction. In E. Cox, T. Bachkirova, & D. Clutterbuck (Eds.), *The complete handbook of coaching* (2nd edn.) (pp. 1–18). London, CA: Sage.

Baugh, S. G. & Fagenson-Eland, E. A. (2007). Formal mentoring programs: A "poor cousin" to informal relationships. In B. R. Ragins & K. E. Kram (Eds.), *The handbook of mentoring at work: Theory, research and practice* (pp. 249–272). Thousand Oaks, CA: Sage.

Beattie, R. S., Kim, S., Hagen, M. S., Egan, T. M., Ellinger, A. D., & Hamlin, R. G. (2014). Managerial coaching: A review of the empirical literature and development of a model to guide future practice. *Advances in Human Resource Development, 16*(2), 184–201.

Bednall, T. C., Sanders, K., & Runhaar, P. (2014). Stimulating informal learning activities through perceptions of performance appraisal quality and human resource management system strength: A two-wave study. *Academy of Management Learning & Education, 13*(1), 45–61.

Bertolino, M., Truxillo, D. M., & Fraccaroli, F. (2011). Age as moderator of the relationship of proactive personality with training motivation, perceived career development from training, and training behavioral intentions. *Journal of Organizational Behavior, 32,* 248–263.

Blickle, G., Witzki, A., & Schneider, P. B. (2009). Self-initiated mentoring and career success: A predictive study. *Journal of Vocational Behavior, 74,* 94–101.

Borgen, W. A., Amundson, N. E., & Reuter, J. (2004). Using portfolios to enhance career resilience. *Journal of Employment Counseling, 41,* 50–57.

Bozionelos, N., Bozionelos, G., Kostopoulos, K., & Polylchroniou, P. (2011). How providing mentoring relates to career success and organizational commitment: A study in the general managerial population. *Career Development International, 16*(5), 446–468.

Brown, D. (2012). *Career information, career counseling, and career development* (3rd edn.). Upper Saddle River, NJ: Pearson.

Careete, B., Anseel, F., & Lievens, F. (2013). Does career timing of challenging job assignments influence the relationship with in-role job performance? *Journal of Vocational Behavior, 83,* 61–67.

Carter, G. W., Cook, K. W., & Dorsey, D. W. (2009). *Career paths: Charting courses to success for organizations and their employees.* Malden, MA: Wiley-Blackwell.

Chandler, D. E., Hall, D. T., & Kram, K. E. (2010). A developmental network and relational savvy approach to talent development: A low-cost alternative. *Organizational Dynamics, 39*(1), 48–56.

Clutterbuck, D. (2012). *The talent wave: why succession planning fails and what to do about it.* London: Kogan Page.

Clutterbuck, D. (2014). Team coaching. In E. Cox, T. Bachkirova, & D. Clutterbuck (Eds.), *The complete handbook of coaching* (2nd edn.) (pp. 271–284). London, CA: Sage.

de Janasz, S. C. & Forret, M. L. (2008). Learning the art of networking: A critical skill for enhancing social capital and career success. *Journal of Management Education, 32,* 629–650.

De Pater, I. E., Van Vianen, A., Fisher, A., & Van Ginkel, W. P. (2009). Challenging experiences: Gender differences in task choice. *Journal of Managerial Psychology, 24*(1), 4–28.

Dickison, S. (2011, January). Networking: A how-to guide for both introverts and extroverts. *Writer 124* (1), 10. Retrieved from http://web.b.ebscohost.com

Dragoni, L., Tesluk, P. E., Russell, J. E. A., & Oh, I. S. (2009). Understanding managerial development: Integrating developmental assignments, learning orientation, and access to developmental opportunities in predicting managerial competence. *Academy of Management Journal, 52,* 731–743.

Eby, L. T. & Lockwood, A. (2005). Protégés' and mentors' reactions to participating in formal mentoring programs: A qualitative investigation. *Journal of Vocational Behavior, 67,* 441–458.

Ellinger, A. D. & Kim, S. (2014). Coaching and human resource development: Examining relevant theories, coaching genres, and scales to advance research and practice. *Advances in Human Resource Development, 16*(2), 127–138.

Feldman, D. C. & Ng, T. W. H. (2008). Motivation to engage in training and career development. In R. Kanfer, G. Chen, & R. D. Pritchard (Eds.), *Work motivation: Past, present, future* (pp. 401–431). New York: Routledge.

Forret, M. L. & Dougherty, T. W. (2004). Networking behaviors and career outcomes: Difference for men and women? *Journal of Organizational Behavior, 25,* 419–437.

Forret, M. L. & Sullivan, S. E. (2002). A balanced scorecard approach to networking: A guide to successfully navigating career changes. *Organizational Dynamics, 31*(3), 245–258.

Garvey, R., Stokes, P., & Megginson, D. (2009). *Coaching and mentoring: Theory and practice.* London: Sage.

Ghosh, R. & Reio, T. G., Jr. (2013). Career benefits associated with mentoring for mentors: A meta-analysis. *Journal of Vocational Behavior, 83,* 106–116.

Gibson, C., Hardy, J. H., III, & Buckley, M. R. (2014). Understanding the role of networking in organizations. *Career Development International, 19*(2), 146–161.

Gorman, C. A., Thibodeaux, C. N., Eisinger, S. E., & Overstreet, B. L. (2012). Selection for training: The forgotten employment decision? In N. P. Reilly, M. J Sirgy & C. A. Gorman (Eds.), *Work motivation: Past, present, future* (pp. 95–105). New York: Routledge.

Grote, D. (2011). Designing a performance appraisal for driving organization success. In L. Berger & D. Berger (Eds.), *The talent management handbook: Creating a sustainable competitive advantage by selecting, developing, and promoting the best people* (2nd edn.) (pp. 45–54). New York: McGraw Hill.

Haggard, D. L., Dougherty, T. W., Turban, D. G., & Wilbanks, J. E. (2011). Who is a mentor? A review of evolving definitions and implications for research. *Journal of Management, 37,* 280–304.

Hazen, B. & Steckler, N. (2014). Career coaching. In E. Cox, T. Bachkirova, & D. Clutterbuck (Eds.), *The complete handbook of coaching* (2nd edn.) (pp. 329–341). London, CA: Sage.

Higgins, M. C. (2007). A contingency perspective on developmental networks. In J. E. Dutton & B. R. Ragins (Eds.), *Exploring positive relationships at work* (pp. 207–224). Mahwah, NJ: Erlbaum.

Higgins, M. C. & Kram, K. (2001). Reconceptualizing mentoring at work: A developmental network perspective. *Academy of Management Review, 26*(2), 264–288.

Hunt, C. M. & Fielden, S. L. (2013). E-coaching as a technique for developing the workforce and entrepreneurs. In S. Vinnicombe, R. Burke, S. Blake-Beard, & L. Moore (Eds.), *Handbook of research on promoting women's careers* (pp. 471–486). Cheltenham: Edward Elgar.

Hurst, C. S. & Eby, L. T. (2012). Mentoring in organizations: Mentor or tormentor? In N. P. Reilly, M. J. Sirgy, & C. A. Gorman (Eds.), *Work and quality of life: Ethical practices in organizations* (pp. 81–94). New York: Springer.

Ibarra, H. & Hunter, M. L. (2007, January). How leaders create and use networks. *Harvard Business Review*. Retrieved from https:HBR.org/2007/01/how-leaders-create-and-use-networks.

Insler, D. & Becom, A. (2011). Conducting performance reviews that improve the quality of your talent base. In L. Berger & D. Berger (Eds.), *The talent management handbook: Creating a sustainable competitive advantage by selecting, developing, and promoting the best people* (2nd edn.) (pp. 65–75). New York: McGraw Hill.

Kim, S. (2013). Networking enablers, constraints and dynamics: A qualitative analysis. *Career Development International, 18*(2), 120–138.

Kram, K. (1983). Phases of the mentor relationship. *Academy of Management Journal, 26*(4), 608–625.

Kram, K. (1985). *Mentoring at work: Developmental relationships in organizational life*. Glenview, IL: Scott, Foresman & Company.

Ladyshewsky, R. (2014). Peer coaching. In E. Cox, T. Bachkirova, & D. Clutterbuck (Eds.), *The complete handbook of coaching* (2nd edn.) (pp. 285–297). London, CA: Sage.

Lankau, M. J. & Scandura, T. A. (2007). Mentoring as a forum for personal learning in organizations. In B. R. Ragins & K. E. Kram (Eds.), *The handbook of mentoring at work: Theory, research and practice* (pp. 95–122). Thousand Oaks, CA: Sage.

Laud, R. L. & Johnson, M. (2012). Upward mobility: A typology of tactics and strategies for career advancement. *Career Development International, 17*(3), 231–254.

Lohman, M. C. (2005). A survey of factors influencing the engagement of two professional groups in informal workplace learning activities. *Human Resource Development Quarterly, 16*, 501–527.

McCall, M. W. (2004). Leadership development through experience. *The Academy of Management Executive, 18*(3), 127–130.

Major, D. A., Turner, J. E., & Fletcher, T. D. (2006). Linking proactive personality and the big five to motivation to learn and development activity. *Journal of Applied Psychology, 91*(4), 927–935.

Maltbia, T. E., Marsick, V. J., & Ghosh, R. (2014). Executive and organizational coaching: A review of insights drawn from literature to inform HRD practice. *Advances in Human Resource Development, 16*(2), 161–183.

Mustapha, M. & Daud, N. (2012). Perceived performance appraisal effectiveness, career commitment and turnover intention of knowledge workers. *International Journal of Business and Social Sciences, 10*, 157–165.

Navarro, A. (2011, January–February). Good networking/bad networking. *PEJ*, 58–60.

Parise, M. R. & Forret, M. L. (2008). Formal mentoring programs: The relationship of program design and support to mentors' perceptions of benefits and costs. *Journal of Vocational Behavior, 72*, 225–240.

Parker, P., Hall, D. T., & Kram, K. (2008). Peer coaching: A relational process for accelerating career learning. *Academy of Management Learning & Education*, 7(4), 487–503.

Parsons, F. (1909). *Choosing a vocation*. Boston, MA: Houghton Mifflin.

Ragins, B. R. & Kram, K. (2007). The roots and meaning of mentoring. In B. R. Ragins & K. E. Kram (Eds.), *The handbook of mentoring at work: Theory, research and practice* (pp. 3–16). Thousand Oaks, CA: Sage.

Ragins, B. R. & Verbos, A. K. (2007). Positive relationships in action: Relational mentoring and mentoring schemas in the workplace. In J. E. Dutton & B. R. Ragins (Eds.), *Exploring positive relationships at work* (pp. 3–28). Mahwah, NJ: Erlbaum.

Rosato, D. (2009, April). Networking for people who hate to network. *Money*, 38(4), 25–26.

Rothwell, W. J., Jackson, R. D., Knight, S. C., & Lindholm, J. E. (with Sang, W. A. & Payne, T. D.) (2005). *Career planning and succession management: Developing your organization's talent—for today and tomorrow*. Westport, CT: Praeger.

Segers, J., Vloeberghs, D., Henderickx, E., & Inceoglu, I. (2011). Structuring and understanding the coaching industry: The coaching cube. *Academy of Management Learning and Education*, 10(2), 204–221.

Singh, R., Ragins, B. R., & Tharenou, P. (2009). What matters most? The relative role of mentoring and career capital in career success. *Journal of Vocational Behavior*, 75, 56–67.

Stokes, J. & Jolly, R. (2014). Executive and leadership coaching. In E. Cox, T. Bachkirova, & D. Clutterbuck (Eds.), *The complete handbook of coaching* (2nd edn.) (pp. 244–255). London, CA: Sage.

Taormina, W. W. & Taormina, R. J. (2014). A new multidimensional measure of personal resilience and its use: Chinese nurse resilience, organizational socialization and career success. *Nursing Inquiry*, 21(4), 346–357.

Tips for successful networking (2013, September). *Sound & Video Contractor*, 31(9), 12.

van Rijn, M. B., Yang, H., & Sanders, K. (2013). Understanding employees' informal workplace learning: The joint influence of career motivation and self-construal. *Career Development International*, 18(6), 610–628.

Werner, J. M. & DeSimone, R. L. (2012). *Human resource development* (6th edn.). Mason, OH: South-Western.

Wolff, H.-G. & Moser, K. (2009). Effects of networking on career success: A longitudinal study. *Journal of Applied Psychology*, 94(1), 196–206.

Wolff, H.-G. & Moser, K. (2010). Do specific types of networking predict specific mobility outcomes? A two-year prospective study. *Journal of Vocational Behavior*, 77, 238–245.

# 5 Career Development Links to Career Psychology

> The only reliable prediction is that we will have to become perpetual learners, more self-reliant and more capable than ever in dealing with surprises of all sorts.
>
> Schein, 1996, p. 88; commentary on the future of career development

Career development has eclectic origins and remains a multidisciplinary field. Recognizing the potential strength in drawing from the research and practice of varied disciplines, researchers have advocated for sharing theories (e.g., Cameron, 2009; Egan, Upton, & Lynham, 2006; McDonald & Hite, 2014), yet collaboration has not been the norm. As we noted in Chapter 1, dissent remains within two of those fields, human resources (HR) and psychology, over emphasis on individual career needs and interests versus those of the organization (known as the contested terrain in HR, Inkson & King, 2011). Both disciplines feel the strain of those internal disputes and that may have hindered an inclination to look to other fields for ideas and insights, or both may simply be following the historic precedent to go it alone. Whatever the reason, the challenging reality of the current career environment should provide a greater sense of urgency to seek out new perspectives.

For its part, HR must recognize the importance of individual agency as it looks to the future of career development and provide supportive initiatives that fit both person and system. The recognition phase has been ongoing, with several researchers noting the need for a resurgence of career development within HRD to address current career issues (see for example, Egan et al., 2006; McDonald & Hite, 2005). However, the implementation seems to have stalled. This chapter offers an introduction to career development theories originating in the career psychology tradition which typically has focused on the quest of the individual to seek out meaningful work. That field's theoretical progression towards a holistic view of the individual as career seeker provides valuable insights for HR.

We will begin with an overview of some key career development and counseling theories to provide a basic understanding; then explore how those theories might better inform HR career development within systems. We will finish by suggesting some next steps to keep up with the changing nature of careers and the evolving needs of individuals pursing them.

## Theories from Career Psychology

There are a myriad of career development theories and varying ways to categorize them. One overarching classification divides theories into two eras, modern and postmodern, each representing a different epistemological perspective. Modern theoretical traditions indicate that "there is a reality 'out there' and that the theory is an attempt to map or to represent that reality" (Richardson, Constantine, & Washburn, 2005, p. 55). Postmodern approaches also recognize reality, but suggest that it is much more fluid and that how it is perceived will vary depending on individual cultural and life experience (Richardson et al., 2005). We will explore both, because, while the postmodern theories seem to fit better with individually driven careers, some of the previous approaches continue to influence current career development. As we explore theoretical constructs, you will see how these methods differ in application.

Some career development theories have proved to have more lasting impact than others, as well as more potential influence on HR, and those will be our focus here. We will explore the theories classified as "modern" first. Researchers (see, for example, Juntunen & Even, 2012; Shoffner Creager & Deacon, 2012) often consider them in three main categories: person–environment (P–E), developmental, and social cognitive. We will use current researchers to give us a valuable retrospective look at each theory to gauge how well they have lasted over time. Let's begin chronologically with the person–environment approach.

### *Person–Environment Fit*

Our previous discussion of the history of careers and career development (Chapter 1) mentioned Frank Parsons (1909) as an early advocate and practitioner. His belief that choosing the appropriate vocation was based on matching individual traits with "factors required for success in a given workplace environment" (Juntunen & Even, 2012, p. 239) is the origin of this approach. Decades after Parsons proposed his plan, the idea of linking people's interests with career requirements led John Holland (1962) to develop a theory that categorized individual personalities into six types, each representing a type of work. It became identified as the RIASEC hexagon (see the box below), because the positioning in the model set similar categories side by side and opposing categories across from one another. Take a moment, as you review the brief descriptions in Textbox 5.1, to consider what RIASEC type or combination comes closest to how you see yourself. The theory has endured, in part because the RIASEC types still appear to cover most/ all potential career-related options. Can you think of any other categories that should be included?

---

### RIASEC

#### RIASEC Categories

- Realistic: "those who do things" (p. 46), showing a preference for hands-on work including working with tools or objects (e.g., skilled trades or service work).
- Investigative: "those who think about things" (p. 46), representing a scientific, problem-solving perspective involving imaginative investigation (e.g., physician, biologist, chemist).
- Artistic: "those who create things" (p. 46), suggesting a flare for artistic, expressive endeavors (e.g., theater, interior decorator, musician).
- Social: "those who help others" (p. 47), with an interest in human interaction that might include social welfare or education (e.g., training, teaching, counseling).
- Enterprising: "those who persuade others" (p. 47), preferring connections that involve persuasion, selling; sense of self as ambitious (business owner, consultant).
- Conventional: "those who organize things" (p. 47), demonstrating skill in "systemic processes, numbers, records, accounting, and clerical occupations" (p. 47) (accountant, administrative assistant).

Source: Shoffner Creager & Deacon (2012)

---

The reasoning behind the RIASEC theory is that determining the type or type combination that best fit a particular person would provide a clear career direction; helping the individual to narrow a vocational search to those jobs that best matched personal interests. The RIASEC system endures as "one of the most prevalently used in research and practice articles" (Sampson et al., 2014), a testament to its influence in the field. However, it is open to criticism, for focusing only on interests to the exclusion of outside factors like economic or cultural limitations (Juntunen & Even, 2012) and for fostering a prescriptive view of career development.

The latter concern has been prompted by the popularity of the use of the RIASEC types in traditional career testing, including the Strong Interest Inventory and Self Directed Search (SDS, developed by Holland), two of the "most frequently used" interest inventories (Dik & Rottinghaus, 2013, p. 331) in the field of career counseling. Other prevalent inventories (e.g., the Campbell Interest and Skill Inventory) use structures similar to Holland's hexagon. While well-validated instruments, the often expressed apprehension is that their use may foster a "test and tell" approach to career development, where the results are presented as definitive determinations of a career rather than as one piece of information in a wide and varied picture of possibilities. A variant of that concern attests to the power of test results that prompts some individuals to see "the answer" in their scores, assuming that the test knows them better than they know themselves. That becomes particularly disconcerting since the SDS (and other less valid options) is readily available on-line, so potential career seekers have easy access. The result is often information without context. As we explore these theories further, the importance of context in career development will be reinforced. It may be useful to note at this point, that caution about relying on testing alone to circumvent a more individually driven, comprehensive career development process is indicative of a larger debate that prompted the postmodern career counseling movement, which we will discuss later in this chapter.

Additional criticisms aimed at Holland's hexagon and the tests based on it are prompted by the potential gender and cultural biases in the RIASEC types. They were originally developed in the 1950s, an era when gender roles were more restrictive and the career-focused workforce was more homogeneous (Einarsdottir & Rounds, 2009). Interest inventories in general have come under scrutiny for gender bias, despite efforts in recent years to update the instruments and include more women in the norming process. Concerns include ongoing gender bias in test materials (Einarsdottir & Rounds, 2009; Hansen, 2005), as well as bigger-picture issues, like the presumed salience of work over other aspects of life (Fitzgerald & Harmon, 2001). Interest inventories (and the RIASEC) have also been called into question for their Western, especially US, conceptualization of careers, severely limiting their adaptability to a global workforce (Fouad, 2002; Watson, 2006; Watson, Duarte, & Glavin, 2005). This limitation becomes exacerbated if the test results are left to interpretation by a career practitioner lacking sufficient understanding of other cultures (Watson, 2006).

Although developed decades after both Parsons and the RIASEC, the primary goal of matching worker and workplace is also reflected in the Minnesota Theory of Work Adjustment (TWA). As the name implies, the TWA "focuses on the process of persons' adjustment to their work environments, including the characteristics of persons that predict their satisfaction with the work environment," as well as how happy the organization is with them (Swanson & Schneider, 2013, p. 30). The predictive aspect of this theory follows the typical P–E fit approach, assessing the person and potential environments to find the appropriate fit. What makes the TWA different and note-worthy is that it also has a process aspect that expects that both the individual and the workplace will change over time and adjust accordingly to maintain the relationship (Shoffner Creager & Deacon, 2012; Swanson & Schneider, 2013). Each entity determines how much variation from the ideal will be tolerated and for how long. So, for example, a system may keep a person on even though skills may be lacking in some area as long as other requirements are being met; or an individual may justify a lack of raises as a tempo-rary step or may adjust personal salary expectations to achieve congruence.

The assessment aspect of TWA prompts apprehension because the instruments designed for this theory are not readily accessible (Swanson & Schneider, 2013), and while others can be used instead, they may bring their own set of difficulties, as noted above. However, research to date suggests that the TWA may work well with diverse populations because its implementation determines personal percep-tions of fit within a work environment (meaning it captures concerns like those we discuss in Chapter 6), making it more individually adapt-able than traditional trait and factor approaches (Juntunen & Even, 2012; Swanson & Schneider, 2013).

### *Developmental*

This category broadens the scope of careers to include the influence of "sequential life experiences, including those of childhood, on subsequent vocational development" (Juntunen & Even, 2012, p. 244), taking the idea of "development" into a more expansive realm. This marks a significant shift in perspective regarding careers, recognizing how life and careers might intersect. Approaches up to this point did not address how early or current life experiences or roles might affect career choices or opportunities. Our current understanding acknowledges the value of putting careers in context, but it was a new idea when these models were created. Two theories represent the developmental approach; both closely identified with their designers, but one clearly viewed as defining the genre. We will begin there with Donald Super's life span, life space theory; early ideas of this theory began in the 1950s but were revised over subsequent decades.

In his overview of the life span, life space theory, Hartung (2013a) explained that the dual concepts in the title signify careers as a synergistic process, building over time through different life phases or roles that reflect how self-concept is entwined with all other aspects of life. He observed:

> Life-span, life-space theory underscores the point that individuals develop not just one but rather constellations of self-concepts, or ideas about themselves, based on experiences in a wide array of life spheres. The primary concern within life-span, life-space theory, of course, is the vocational sphere, wherein the individual rests at the center of career choice, development, and decision making.
>
> (p. 89)

The life span aspect proposes that individuals go through a series of five phases over time, each linked to an age range and a set of experiences or tasks that lead to the next (see the box below for the stages).

**Super's 5 Stages of Career Development**

*Growth:* birth–14

- First exposure to work
- Begin developing self-concept

*Exploration:* 15–24

- Try out work with first jobs
- Explore self-concept and work

*Establishment:* 25–44

- Find a place in your field
- Seek advancement, recognition

*Maintenance:* 45–64

- Stay the course
- Adapt as needed to be relevant

*Disengagement:* 65–death

- Winding down; retirement
- Engage with roles outside work

Source: Shoffner Creager & Deacon (2012)

The stage progression of Super's model is both a hallmark of this theory and a focus of criticism. As you look at his proposed phases of career life, you may join the critics in observing that rigid representation of career progression may have fit traditional career paths decades ago, but it does not fit for you or others you know. It seems to ignore gender and cultural differences in life roles and the possibility that other aspects of life or society might impose on the closely prescribed pattern. Super reportedly added samples of women in his later research (Hartung, 2013a; Juntunen & Even, 2012), but remnants of gender bias lingered. While the theory remained the same, there are indications that Super acknowledged that circumstances might lead individuals to deviate from the linear progression and revisit some earlier stages as they pursued career changes or transitions (Hartung, 2013a; Juntunen & Even, 2012). How closely do Super's stages fit your own career path so far? What would you change to make this stage model more applicable to current careers?

Although the theory has waned in influence over time, the life span, life space theory is noted for bringing two key ideas into the ongoing career development discourse (Hartung, 2013a; Juntunen & Even, 2012):

- career maturity, readiness to make career-related decisions (i.e., investment in career planning, understanding of self and work);
- career adaptability, flexibility in pursuing a career path so that one can respond effectively to unexpected circumstances or make the transition from one phase to another.

Another development approach, Gottfredson's Theory of Circumscription and Compromise, appeared in 1981. While it is also categorized as a developmental theory for its use of lifelong career influences and stage-based orientation, it has no other links to Super; and it has received much less attention. It proposes four stages, spanning from early childhood beyond age 14. At each successive stage, children circumscribe their career options by eliminating occupations that seem inappropriate, leaving a smaller subset of "acceptable alternatives" after each progression (Gottfredson, 1981; Juntunen & Even, 2012; Shoffner Creager & Deacon, 2012). Successive limitations imposed start with differences between fantasy and reality and the power of being an adult, at ages 3–5 (i.e., recognizing the difference between children and adults and seeing work as something adults are supposed to do); then gender roles, at ages 6–8 (i.e., what jobs are considered gender appropriate); then occupational prestige and difficulty, at ages 9–13 (i.e., status of a particular occupation versus the effort required to get there); and finally congruence with personal interests and abilities, at age 14 and beyond (i.e., seeking what careers fit personal preferences and skills from the acceptable options determined to date; Gottfredson, 1981; Hutchinson & Niles, 2009; Juntunen & Even, 2012). The compromise aspect comes into play when options on the acceptable list according to the circumscription process are not accessible. Then the individual begins to forfeit some of the options, backing away from those initial possibilities towards something within reach. This process typically moves in reverse order of the circumscription process, sacrificing interests first; then, if necessary, giving up prestige; and, finally, abandoning gender roles to come up with viable choice (Gottfredson, 1981; Juntunen & Even, 2012; Shoffner Creager & Deacon, 2012).

Before we move to the next set of theories, consider another difference between Super and Gottfredson. While the life span, life space approach may seem overly prescriptive and perhaps outdated, it can be perceived as seeing careers in an optimistic light, as one plans for and supposedly achieves career opportunities. In contrast, Gottfredson's theory is about reigning in expectations, making do with what is feasible as society or life circumstances dictate options. It is difficult to grasp the meaning of that theory and not see implications for children growing up in poverty or without role models or advocates that would push them to consider non-traditional careers or continuing their education. Some might say that it is the more realistic view, recognizing that we all live within certain parameters. The next theory moves the idea of environmental influences on careers to a higher level.

### Social Cognitive

Social Cognitive Career Theory (SCCT) first appeared in the mid-1990s, created by Lent, Brown, and Hackett, and it has continued to be updated and augmented over the years, making it "one of the most comprehensive and popular theories in the contemporary counseling psychology literature" (Juntunen & Even, 2012, p. 251). The SCCT incorporates elements of both P–E fit and developmental theories, but refines them to address the interaction between individual thoughts and actions and the life experiences that may support or hinder career planning and development. The result is a theory that works well for a diverse workforce in a changing career environment. The title refers to the focus on cognition and resulting behaviors that stem from Bandura's social learning theory and are contextualized through three "cognitive-person variables" (Lent, 2013, p. 118). They are:

- self-efficacy: how individuals perceive their capabilities relative to specific tasks;
- outcome expectations: what one believes about the potential consequences of a career path;
- personal goals: intention to follow through, both in terms of what to do and a commitment to how well a task will be completed.

These components interplay throughout the four overlapping models that make up SCCT, focusing on: how career interests develop; factors that affect career choice; task performance, including influences that determine performance quality and persistence in the face of obstacles; and achievement of work satisfaction or well-being (Lent, 2013; Lent & Brown, 2006). Throughout the four models, multiple elements are addressed, recognizing potentially supportive or complicating aspects in each, and keeping the perspective of a lifelong career journey. For example, the two types of environmental influencers included in the career choices model represent a long-term progression. The term *distal* refers to factors that one encounters while still developing self-efficacy and outcome expectations, like support received for participating in educational activities or having access to career role models. In contrast, *proximal* factors typically come later in the career process, and may pose barriers to career opportunities, like quality of one's networks or encounters with discrimination in hiring (Lent, Brown, & Hackett, 2000).

HR professionals might be most interested in the models on task performance and work satisfaction, since they are more focused on the experiences of individuals already in the workforce. For instance, the model highlighting work satisfaction includes five variables, some originating from the individual, others systemically based: "working conditions and outcomes, goal-directed behavior, self-efficacy, goal and efficacy relevant supports and obstacles, and personality and affective traits" (Juntunen & Even, 2012, p. 253; Lent & Brown, 2006). While some aspects are within the individuals' power to change, others clearly point to HR as potential contributors to the process. Coaching on goals, "job redesign or change, social support, mentoring, or other environmental methods (e.g., advocacy) may also offer useful tools for reducing dissatisfaction or promoting satisfaction" (Lent & Brown, 2006, p. 244). While the next section highlights the more person-centered approaches coming out of the career counseling field, the SCCT remains a well-supported theory that offers insights for HR into the career development process.

### *Introduction to Constructivist Approaches*

The divide between modern and postmodern approaches to career development can be defined in various ways, but it is essentially a break between theories that rely on objective outside sources (e.g., tests, historical patterns) to define career parameters for people and those that encourage each individual to create his/her own career reality through self-discovery.

The former has been labeled "logical positivist," suggesting over-reliance on the role of logic, precedents, and sequential career progress. It has been called into question in a contemporary career environment that is characterized by change and unpredictability. Recognizing the need for a less prescriptive approach for an era when career development is driven by individual agency, the postmodern or constructivist worldview:

> views the person as an open system, constantly interacting with the environment, seeking stability through ongoing change. The emphasis is on the process, not on an outcome; there is no completion of a stage and the arrival at the next stage.
>
> (Patton & McMahon, 2006a, p. 4)

However, in contrast to the specificity of more objectively based approaches, constructivism has been described as a "way of thinking or a set of values," rather than a designated framework or set of steps, leaving its application open to practitioner acceptance, understanding, and implementation of the mindset and principles (Patton & McMahon, 2006a, p. 10). "Constructivists believe that there is no absolute truth, that truth lies where individuals are and in how they derive meaning from their environment and their experiences with others" (Watson, 2006, p. 46).

The open structure plays into both the complexity and the flexibility of constructionism. One of its strengths is recognizing and capturing the influence of environment (e.g., social, cultural, economic) on individual career planning and implementation, making it potentially adaptable across cultures. However, its successful application in multicultural settings is also dependent on the practitioner being aware of his/her own potential cultural biases when facilitating the process (Watson, 2006).

### Theory of Career Construction

In our discussion, we will explore a few of the better known theoretical frameworks that ascribe to the constructionist view. We will begin with one that takes its name from the genre itself and was developed by one of the key scholars in the constructivist approach, Savickas's theory of career construction, which:

> asserts that individuals construct their careers by imposing meaning on their vocational behavior and occupational experiences. Whereas the objective definition of career denotes the sequence of positions occupied by a person from school through retirement, the subjective definition used in construction theory is not the sum of work experience but rather the patterning of these experiences into a cohesive whole that produces a meaningful story.
>
> (Savickas, 2005, p. 43)

While clearly adhering to the tenets of the constructionist view, this theory does not summarily discount all of the elements of logical positivist theories, but instead may use them in context, as smaller parts of a larger, holistic, ongoing journey of development (Savickas, 2005). This would manifest in different types of career development interventions. P–E fit interventions can be helpful for expanding knowledge about self and work options when individuals need to revisit occupational choices or make decisions about additional education. The developmental perspective may be useful when taking stock of one's career to date, preparing for transitions, and building competencies. The constructivist approach then comes in when the goal is to "clarify our identities, purpose and direction in life and how we may use work to become more complete" (Hartung, 2013b, p. 47; Savickas, 2013).

The life-design framework puts constructivist theory goals into practice. Designed to highlight "flexibility, employability, commitment, emotional intelligence, and lifelong learning" (Savickas, 2012, p. 14), it describes a career counseling intervention that takes an individual on a progressive narrative journey. It begins with constructing an individual perspective of career through capturing personal stories, continues through deconstructing those stories (to expose "self-limiting ideas, confining roles and cultural barriers"), then building a new vision of a self and career, and finally settling on a plan of action to go forward and embrace the next career transition (Savickas, 2012, p. 16). The elements of this framework fit well with the current career environment, so it may be particularly useful for HRD. A critical aspect of enacting this intervention is a mainstay of all constructionist approaches: the narrative—our next topic.

*Narrative*

The narrative is a ubiquitous part of constructivism. It is integral to the process defined in all theories attributed to this genre, because it is the key to capturing an individual's unique story about his/her life and work. More than a simple interview or conversation about careers, a narrative offers the individual an extended opportunity to relate life stories, complete with all the contextual factors (e.g., past work, education, family, culture, values) that create a unique picture of one person's past, present, and goals for the future. While some earlier theories may have made reference to the interaction between person and environment related to careers, the narrative process illustrates the inherent complexity of an individual life, while providing a backdrop for what might come next.

Given its crucial role in the career development process, some researchers have also described "narrative" as its own constructivist approach (e.g., McIlveen & Patton, 2007; Sharf, 2013), rather than one component of another theory. Whether as theory or method, the basic intention remains the same, to foster self-understanding through artic- ulation of and reflection upon one's own experience that can help build lifelong career adaptability. To capture the potential breadth of the narrative, McIlveen and Patton (2007) listed some of the techniques that would be categorized as part of the narrative process. They included some predictable possibilities, like storytelling or written auto- biographies, but they also added less expected options like guided fantasies (about future career/life), life-lines (capturing significant points on a time line), or card sorts (moving 50–100 cards "with an occupation, skill, or value" on each into categories; Chope, 2015, p. 74). In the spirit of lifelong learning, all are designed to foster self-understanding and insights that may be applied to current and future endeavors.

### *Chaos and Happenstance*

While career models often have taken the stance that knowledge (of self and work), insight, and planning are a part of navigating careers, two constructivist theories add a different perspective, emphasizing the influence of the unpredictable and the unexpected. These brief descriptions will not fully do them justice but can serve as an introduction. Chaos theory seeks to address the inherent complexity in individual career paths. Pryor and Bright (2006) observed that, while some general patterns may exist regarding careers, predictability is illusive, because any one person's unique qualities, in conjunction with myriad environmental factors and combinations of factors (social, economic, cultural), might yield vastly different results. Additionally, career "decision makers both change and can be changed by the influences on them in an ongoing, interactive way" (Pryor & Bright, 2006, p. 4). The overall result is a good deal of uncertainty, regardless of effort, knowledge, retrospection, or planning. The idea in building awareness of this potentially disturbing thought is to help individuals realize the importance of remaining flexible and adaptable and to help them develop the skills and mindset that they will need in their career journey. A variation on this theme is behind the Happenstance Learning Theory, which suggests that careers are subject to a lifetime of unexpected situations and opportunities, and it is unrealistic to think otherwise (Krumboltz, 2009). These two theories epitomize a key point of the postmodern view of careers, that career decision making is both highly individualized and an on-going process, not a single event. Both should resonate with HR professionals as they explore how to support career development in organizations.

### *Systems Theory Framework*

To summarize some of the key aspects of constructionist theories, we will wrap up our exploration of these approaches with an overarching view. Patton and McMahon's Systems Theory Framework (STF) (2006b) was proposed as a way to capture the range and depth of various career development theories that adhere to the constructionist mindset. STF was not designed to be a developmental theory itself, but rather "an overarching framework" illustrating the multiple "interpersonal and contextual" influences on individual career development represented in other theories (p. 196). The designated key features of career development influence are characterized as:

- the individual (e.g., gender, age, ability, aptitudes, etc.), a primary focus in all constructionist theories;
- the environment, including:
  - social systems (e.g., community, school, family, peers) that may change over time;
  - environmental–societal systems (e.g., socioeconomic status, globalization, employment markets) that have a less direct, but still pervasive impact.

Patton and McMahon (2006b, p. 197) further determined that those elements are subject to the influence of three processes:

- recursiveness, representing the ongoing multidirectional interaction among individual and environmental influences that signify open systems;
- changes that may occur over time throughout the systems (recognizing the enduring value of viewing career development as a life-spanning concept);
- chance, an unpredictable but inevitable influence on career development.

This overview provides a concise way to capture the basic components of the constructivist approach.

## HR and Career Psychology

Our goal in the previous section was to provide an introduction to the theoretical constructs behind some current career psychology initiatives. Career development for the twenty-first century will require ingenuity and insight, and HR scholars and practitioners will need to draw on varied sources for information and ideas. For example, while current wisdom exposes the weaknesses in some of the logical positivist approaches, like P–E fit and developmental models, they expand our current understanding about the appropriate use of testing or the potential influences of early life experiences on career agency. The SCCT framework series serves as a reminder of the complex interactions of environmental influencers that affect career development for individuals (including some of the barriers that we address in Chapter 6). Beyond fostering understanding of career motivations and limitations, recognition of the influencers that are part of the workplace can guide change as systems strive to improve career development processes.

While the logical positivist theories do not have an identifiable parallel in the history of career development in HR, the progression to the postmodern constructivist view illustrates the challenges of the current career environment in HR. A diverse workforce requires a more individualized approach to career development, but developing a systemic structure to accommodate unique needs can be a daunting task. Both career psychology and HR are struggling with this transition (see the box below for some examples). We will explore potential organizational and individual initiatives to address these concerns after addressing two overarching concepts that span constructivist career psychology and career development in HR.

### Common Concerns: HR and Career Psychology Practitioners

The two fields have rarely collaborated, but they have some common concerns regarding twenty-first-century career development:

- Better integration of theory and practice: so that practitioners are working with solid foundations.
- A contested terrain: both HR and psychology face organizational versus individual career dichotomies; both see middle ground but struggle to attain it.
- New roles for career practitioners as individual agency becomes the focus: less "expert," more "facilitator."
- Educating and training professionals with the competencies they need for career development work in the twenty-first century
- Measuring results when objective goals give way to more subjective goals.

Sources: Patton & McMahon (2006b); Tang (2003); Watson (2006)

The first is lifelong learning. In a chapter appropriately titled "Lifelong career development learning," Patton and McMahon (2006b) reiterated that the new job security is in developing employable skills that translate into marketability elsewhere. They observed, "most individuals will not only have to find and hold a job once, they will have to do it repeatedly during their lifetime" (p. 229). Rottinghaus and Van Esbroeck (2011) reinforced the need for lifelong learning and the ideas behind chaos and happenstance theories when they observed, "individuals must now construe their careers as an unpredictable, life-long evolution" (p. 45). Historically, career decision making was largely confined to those starting their careers, but it has now become a skill to be honed on a regular basis, requiring ready access to career information and training on job search skills (Feller & Peila-Shuster, 2012; Patton & McMahon, 2006b). The reality of a lifelong career search and decision-making process means expanding the role of career development for HR.

The constructivist emphasis on individual agency also highlights career self-management as another skill set to be mastered in the workplace. HRD research has acknowledged that the current career environment dictates a shift away from a focus on system-controlled career development to include individually driven development (e.g., Doyle, 2000; McDonald & Hite, 2005), but movement in that direction has been slow. One way to begin would be to prepare individuals for self-managing their careers (Patton & McMahon, 2006b). Taking control of one's own career requires knowledge, an adaptive mindset, and system support.

Knowledge needs will be primarily dependent upon the individual's background, education, and work experience acquired so far. Younger employees likely will require more assistance to learn about themselves and about career planning (e.g., tapping into their own strengths, how to gather career information, choose appropriate education and training, develop a network; King, 2004). Their more experienced colleagues will need support for learning how to augment their employability or find new challenges. Helping individuals identify those learning needs and meet them is part of the HR career development process.

Savickas (2005) defined career adaptability as "a psychosocial construct that denotes an individual's readiness and resources for coping with current and imminent vocational development tasks, occupational transitions, and personal traumas" (p. 51). This definition combines Super's constructs of career maturity and adaptability, noted earlier in this chapter. Adaptability is conceptualized as demonstrating career concern, control, curiosity, and confidence (see Chapter 3 for more on adaptability).

The combination of self-efficacy and motivation to plan, take initiative, and explore career possibilities is essential for career management, but career development interventions are needed to accomplish proficiency in each of those. For example, efficacy comes with experiences of successful fulfillment of challenging tasks (Savickas, 2005), but learning to choose those wisely and gaining access to them involves career development. Similarly, motivation may vary, based on environmental influencers that interact with individual interests (see the SCCT mentioned earlier or Chapter 6). HR's role in nurturing an adaptive mindset will likely combine advocacy (e.g., for policies ensuring equal access) with more traditional initiatives (e.g., training, mentoring programs).

HR advocacy and initiatives leads to the final point, system support. King (2004) suggested that, even within career self-management, "people do not have full decision latitude over their desired career outcomes" (p. 118), because decisions about issues such as salary, maintaining employment, or access to opportunities are typically made by someone else in the organization. However, when individuals perceive that an organization is invested in their career development, they may decide to join, to stay on or simply to be more invested in their work (Arnold & Cohen, 2013). For example, a 2006 Dutch study summarized by stating:

> An important conclusion for the field of human resource management and development concerns the relation between career competencies and career support at the workplace. Employees who experience career support at work show more career competence than employees who experience less career support.
> (Kuijpers & Scheerens, 2006, p. 317)

The system support factor puts the responsibility on the organization to review policies and practices for their impact on career development in general and career self-management in particular. It also reinforces the strategic power of a comprehensive career development system within HR (see Chapter 4 for examples of specific career development interventions).

## Organizational Action

Other chapters in this volume highlight systemic career development interventions that will be part of the comprehensive career development support within an organization. See Chapter 4, for example, for information on mentoring, coaching, stretch assignments, succession planning, and career paths. Here we will focus primarily on additional initiatives that most directly relate to individual agency in career development.

Interestingly, career management may be the bridge that crosses the contested terrain in HR. Arnold and Cohen (2013) observed that, while

> there is a tendency to consider organizational and individual perspectives on career as being in conflict ... there is accumulating evidence that when it comes to career management interventions, individual and organization can operate in harmony, or at least in cooperation.
> (p. 294)

They based this assessment on research that, similar to the Kuijpers & Scheerens (2006) study mentioned earlier, found synergy between organizational career support and career self-management, each benefitting the other. A different study reinforced the potential for mutual benefits, indicating that organizational career support "encourages employees to improve both their internal and their external employability," although the effect is stronger for internal employability (Verbruggen, Sels, & Forrier, 2007, p. 79). Of course, the usual caveats apply, for example if systems condone restricting access to certain opportunities or using data gathered for individual feedback to fast track some individuals over others under the guise of career development, they will undermine any trust they might have gained (Arnold & Cohen, 2013). So the first recommendation is the most comprehensive and lays the foundation for the rest:

- Create a transparent and open developmental culture with policies and procedures that support career access and opportunity.

Our discussion of lifelong learning and the need for recurring career decision making sets the stage for some logistical support initiatives, those that provide information about self and occupational opportunities within and outside the organization. Some of these would fall under the heading of targeted training, such as career planning workshops, that might include individual assessments as well as skill building. Workshops would work well in conjunction with career resource centers offering information that fosters individual exploration, either on-site or via the Internet (Arnold & Cohen, 2013). Cautions and capabilities abound regarding on-line career development, so we will address them briefly here.

Not surprisingly, Internet sources for career development have expanded and advanced in recent decades. They now include assessment and interpretations, and a range of career information (e.g., O*NET, an extensive database, and the on-line version of the *Occupational Outlook Handbook*, a mainstay of career data), as well as complete computer-assisted career guidance systems (Sampson & Osborn, 2015). As expected, the main benefits are ease of access to information and learning opportunities, lower costs, and anonymity. Unfortunately, the limitations are critical ones, including uneven quality of information or assessments, potential breaches of confidentiality, and lack of professional assistance when it might be needed (Sampson & Osborn, 2015).

Other resources might include development centers focused on helping individuals access personal strengths and goals for improvement, or personal development plans to build individualized career paths that match goals for success (Arnold & Cohen, 2013). So the next recommendation is:

- To develop logistical support interventions that offer both general resources for use by anyone in the system and individualized feedback and planning.

The concern about professional assistance noted above taps into a larger issue about this era of career development: competencies for career development professionals. We addressed general competencies in Chapter 1, but our discussion about career psychology theories and practices suggests new challenges. The complexity of current careers may require more support than HR professionals can offer. Consider implementation of the constructivist theories that we covered earlier. The extensive narrative approach demands a particular type of knowledge and expertise that is not part of human resource development or human resource management curricula. It is different from, yet complementary to, other career development initiatives. As employees continue a lifelong journey to further their self-knowledge and career self-efficacy, they are likely to both need and want this type of career development intervention. In response, some organizations are incorporating career counseling into their career development process (see box below).

### Next Step: Career Counseling

According to the *Wall Street Journal*, several large companies are adding career counselors to their payrolls. Aflac, Genentech, and American Express were among those listed as taking this step as companies strive to reduce staff turnover through career development initiatives. The counseling services often are part of a larger effort including career centers and targeted training initiatives.

Source: Silverman (2015)

Depending on the needs of the system, career counselors may be added to the HR staff or outsourced so that they remain external to the organization. Verbruggen et al. (2007) considered external career counseling as part of a larger study (using the assumption that counselors not affiliated with the organization might be more impartial) and found that employees benefitted from having that resource available. Arnold and Cohen (2013) suggested that either could work. An alternative that organizations may want to consider is to have HR staff trained as career development facilitators. The 120-hour training program sponsored by the National Career Development Association (NCDA) addresses 12 competencies, including assessment comprehension and use, understanding of career development models and theories, and following the professional code of ethics. Research also suggests training line managers to be more knowledgeable about career development, since individuals may approach them first for guidance. This leads to the final recommendation for organizations:

- Add career counseling professionals to your career development system.

**Individual Actions**

Recommendations in this section risk being repetitive of what we have suggested throughout the book, suggesting both consistency in research findings and clarity for those pursuing career development. Lips-Wiersma and Hall (2007) looked at the new career parameters within the context of organizations and suggested several actions that individuals can take. We begin with a representative sample from their study that reinforces advice from other sources and then add two others that particularly fit career self-management:

- Be proactive—we have noted this before, indicating how foundational it is to the entire pursuit of careers in the twenty-first century.
- Pursue opportunities to augment your skills—in Chapter 4 we discussed stretch assignments as key to building employability and visibility; succeeding in new endeavors also boosts your career self-efficacy.
- Communicate your career goals—once others know your aspirations, they can assist you in reaching them.
- Seek honest feedback—show that you are open to learning; go beyond your performance appraisal to gather additional input about potential career opportunities or changes.
- Build career resilience—remember that a career is a journey, not a single destination. Adopt a lifelong learning perspective; prepare to remain flexible and open to change (Casio, 2007; see Chapters 3 and 7 for more on resilience).
- Diversify your work experience—look for opportunities to work in different contexts to build range as well as depth in your career portfolio (Arnold & Cohen, 2013; Karaevli & Hall, 2006).

## Summary

This chapter began by reinforcing the value of exploring knowledge outside of HR to better inform career development in organizations. The theories from career psychology reinforced the individual agency aspect of twenty-first-century careers and provided insights applicable to lifelong learning and career self-management. Those insights led to recommendations for systems and individual career managers. It is our hope as authors that organizations build career development systems that reflect a wide range of knowledge and that serve both the system and the individuals within it well.

## References

Arnold, J. & Cohen, L. (2013). Careers in organizations. In W. B. Walsh, M. L. Savickas, & P. J. Hartung (Eds.), *Handbook of vocational psychology: Theory, research, and practice* (4th edn.) (pp. 273–304). New York: Routledge.

Cameron, R. (2009). Theoretical bridge building: The career development project for the 21st century meets the new era of human resource development. *Australian Journal of Career Development*, *18*(3), 9–17.

Casio, W. F. (2007). Trends, paradoxes, and some directions for research in career studies. In H. Gunz & M. Peiperl (Eds.), *Handbook of career studies* (pp. 549–557). Los Angeles, CA: Sage.

Chope, R. C. (2015). Card sorts, sentence completions, and other qualitative assessments. In P. Hartung, M. Savickas, & W. B. Walsh (Eds.), *APA handbooks in psychology: Vol. 2 Applications. APA handbook of career interventions* (pp. 71–84). Washington, DC: American Psychological Association.

Dik, B. J. & Rottinghaus, P. J. (2013). Assessments of interests. In K. F. Geisinger (Ed.), *APA handbook of testing and assessment in psychology: Vol 2. Testing and assessment in clinical and counseling psychology* (pp. 325–348). Washington, DC: American Psychological Association.

Doyle, M. (2000). Managing careers in organisations. In A. Collins & R. A. Young (Eds.), *The future of careers* (pp. 228–242). Cambridge: Cambridge University Press.

Egan, T. M., Upton, M. G., & Lynham, S. A. (2006). Career development: Load-bearing wall or window dressing? Exploring definitions, theories, and prospects for HRD-related theory building. *Human Resource Development Review*, *5*(4), 442–477.

Einarsdottir, S. & Rounds, J. (2009). Gender bias and construct validity in vocational interest measurement: Differential item functioning in the Strong Interest Inventory. *Journal of Vocational Behavior*, *74*, 295–307.

Feller, R. W. & Peila-Shuster, J. J. (2012). Designing career development plans with clients. In D. Capuzzi and M. D. Stauffer (Eds.), *Career counseling: Foundations, perspectives, and applications* (2nd edn.) (pp. 223–252). New York: Routledge Taylor & Francis.

Fitzgerald, L. & Harmon, L. (2001). Women's career development: A postmodern update. In F. Leong & A. Barak (Eds.), *Contemporary models in vocational psychology* (pp. 207–230). Mahwah, NJ: Lawrence Erlbaum.

Fouad, N. (2002). Cross-cultural differences in vocational interests: Between-groups differences on the Strong Interest Inventory. *Journal of Counseling Psychology, 49*(3), 283–289.

Gottfredson, L. S. (1981). Circumscription and compromise: A developmental theory of occupational aspirations (monograph). *Journal of Counseling Psychology, 28*(6), 545–579.

Hansen, J. C. (2005). Assessment of interests. In S. Brown & R. Lent (Eds.), *Career development and counseling: Putting theory and research to work* (pp. 281–304). Hoboken, NJ: Wiley.

Hartung, P. J. (2013a). The life-span, life-space theory of careers. In S. Brown & R. Lent (Eds.), *Career development and counseling: Putting theory and research to work* (2nd edn.) (pp. 83–114). Hoboken, NJ: Wiley.

Hartung, P. J. (2013b). Career as story: Making the narrative turn. In W. B. Walsh, M. L. Savickas & P. J. Hartung (Eds.), *Handbook of vocational psychology: Theory, research, and practice* (4th edn.) (pp. 33–52). New York: Routledge.

Holland, J. L. (1962). Some explorations of a theory of vocational choice: I. One- and two-year longitudinal studies. *Psychological Monographs: General and Applied, 76*(26, Serial No. 545), 1–49.

Hutchinson, B. & Niles, S. G. (2009). Career development theories. In I. Marini & M. Stebnicki (Eds.), *The professional counselor's desk reference* (pp. 467–476). New York: Springer.

Inkson, K. & King, Z. (2011). Contested terrain in careers: A psychological contract model. *Human Relations, 64*(1), 37–57.

Juntunen, C. L. & Even, C. E. (2012). Theories of vocational psychology. In N. A. Fouad (Ed.), *APA handbook of counseling psychology: Vol. 1. Theories, research, and methods* (pp. 237–267). Washington, DC: American Psychological Association.

Karaevli, A. & Hall, D. T. T. (2006). How career variety promotes the adaptability of managers: A theoretical model. *Journal of Vocational Behavior, 69*, 359–373.

King, A. (2004). Career self-management: Its nature, causes and consequences. *Journal of Vocational Behavior, 65*, 112–133.

Krumboltz, J. D. (2009). The happenstance learning theory. *Journal of Career Assessment, 17*(2), 135–154.

Kuijpers, M. A. C. T. & Scheerens, J. (2006). Career competencies for the modern career. *Journal of Career Development, 32*(4), 303–319.

Lent, R. W. (2013). Social cognitive career theory. In S. Brown & R. Lent (Eds.), *Career development and counseling: Putting theory and research to work* (2nd edn.) (pp. 115–146). Hoboken, NJ: Wiley.

Lent, R. W. & Brown, S. D. (2006). Integrating person and situation perspectives on work satisfaction: A social-cognitive view. *Journal of Vocational Behavior, 69*, 236–247.

Lent, R. W., Brown, S. D., & Hackett, G. (2000). Contextual supports and barriers to career choice: A social cognitive analysis. *Journal of Counseling Psychology, 47*(1), 36–49.

Lips-Wiersma, M. & Hall, D. T. (2007). Organizational career development is *not* dead: A case study on managing the new career during organizational change. *Journal of Organizational Behavior, 28*, 771–792.

McDonald, K. S. & Hite, L. M. (2005). Reviving the relevance of career development in human resource development. *Human Resource Development Review, 4*(4), 418–439.

McDonald, K. S. & Hite, L. M. (2014). Contemporary career literature and HRD. In N. E. Chalofsky, T. S. Rocco, & M. L. Morris (Eds.), *Handbook of human resource development* (pp. 353–368). Hoboken, NJ: Wiley.

McIlveen, P. & Patton, W. (2007). Narrative career counselling: Theory and exemplars of practice. *Australian Psychologist, 42*(3), 226–235.

Parsons, F. (1909). *Choosing a vocation.* Boston, MA: Houghton Mifflin.

Patton, W. & McMahon, M. (2006a). Constructivism: What does it mean for career counselling? In M. McMahon & W. Patton (Eds.), *Career counseling: Constructivist approaches* (pp. 3–15). London: Routledge.

Patton, W. & McMahon, M. (2006b). *Career development and systems theory: Connecting theory and practice.* Rotterdam, Netherlands: Sense.

Pryor, G. L. & Bright, J. E. (2006). Counseling chaos: Techniques for practitioners. *Journal of Employment Counseling, 43*, 2–16.

Richardson, J. S., Constantine, K., & Washburn, M. (2005). New directions for theory development in vocational psychology. In W. B. Walsh & M. L. Savickas (Eds.), *Handbook of vocational psychology: Theory, research, and practice* (3rd edn.) (pp. 51–84). Mahwah, NJ: Earlbaum.

Rottinghaus, P. J. & Van Esbroeck, R. (2011). Improving person–environment fit and self-knowledge. In P. J. Hartung & L. M. Subich (Eds.), *Developing self in work and career: Concepts, cases, and contexts* (pp. 35–52). Washington, DC: American Psychological Association.

Sampson, J. P. Jr., Hou, P.-C., Kronholz, J. F., Dozier, V. C., McClain, M.-C., Buzzetta, M., Pawley, E. K., Finklea, J. T., Peterson, G. W., Lenz, J. G., Reardon, R. C., Osborn, D. S., Hayden, S. C. W., Colvin, G. P., & Kennelly, E. L. (2014). A content analysis of career development theory, research, and practice—2013. *The Career Development Quarterly, 62*, 290–326.

Sampson, J. P. & Osborn, D. S. (2015). Using information and communication technology in delivering career interventions. In P. Hartung, M. Savickas, & W. B. Walsh (Eds.), *APA handbooks in psychology: Vol. 2 Applications.*

*APA handbook of career interventions* (57–70). Washington, DC: American Psychological Association.

Savickas, M. (2005). The theory and practice of career construction. In S. Brown & R. Lent (Eds.), *Career development and counseling: Putting theory and research to work* (pp. 42–70). Hoboken, NJ: Wiley.

Savickas, M. (2012). Life design: A paradigm for career intervention in the 21st century. *Journal of Counseling and Development, 90*, 13–19.

Savickas, M. (2013). Career construction theory and practice. In S. Brown & R. Lent (Eds.), *Career development and counseling: Putting theory and research to work* (2nd edn.) (pp. 147–183). Hoboken, NJ: Wiley.

Schein, E. H. (1996). Career anchors revisited: Implications for career development in the 21st century. *The Academy of Management Executive, 10*(4), 80–88.

Sharf, R. S. (2013). Advances in theories of career development. In W. B. Walsh, M. L. Savickas, & P. J. Hartung (Eds.), *Handbook of vocational psychology: Theory, research, and practice* (4th edn.) (pp. 3–32). New York: Routledge.

Shoffner Creager, M. F. & Deacon, M. M. (2012). Trait and factor, developmental, learning, and cognitive theories. In D. Capuzzi & M. Stauffer (Eds.), *Career counseling: Foundations, perspectives, and applications* (2nd edn.) (pp. 43–79). New York: Routledge.

Silverman, R. E. (2015, January). Careers: Climbing career ladder with help. *Wall Street Journal*, Eastern edition, B.6. Retrieved from http://search.proquest.com.ezproxy.library.ipfw.edu/docview/1645012662?

Swanson, J. L. & Schneider, M. (2013). Minnesota theory of work adjustment. In S. Brown & R. Lent (Eds.), *Career development and counseling: Putting theory and research to work* (2nd edn.) (pp. 29–54). Hoboken, NJ: Wiley.

Tang, M. (2003). Career counseling in the future: Constructing, collaborating, advocating. *The Career Development Quarterly, 52*, 61–69.

Verbruggen, M., Sels, L., & Forrier, A. (2007). Unraveling the relationship between organizational career management and the need for external career counseling. *Journal of Vocational Behavior, 17*, 69–83.

Watson, M. B. (2006). Career counselling theory, culture and constructivism. In M. MaMahon & W. Patton (Eds.), *Career counseling: Constructivist approaches* (pp. 45–56). London: Routledge.

Watson, M., Duarte, M. E., & Glavin, K. (2005). Cross-cultural perspectives on career assessment. *The Career Development Quarterly, 54*(1), 29–35.

# 6 Career Development Barriers and Diverse Populations

> Overall, a career-development strategy that enables organizations to adapt to rapidly changing environments and to maintain their employees' employability needs to be based on the diversity of the organization's workforce.
>
> Voelpel et al. 2012, p. 509

It has now become almost a cliché to say "we live and work in a diverse global society." Researchers no longer refer to a diverse workplace as an emerging idea, but acknowledge it as a certainty. Systems also grasp this reality and may be drawn to considering diversity as a means to:

- maintain global competitiveness (appealing to niche markets, harnessing the creativity of multiple perspectives);
- attract and retain the best employees (noting the changing demographics of the workforce);
- enhance their image in the industry or community as good partners (doing well by doing good), or perhaps simply to be ethically responsible citizens (Mor Barak, 2014; Thomas, 2005).

Yet, despite this recognition, many organizations still seem to struggle with building inclusive cultures that actually embrace and integrate differing practices and procedures into their traditional ways of operating. For example, many have become more adept at recruiting a diverse workforce (sometimes with the push of legislation; sometimes by choice), but not necessarily more skilled at retaining those new recruits or knowing how to use that diversity to strengthen the organization. This dilemma has prompted an interest in engaging diversity at a different level, as systems recognize:

that the mere presence of a diverse group of employees in an organisation does not guarantee that the organisation is necessarily welcoming of cultural or other differences. Nor does a diverse employee base necessarily indicate that a company is making use of its diversity in a way that enhances organisational performance.

(Bristol & Tisdell, 2010, p. 225)

One of the ways that systems can build more inclusive organizational cultures is to review and revise their career development so that it maximizes opportunities for their entire workforce (traditional majority *and* under-represented members), which in turn can enhance system performance.

Career development has never been a "one-size-fits-all" construct, although historically systems were much less focused on individual needs and more invested in how employees could be developed to sustain the growth and continuity of the organization. Coincidently, that singularly directed view of careers flourished when the workforce being considered for career development was also narrowly defined as a largely White, male majority. As we have noted earlier in this book, the current climate of careers negates such an organizationally driven, system-serving approach. Similarly, the view must expand to address career development for employees that represent a multiplicity of differences. Research confirms that individuals from under-represented groups "encounter tremendous obstacles in their career development" (Niles & Harris-Bowlsbey, 2013, p. 130). As individuals become more invested in guiding their own career paths, human resources (HR) and the systems that they assist must not only adapt to a new way of supporting career development as a function, but also recognize and address the barriers to career development of a diverse workforce. In this chapter, we will explore some of the key barriers, examining them from a systems and an individual level. We will also discuss potential initiatives for building a more inclusive career culture as well as options for individuals from under-represented groups to enhance their own career development possibilities.

A caveat before we continue: in determining how to approach this chapter, we recognized two factors:

- Proportionally, more workplace diversity research has been devoted to gender than to other types of differences (Ryan & Haslam, 2007). Not surprisingly, this also tends to be the case in the subset of literature devoted to career development. That is not to imply that we have resolved gender issues in the workplace, just that researchers have explored it more than other types of diversity. It seems to be the aspect of difference that organizations and society as a whole are most comfortable addressing. Also, while other non-dominant groups remain very much in the minority in many organizations, White women make up a higher proportion of many workplaces, providing greater numbers to study. However, their increased presence has not resulted in equal career opportunities. They remain under-represented in positions of power. While we may extrapolate some from gender research to identify issues for other under-represented groups, those studies are inadequate to capture all diversity issues. Each under-represented group experiences some unique barriers that we cannot address in full here.

- While the nature of research often compels us to study diversity in discrete segments that propose to be singular in nature (e.g., gender, race, age), there are few singularities in reality. The concept of intersectionality reminds us that, as humans, we are mosaics of various types of identities (e.g., Black lesbian, deaf man over 50). Intersectionality also means that barriers that may exist as a result of one aspect of difference from the majority are potentially exacerbated when several variations are compounded (Shore et al., 2011). In any situation or for any individual, one aspect of identity may be more salient than the others or may prompt stronger reactions, but there is always the dynamic of a compounded effect.

Since we have only a chapter to address career development barriers for a diverse workforce, we decided to frame our discussion by types of barriers that impact non-majority employees, rather than addressing each group separately. Consider references cited here as a springboard to delve more deeply into issues that limit career development for members of particular groups.

## System-level Barriers

While many of the system-level barriers to career development for under-represented groups reflect organizational culture, some are carry-overs from the external environment (Thomas, 2005). In addition to those identified in earlier chapters, these particularly affect non-majority group members.

### Societal Influences

The term "stereotype" is well-known, but a brief definition seems in order to begin. While Thomas was clearly not the first to define this concept, we will use her definition as our starting point. "Stereotypes are (often negative) generalizations that are based upon group membership" (Thomas, 2005, p. 78). It is human nature to gravitate towards using stereotypes. They provide a way for us to apply our limited knowledge to interactions with others so that we feel more comfortable (Mor Barak, 2014). The insidiousness of stereotypes is that they are often based on broad, oversimplified generalities and that they deny individual differences, lumping everyone of a particular group into one large, amorphous category. So that means that even stereotypes that may appear to be positive on the surface (e.g., Asians are smart in math) can be damaging (Thomas, 2005).

Bell (2012) observed another concern about stereotypes and career development: they "can lead to prejudice, which in turn can lead to discrimination" (p. 43). Like stereotypes, prejudices are based on flawed generalizations that are often stubbornly held despite evidence to the contrary (Allport, 1979; Bell, 2012). Prejudice uses those generalizations to pre-judge someone, usually negatively, for no reason other than his/her membership in a particularly group (Mor Barak, 2014). As with stereotypes, people are more likely to apply negative attributes to people unlike themselves and more positive ones to those most like themselves. Acting on those perspectives results in discrimination that may be described as "isms" (e.g., sexism, racism, heterosexism, ableism, ageism, classism). While research indicates that it is human nature to hold some prejudices, as it is to stereotype, the challenge becomes recognizing and combating those tendencies so they are not acted on unconsciously, hurting the career chances of others. However, our own image management makes it difficult for many to admit that they hold these biased views. Think of how many times you have heard someone say "I'm not prejudiced." Ironically, that phrase usually accompanies a statement or action that suggests the opposite.

Similarly, it is not uncommon for individuals who see themselves as open to different cultures to not realize that they are judging other national or regional customs and values as inferior to their own. This ethnocentric viewpoint uses one's own culture as the norm or as the standard and sets expectations accordingly (Thomas, 2005). It is also a human tendency. We naturally think our culture is the best, so the further from our own cultural practices that others seem to be, the more unusual or unsuitable they appear. This restricted perspective of correct behaviors and ideals may simply be the result of limited cultural intelligence, or it may indeed be a stubbornly held narrow view of what is deemed appropriate. In any event, it can lead to poor ratings or ostracism for employees whose cultural principles do not fit the standard, if those in power remain unaware or unconcerned about their own limited outlook. This has negative career ramifications for those individuals.

Societal biases and stereotypes can have a profound impact on organizational culture and, as a result, on career development, potentially derailing careers with the power of assumptions. Descriptive stereotypes define what members of a particular group are like, based on generally held beliefs (Caleo & Heilman, 2013). Common descriptive stereotypes suggest for example that women lack the qualities required of leaders (Caleo & Heilman, 2013), that older workers cannot or will not embrace new technology (Wang, Olson, & Shultz, 2013), or that they are disinterested in career development (Ng & Feldman, 2012), or that hiring employees with disabilities will result in less productivity (Rocco, Bowman, & Bryant, 2014). These pervasive misperceptions often carry over into organizations and may influence decisions about hiring, training and development, mentoring options, or assignments to key projects, choices that directly impact career development.

Often stereotypes come with a set of pre-determined expectations. If not met, these prescriptive stereotypes result in a negative evaluation (Caleo & Heilman, 2013). For example, Fernando and Cohen (2014) described the dilemma of women in Sri Lanka who are expected to uphold a societal ideal of "respectable femininity" that conflicts with the requirements for career accomplishment and advancement. So activities such as cultivating a professional network by attending after-work social events, while considered essential for one's career, present a challenge to retaining one's feminine respectability as defined by the cultural norms. Navigating compromises to uphold both sets of expectations takes additional time and energy that their male counterparts can apply elsewhere. In a US variation, Mor Barak (2014) referred to a court case where a woman leader was denied a promotion because her interpersonal style was considered too aggressive, apparently not upholding someone's stereotype of appropriate behavior for a female in leadership. Recognition that women may be chastised for leadership behaviors typically praised in their male counterparts points out the inherent double standard (Caleo & Heilman, 2013). Although we often think of gender examples first when discussing prescriptive societal stereotypes, others are not immune. For example, when workplaces expect people with disabilities to be grateful just to have a job rather than to seek promotions or assume that Asian employees prefer non-leadership roles, they are reinforcing narrowly defined societal stereotypes that thwart career opportunities.

HR professionals need to be particularly cognizant of stereotypes and prejudices that they hold, since they may be making decisions about hiring or selection for career development opportunities. They also are in the position to guide managers and supervisors making those key career-related choices for their subordinates. Biases often become part of our subconscious from such an early age that we fail to recognize them for what they are. For example, in a study conducted by one of the authors, both White and Black women were mindful of gender inequities regarding careers; but White women were unaware of the additional injustices experienced by women of color (Hite, 2004). What stereotypes or prejudices might you hold and how can you minimize their impact on your work?

### Organizational Culture

Scholars and practitioners recognize that organizational culture is a large and complex entity that defines how work is accomplished and how employees interact with one another in the system. Some systems are more open to embracing workplace diversity than others, and as integral as that discourse is for HR, that is not our focus here. In this section, we will address three aspects of organizational culture that relate particularly to career development for members of under-represented groups: structural integration, social integration, and institutional bias.

### Structural Integration

It is very likely that you have seen evidence of structural integration, perhaps experienced it yourself. As we discuss it further, you will certainly recognize some of the ideas that it includes. Structural integration is the proportional representation of diversity throughout the organization (Cox, 1993; Thomas, 2005). It may be characterized as "the higher, the fewer," meaning that, if you observe the system hierarchically, diversity diminishes as you look higher. It is another way to address the distribution of power in the organization. If most of the under-represented group members are clustered in lower-level positions and the "majority rules" as you approach the upper management, you are seeing lack of structural integration. Occasionally there will be a token non-majority group member in the upper echelon, but that exception does not sufficiently alter the skewed proportionality.

Structural integration is not simply a descriptive term but also a career development issue that prompts the question of access to higher-level positions. This is where some additional concepts come into play. The most well known is probably the glass ceiling, that invisible barrier that members of under-represented groups can see through, but rarely move beyond, to upper-level positions (Bell, 2012; Thomas, 2005). The underlying meaning is that under-represented group members have the "motivation, ambition, and capacity for positions of power and prestige, but invisible barriers keep them from reaching the top" (Sagrestano, 2004, p. 135). Fueled in part by some of the stereotypes and prejudices discussed in the previous section, the glass ceiling is an example of a concern that has received both scholarly and popular press attention over decades, but recognition has not led to resolution. There is some evidence that the ceiling, while still firmly in place, has risen for White women, letting some of them get closer to the executive levels of systems; that is not the case for other non-majority group members (Bell & Nkomo, 2001). Researchers have also offered that the metaphor of a sticky floor may more accurately describe the plight of those under-represented groups who are so far down in the hierarchy of power that the ceiling is not even within sight (Bell, 2012).

A related concept may be described as glass walls (Bell, 2012), "invisible horizontal barriers" (p. 309), apparent when a particular department or job category is almost entirely homogeneous. This occupational segregation typically relegates non-dominant group members to staff (support functions) rather than line (key to service or product) positions, consigning them to functional areas that rarely lead to the highest levels of power and responsibility (Bell, 2012). This type of scenario leads to another career development concern when disproportionate power is involved, such as a group of female nurses headed by a male director. The rapid ascendency to power positions for majority group members who enter fields dominated by under-represented groups is referred to as the glass escalator (Bell, 2012; Thomas, 2005). This rather self-explanatory phrase leads us to explore other career hurdles that non-dominant groups encounter.

Yet another barrier using the medium of glass as a metaphor is the concept of glass cliffs. Ryan and Haslam (2005) described glass cliffs particularly in terms of gender, noting that, when women are promoted to leadership positions, it is typically because the organization is experiencing difficult times. This places the female leader in a precarious position, setting her up for a challenging task with the risk of hurting her own career if her efforts do not result in bringing the organization back to health. The rationale for this selection pattern has not been definitively determined, although most of the potential reasons lead to the conclusion of discrimination or stereotyping (Ryan & Haslam, 2007). Cook and Glass's (2014) study of Fortune 500 companies over a 15-year span built on the idea and proposed that: "occupational minorities are more likely than white men to be promoted CEO of weakly performing firms; and when firm performance declines during their tenure, occupational minority CEOs are likely to be replaced by white men" (p. 1081). They observed that, not only does the glass cliff phenomenon prove risky for the individual leader, by "creating greater obstacles to successful leadership than their white male peers" (p. 1087), but it also may reinforce old stereotypes that non-majority employees are not suited for leadership. As Ryan and Haslam (2007) concluded, the study of glass cliffs reinforces two points: "that opportunity is not the same as equal opportunity and that having a more inclusive playing field does not necessarily mean that the field is any more level" (p. 566).

Additional barriers have been identified for Black and Latina women (Bell & Nkomo, 2001; Cocchiara, Bell, & Berry, 2006). The term *concrete wall* was originally noted by Bell and Nkomo (2001) as a way to envision the double career obstacle of "racialized sexism" as a "two-dimensional structure: a concrete wall topped by a glass ceiling" (p. 137). While manifested in multiple ways, concrete walls have been described as "intense resistance from members of the dominant group once minorities achieve high organization levels" (Cocchiara et al., 2006, p. 279). It typically results in stalling, or in some cases derailing, career progression. While this research has been limited to the intersection of race and gender, it is likely that this phenomenon might be applicable to others representing multiple aspects of minority status.

We acknowledge that career goals differ greatly, certainly across diverse groups. Yet some still seek the objective success of advancement, and even those not focused on moving up in one system might find their employability is enhanced by showing progressive career movement. Whether by design or by inadvertent neglect on the part of the system, barriers to advancement that target under-represented groups are a manifestation of discrimination. The result costs diverse employees career opportunities and hobbles organizations hoping to gain from workforce diversity. Structural integration is a clue for HR practitioners to look deeper into this aspect of career development.

*Social Integration*

Structural integration often prompts insufficient social integration, minimizing opportunities for under-represented employees to interact with those in power positions and consequently to build relationships throughout the organization that could benefit their careers (Combs, 2003). Yet, as we observed in an earlier chapter, research confirms the career advantage of building and maintaining strong connecting relationships. Mor Barak (2014) chose the phrase "social exclusion" to describe this barrier, when she observed:

> Though diversity groupings vary from one culture or country to the next, the common factor that seems to transcend national boundaries is the experience of social exclusion, particularly in the workplace. Individuals and groups are implicitly or explicitly excluded … because of their actual or employer-perceived membership in a minority or disfavored identity group.
>
> (p. 6)

This experience of exclusion affects career development opportunities on multiple levels. For example, Naraine and Lindsay (2011) addressed the challenges that blind or low vision (B/LV) employees face engaging in informal social events with work colleagues, from navigating in a strange environment to struggling to build rapport when they could not make eye contact. Their conclusion was that these barriers yielded "an adverse impact for B/LV employees because these important informal social networks are delayed in developing or do not develop at all" (p. 399).

Sometimes employees' efforts to build connections are hindered by the effects of stigma about who they are and what they represent that supersedes their career potential. Combs (2003) described the stigma surrounding employees presumed to be Affirmative Action hires, individuals from non-dominant groups who are assumed to be less qualified than their majority peers and hired simply to fulfill legislative requirements. Other researchers (Gedro, 2009; Kaplan, 2014) have observed that LGBT employees, if out at work, may be subject to such negative reactions that their skills are overshadowed by acknowledgment of their sexual orientation. Similarly, Wilson-Kovacs, Ryan, Haslam, & Rabinovich, (2008) found that people with disabilities were often defined "solely in terms of their condition, rather than in terms of their abilities" (p. 713). Some groups are discounted not for who they are, but for where they are in the organization. For example, Bullock (2004) commented on the stigma surrounding class differences at work, noting that: "Judgments of occupational prestige not only reflect widely shared cultural beliefs about the relative value of different types of labor, but also justify differential rewards and treatment in the workplace by valuing some workers and skill sets over others" (p. 229). The "unvalued" are not expected to move from their current status in the system, regardless of their potential. In each instance noted above, informal socialization may suffer since these employees are assumed to be less deserving of time and attention than their counterparts, and as a result are subjected to career limiting, discrimination-based exclusion.

Access to connecting relationships like mentoring and networking are also included in social integration. We discussed these initiatives earlier in this book, noting their value in career development. Here we will focus on aspects of these relationships that are particularly relevant for under-represented groups.

Interpersonal connections are essential in helping members of non-dominant groups to build the social capital they need to progress in their careers, yet establishing them is more challenging if you are not part of the majority (Baruch & Bozionelos, 2011). Those in the minority often enter the organization defined as "the other," more recognizable for their obvious differences from the traditional majority than for their expertise. Being part of a non-dominant group, they could clearly benefit from building key relationships that would help acculturate them into the system and perhaps provide advocacy and advice. However, research reminds us that there is a strong tendency for the majority of senior leadership to "consciously or unconsciously select individuals who resemble themselves" because that makes them feel most comfortable (Bristol & Tisdell, 2010, p. 227). As a result, it is difficult for anyone who is not part of the dominant group to gain entry into the very networks likely to help them the most.

One suggestion might be to establish a homogenous network, seeking out others from one's identity group. However, Cocchiara et al. (2006) confirmed that the limited number of diverse others in most organizations makes that challenging as well, requiring a more extensive and wide-ranging search to get the level of assistance so readily available to dominant group members. Additionally, Kulkarni (2012) warned that focusing primarily on similarity-based networks may further isolate and marginalize non-dominant group members from the majority, hindering career development opportunities. Attempting to formalize informal networks seems counterintuitive, so HR practitioners and researchers will need to be creative in helping under-represented group members to access and grow their career networks.

Mentoring relationships are another way to build social capital. While gender and race represent only two of multiple aspects of difference, there is a dearth of research addressing mentoring with other non-dominate groups (Ragins, 2007), so we often rely on the gender and race studies and attempt to extrapolate to other groups. That is the approach we are taking here. We recognize that members of under-represented groups face multiple complexities in mentoring relationships. As a demographic minority in an organization or profession, one is not only less likely to be selected as a protégé by majority members of upper management but, as we noted earlier, there are typically few, if any, non-majority members in positions of power. Those who are at that level likely have been inundated with requests to mentor, so they are unavailable, leaving potential protégés to fend for themselves. While formal mentoring often can provide a match and access to leadership, the dynamics of mixed gender or mixed race mentoring can make those relationships more of a challenge. For example, a risk identified early in cross-gender mentoring is the appearance or assumption of sexual involvement, either of which could be damaging to mentor and mentee (Ragins, 1996). However, a recent study conducted in Taiwan concluded that "career mentoring positively influenced resilience levels of protégés in cross-gender mentoring relationships" (Kao, Rogers, Spitzmueller, Lin, & Lin, 2014, p.199), suggesting an unexpected benefit of mixed mentoring relationships.

The inherent power disparity of a traditional mentoring relationship complicates both cross-gender and cross-race relationships. Since issues of racial power imbalances have both historic significance and current resonance, White mentors and their protégées of color work in a context already fraught with hurdles. This is particularly challenging for women of color, since their experiences combine concerns involving gender and race, making them twice removed from the traditional majority (Combs, 2003). To increase the likelihood of a connection that will yield career benefits, Murrell, Blake-Beard, Porter, & Perkins-Williamson (2008) advised that cross-race formal mentoring matches "must also be about creating access to power and the development of trust among those who traditionally have been excluded from the knowledge and resources that will support their success and the success of their organization" (p. 277). In response to systems that lack enough non-dominant group members to serve as mentors, they suggested spanning organizations in creating mentoring relationships for members of under-represented groups, "providing people of color access to both career and psychosocial support that may not be afforded by traditional formal mentoring efforts within a single organization" (Murrell et al., 2008, p. 277).

*Institutional Biases*

Some barriers to career development for under-represented group members are the result of organizational policies and practices. It should be noted that, often, these barriers were not designed to exclude non-dominant group members, but they became established in the culture at a time when the workforce was more homogeneous. While those regulations and routines were acceptable for personnel of the past, they inadvertently hinder career development for the current, more diverse workforce. Cox (2001) identified three categories to explore as potential system barriers: time, space, and people.

Time includes factors like workday length and the use of overtime, time-off policies and schedule flexibility (Cox, 2001). Long work-days with regular overtime expectations, limited time off or restricted schedule flexibility can negatively impact the career prospects of workers with other life concerns (e.g., single parents, care-givers, people with disabilities) or priorities (volunteer work, family time; Holvino, Ferdman, & Merrill-Sands, 2004; O'Neil, Hopkins, & Bilimoria, 2013). They risk being seen as less reliable or less committed to their work if they do not uphold the traditional standard, limiting their career progress.

Space factors are often related to manifestations of class and hierarchy (Bullock, 2004; Cox, 2001) that may limit opportunities for interacting with a range of employees (e.g., location of upper management offices and availability of their occupants). Other aspects can suggest subtle or overt biases (e.g., accessibility of work spaces, access to off-site events, or even location of gender-appropriate restrooms). While the latter may seem unrelated to career development, they are physical representations of exclusion or inclusion and therefore of potential opportunity.

People factors include a wide range of policies that can help or hinder career opportunities, starting with recruitment (i.e., you can't win if you can't play), through promotion and performance appraisal practices (i.e., gateways to other possibilities), to succession planning (i.e., who should make it to the top) (Cox, 2001). If the parameters of these policies are narrowly prescribed to fit a traditional majority ideal, members of under-represented groups have little chance of being recommended for career development opportunities. This lack of preparation makes them ineligible for taking on positions of power in that system or for building their own employability to move up in another organization. Ibarra, Ely, & Kolb (2013) have suggested that these policies and the practices they foster are the result of second-generation bias, assumptions that are not intentionally set to exclude, but that yield an environment where women (and potentially other non-dominant group members) "fail to thrive or reach their full potential" (p. 64).

While institutional bias in many systems is inadvertent, the result of a traditional culture that was never questioned or reviewed, some organizations perpetuate deeply embedded purposeful means of keeping under-represented group members from finding career success. For example, in their study of career advancement for Lebanese women, Tlaiss and Kauser (2010) described the practice of *wasta*, the use of a powerful intercessor to speak on one's behalf, to determine who gets career opportunities in Arab organizations. Those who lack those key connections to power and privilege find their career opportunities stunted.

Often these policies and practices fall under HR, so HRD can take a leading role in examining if or how they might be inadvertent barriers to career growth for a diverse workforce. It is not easy to change cultural norms about the timing of work, accessibility and access, and employee selection and evaluation. However, as systems increasingly recognize that they are no longer master planners, but now mutual partners in employee career development, the motivation to make these transitions is likely to be evident.

This section has explored some of the systemic factors that affect career development opportunities for members of under-represented groups. The next will focus on individual factors that also influence career progress for diverse others.

## Individual Factors

We have noted frequently so far that career development of the future will be much more driven by the individual than by the organization. While research indicates that most of the barriers to career development for diverse employees are societal or system-based, it is valuable to explore how individual factors may also hinder or help career progress. Individual inclinations and perceptions will certainly influence how career decisions are made and implemented. This section will examine how those might affect members of under-represented groups differently than their majority peers.

### External–Individual

Just as there are some societal factors that impinge on organizations, under-represented individuals come into the workplace carrying their own external influences that will impact how they approach career development. So, despite the trend towards more individually driven career goals, they may feel much less freedom to choose their own paths (Duffy & Dik, 2009). Family and life circumstance are two powerful external factors (Duffy & Dik, 2009).

Family expectations, values, and needs may be particularly salient for under-represented group members (Duffy & Dik, 2009). For example, members of collectivist cultures may feel they cannot move away from extended family to take promotions that could benefit their careers (Stone & Stone-Romero, 2004). Some women live with cultural mores that prohibit their careers from taking on more importance than their families (Fernando & Cohen, 2014). Similarly, single parents often cannot change cities and leave child-support networks behind to take on positions that require overtime hours or extensive travel, despite their own career hopes (Abele, Volmer, & Spurk, 2012).

Life circumstances include a wide range of factors, including "poverty, marginalization, and stigmatization" (Duffy & Dik, 2009, p. 33), which will vary in salience depending on the individual. For example, we often discuss salary as an objective measure of success, but salary can also be an economic constraint, one that determines if one can meet immediate financial obligations (e.g., rent, bills) and still take career risks. Similarly, the career literature that addresses the new climate of individual free agency rarely includes the caveat that protean and boundaryless careers are largely reserved for those whose expertise, profession, or industry affiliation supersedes economic downturns. Even the type of careers that one considers often is restrained by economic status. Early access to role models, mentors, networks, and good education can have a profound impact on long-term career possibilities (Bullock, 2004). As Blustein, Coutinho, Murphy, Backus, & Catraio (2011) explained: "the vision of self as originator of action and driver of career exploration and development may not be viable for individuals residing in communities in which opportunities are limited" (p. 220).

Other external barriers relate to a different aspect of life circumstances. We addressed some aspects of marginalization and stigma from a systems perspective, but there is a potential individual component as well. Unlike majority group members who tacitly sense that they will fit in wherever they go, members of under-represented groups may face a more difficult scenario that adds a different dimension to their career planning. For example, LGBT individuals often need to consider how well they will be accepted if they relocate to a certain country or community, if they choose to be out in a new organization, or if they select a particular career path (Gedro, 2009). Older workers must contemplate if they can change organizations or vary their career paths after a certain age, or if they will be judged too old to be considered viable candidates. People with disabilities are obliged to determine if their skills will be overshadowed by their conditions, or if potential employers will provide the resources they need (Wilson-Kovacs et al., 2008). For members of these under-represented groups and others, career self-direction often is tempered by the realization that they need to overcome bigger societal and systemic hurdles than their majority counterparts. HR practitioners need to be aware of these potential barriers and how they might impact individual career planning.

### Internal–Individual

While individual tendencies and personality have always influenced career goals to some degree, these internal aspects take on a larger role when career development responsibilities become more individually driven. There are a myriad of factors that could be considered here (e.g., the Big 5, locus of control), each with their own body of literature. We chose to focus on three potential barriers that particularly resonate with the interactive career development process between systems and under-represented individuals.

### Occupational Disidentification

In their studies of female surgeons, Peters, Ryan, Haslam, & Fernandes (2012) determined that "people's perceptions that they fit in with the dominant identity in their occupation play an important role in their occupational identification and that these identity fit dynamics may have especially negative implications for women in male-dominated occupations" (p. 156). On the surface, the idea of "fitting in" may seem rather inconsequential initially. It is not uncommon for most people to recall an awkward moment of feeling like the outsider in a group. However, coping with those situational incidents is like going over a speed bump compared to the steep mountain climb of feeling that one is profoundly different from the norm in a particular profession: a norm that is defined by the majority currently dominating that career. The result is likely to be a pervasive sense of incongruence between the individual and what s/he perceives as the necessary characteristics to succeed in a certain field or role (e.g., leadership) that may influence non-dominant group members to opt out (Peters, Ryan, Haslam, 2013). While some may persevere despite the odds, many will determine that the stretch is too far from their own social identity to be reconcilable. This sets up a cyclical dilemma, since having more varied individuals in a profession or at a particular organization level (e.g., senior management) minimizes the perception of disidentification for non-dominant group members.

### So, How Brilliant Do You Feel?

A recent study, based in an academic setting, indicates that the lack of diversity in certain fields may be connected to how that discipline is perceived. The researchers have determined that "the extent to which practitioners of a discipline believe that success depends on sheer brilliance is a strong predictor of women's and African Americans' representation in that discipline" (Leslie, Cimpian, Meyer, & Freeland, 2015, p. 265). An example of the power of negative stereotypes, members of those under-represented groups are presumed to lack the "innate intellectual talent" (p. 265) required to succeed in these particular fields, so they are not encouraged to pursue those careers. Similarly, to the extent that women and African-Americans accept those stereotypes, they opt out of those disciplines. The recommendation offered for specialties wanting to diversify is to minimize the perceptions of requisite brilliance and instead to focus on the role of persistence in success.

### Stress

A related, but different potential internal career barrier for individuals is stress. HR literature often addresses workplace stress as it relates to workload, working conditions, or lack of job security (Thomas, 2005). Here we will focus on additional work-related stressors for members of under-represented groups. Consider the previous paragraph, for example. Those who persevere despite a sense of disindentification will be likely to experience stress as they struggle to negotiate how to fit into the work roles they are pursuing while remaining true to their own identities (Heppner & Fu, 2011). Stress may also be prompted by incidents of discrimination, prejudice, or harassment at work, whether the actions of a few individuals or tacitly perpetuated by the organizational culture (Sagrestano, 2004; Thomas, 2005). Earlier in this chapter, we discussed structural and social integration as organizational barriers. At the individual level, those concepts manifest as stressors when they result in feeling alone, discounted, or targeted. For example:

- being in a solo or token role, where you are the only non-dominant group member (in your organization, department, or level);
- being excluded by majority group members who fear being stigmatized by association or who avoid interaction to compensate for their own discomfort;

- being subjected to overt and covert discrimination on a regular basis.
(Kulik, Bainbridge, & Cregan, 2008; Mohr & Fassinger, 2013; Sagrestano, 2004; Thomas, 2005)

These stressors may have varying salience for different under-represented groups. Similarly, each group may have added stressors unique to their positions. For example, LGBT employees must determine whether coming out at work will jeopardize their continued employment or their career options (Gedro, 2009). Employees with disabilities often must depend on others for assistance, risking appearing dependent and incapable of taking on higher-level positions. Black women describe a life of constant boundary-spanning, transitioning between Black and White worlds as they go from work to home responsibilities and relationships (Bell & Nkomo, 2001; Thomas, 2005). Individuals working outside their countries of origin while still maintaining their cultural roots at home are likely to encounter similar boundary-spanning stress. Stress takes energy and focus away from performing well at work and takes a long-term toll on one's physical and emotional health (see Chapter 7). Recognizing that members of under-represented groups experience added stressors beyond those faced by others in the workplace can help human resource (HR) profes-sionals acknowledge and address the significance of this career barrier.

*Perceptions of Unfairness*

An additional potential stressor for non-dominant group members is a sense of unfairness or injustice. As we noted in Chapter 3, fairness (or lack of it) is inherent in determining who is selected for career devel-opment (Wooten & Cobb, 1999), an idea reinforced earlier in this chapter in the discussion of organizational barriers. Interestingly, while dispar-ities in access and opportunities for under-represented employees have been readily acknowledged (see for example Bell & Nkomo, 2001; Cokley, Dreher, & Stockdale, 2004; Giscombe & Mattis, 2002; Hite, 2004; Villanueva-Flores, Valle-Cabrera, & Bornay-Barrachina, 2014), individual perceptions of fairness are rarely overtly addressed in the discourse on workforce diversity and careers. However, it is reasonable to assume that the perception that one's organization condones unfair treatment adds insult to the injury of discrimination and may lead to actions (e.g., choosing to leave) and reactions (e.g., decreased work motivation) that can hurt individual careers and systems.

The limited research linking career development and perceptions of fairness indicates that non-dominant employees may have negative perceptions of how career development opportunities are distributed, yielding less trust, lower job satisfaction, and a higher risk of a "careerist" orientation (individuals working to advance their own careers regardless of the cost to others; Crawshaw, 2006; Crawshaw & Brodbeck, 2011). Given the societal and systemic barriers that we have discussed in this chapter, the potential to see disparity in career development is high among members of under-represented groups. While the causes of those disparities may originate in society or within the organization, the resulting sense of unfair treatment can negatively affect individual career trajectories. HR professionals are in a position to recognize the power of those perceptions and to help minimize the causes.

**Organizational Initiatives**

Over 20 years ago, Cox (1993, p. 7) observed that an organizational climate rife with prejudice, stereotyping, limited structural and social integration, and institutional biases would negatively impact the career outcomes of non-dominant group members. He noted that it would limit their satisfaction, work involvement, performance appraisals, and promotion opportunities, and that, ultimately, the effectiveness of the system would suffer. Current research suggests that we have not made much progress in minimizing the career barriers for under-represented group members, so the negative ramifications continue for individuals and organizations. In this section, we will focus on how HR can take a more active role in fostering a better career environment for a diverse workforce.

We should begin by recognizing that some systems make a concerted commitment to becoming more inclusive across the board, including career development, and they devote significant time and resources to that endeavor. Others may be less willing to undergo such an extensive transformation, but might be interested in improving access to career development as a way to recruit and retain a strong workforce. The recommendations here are intended to assist any system wanting to minimize career barriers for all their employees. Each requires that HR practitioners take an active role in assisting with this process.

Early in this exploration, we started with factors outside the organization that foster career barriers for diverse employees. While societal change is a slow and on-going process, organizations are not destined to be powerless in combating stereotypes, prejudices, ethnocentrism, and other biases that seep into the system through myths, misinformation, and misguided intentions. Their effects can be minimized through a multifaceted approach focused on individual awareness and change (Holvino et al., 2004) including:

- implementing well-constructed, on-going, comprehensive training, education, and learning opportunities that go beyond creating awareness to helping employees build skills to work with diverse others and to apply their knowledge (Bristol & Tisdell, 2010; Cox, 1993, 2001; Holvino et al., 2004; Kaplan, 2014; Kulkarni, 2012; Mor Barak, 2014; Thomas, 2005). Make the training part of a strategic diversity initiative, not a stand alone event. Note: poorly designed training can actually reinforce biases, so this must be approached carefully.
- providing coaching for individual leaders and decision makers to identify their own biases and determine how to address them (Holvino et al., 2004). "Individuals who have not progressed in their own identity development are unable to create work contexts in which diverse workers are engaged in their work and feel open to contribute in novel ways" (Thomas, 2005, p. 193).
- initiating multicultural team building that helps members build their own skills (Holvino et al., 2004), recognize the expertise and abilities of their diverse counterparts, and get to know them as individuals, making it harder to stereotype or stigmatize them.

Other organizational barriers typically are embedded into the culture of the system. They may be difficult to identify and challenging to change, because they are perpetuated by practices that have become ingrained into daily work. However, lack of structural integration offers a clue. If career development is working well for everyone in the organization, diverse individuals should be represented throughout the system, at all levels and in different departments or functional areas. If that is not evident, begin by reviewing representation for signs of where structural barriers (e.g., glass ceilings, escalators, concrete walls) are most active.

- Seek leadership support for examining career barriers and implementing initiatives to minimize them (Bristol & Tisdell, 2010; Cox, 1993, 2001; Thomas, 2005). Be prepared to educate them about why inclusive career development matters.
- Consider a culture audit to gather more complete information about which initiatives to implement and where to focus in the system (Holvino et al., 2004; Kulkarni, 2012; Mor Barak, 2014). Examine

enclaves of homogeneity as potential areas of concern (i.e., fostering disidentification for non-dominant group members).

- Establish formal mentoring programs that are accessible to all employees at every level and incorporate metrics to measure effectiveness (Nugent, Dinolfo, & Giscombe, 2013). Consider alternatives such as mentoring circles or peer mentoring to minimize concerns that arise from mixed gender/race pairs or a dearth of diverse mentors, and explore reverse mentoring to keep older workers engaged (Chaudhuri & Ghosh, 2012). See Chapter 4 in this book for more on mentoring specifics.

- Encourage employees to establish heterogeneous and homogeneous career networks that span inside and outside the organization. Consider system-wide employee resource groups, in-house homogeneous networks (e.g., women managers, LGBT employees) that provide peer support (Ibarra et al., 2013). Tread cautiously however. Some fear resource group network membership will segregate them further in the larger system; others express concerns that the networks might be used to reinforce the power structure status quo (O'Neil, Hopkins, & Sullivan, 2011). See Chapter 4 for more networking specifics.

### Best for Employee Resource Groups

Annually, DiversityInc chooses its top 10 companies for Employee Resource Groups based on several criteria, including if the company uses its resource groups to assist with recruiting, employee development, and mentoring, and if the resource group program includes retention and career development as measures of success. PricewaterhouseCoopers came in as number one in 2014 because it met the criteria above and in addition it has solid support for the program from company leadership (upper management members are in sponsoring roles), and a large number of employees (38 percent) are involved in one of the 9 groups (with 80 chapters) in the US or their global affiliates.
(Retrieved from www.diversityinc.com/top-10-companies-employee-resource-groups)

- Review formal policies and procedures for potential institutional bias related to diverse career development (Cox, 1993, 2001; Holvino et al., 2004; Kulkarni, 2012). Study work scheduling for unnecessary rigidity. Scrutinize recruiting routines, performance appraisals, succession plans, and criteria for identifying high-potential candidates for promotion to determine if there are built-in barriers for non-dominant group members.

- Examine formal and informal practices regarding career development recommendations (for training, stretch assignments, etc.; O'Neil et al., 2013). Explore how those decisions are made and suggest ways to ensure under-represented group members have equal access to career opportunities (e.g., evaluating managers and supervisors on how well they develop all their employees). Remain cognizant of perceptions of justice and fairness in suggesting and implementing change.
- Ensure that HR professionals become knowledgeable about the career development barriers that specific under-represented group members face (Gedro, 2009). While some obstacles are not within their power to change (e.g., employee economic status or family obligations), HRD can advocate for individuals by understanding the factors that will influence their career development and by taking an active role in making the organizational culture more career inclusive.

## What Can Organizations Do To Keep Women from Leaving Engineering Jobs?

The dearth of women in STEM (science, technology, engineering, and mathematics) fields remains a persistent concern. A recent report titled "Stemming the Tide: Why Women Leave Engineering" (Fouad, Singh, Fitzpatrick, & Liu, 2012) demonstrates that the difficulty goes beyond just encouraging women to study in those fields. The researchers surveyed over 5,500 women with bachelor's degrees in engineering. The respondents include women who never entered engineering, those who left, and those who stayed. Based on the data, the authors concluded that systems wanting to improve their odds of keeping qualified women in engineering positions should:

- develop clear paths to advancement by
  - being transparent about the criteria for promotion
  - basing promotions on performance
  - providing lots of opportunities to move up;
- offer training and development opportunities (e.g., stretch assignments) to build leadership skills as well as technical expertise;
- be clear about goals, work tasks, and expectations and provide the resources needed to accomplish the work (i.e., keep assignments from growing out of control, requiring overtime and rushed work to meet deadlines);
- build an inclusive culture that
  - demonstrates that it values all employee contributions
  - has zero tolerance for incivility and belittling behaviors
  - fosters a climate of support from supervisors and peers
  - encourages formal and informal mentoring
  - supports work–life through initiatives and expects employees to use them without repercussions.

**Individual Initiatives**

In the diversity literature, researchers periodically chastise studies that include how members of under-represented groups can adapt to organizational expectations to succeed. The idea is that qualified individuals should not have to adjust; the burden should be on systems to become more inclusive. As we acknowledged in the previous section, systemic barriers do need to change, and revisions at that level can have a dramatic impact on career opportunities. However, individuals remain responsible for their own career paths and plans, and there are initiatives that they can take to claim their power in this process. The items on the list are fit for any career seeker, but they are particularly important for non-dominant group members who may need to push harder to be recognized as ready or to be chosen. These include:

- Be proactive (Thomas, 2005; van Veldhoven & Dorenbosch, 2008). This is a repeating theme in the career development literature and it should be a priority for non-dominant group members, who may be passed by if they wait to be acknowledged or chosen.

### Proactivity or Karma?

Research tells us that women often are less likely than their male counterparts to ask for raises or promotions and, as a result, their salaries and advancement opportunities may lag behind their peers. An interviewer's efforts to get a CEO's advice for women in this situation resulted in some backlash for the CEO. In October 2014, during an interview, Microsoft Chief Executive Satya Nadella gave this response:

It's not about asking for the raise, but knowing and having faith that the system will actually give you the right raises as you go along. ... And that, I think might be one of the additional superpowers that quite frankly women who don't ask for a raise have. Because that's good karma.

Following swift and clear negative feedback about his suggestion that women trust "karma" to reward their work, he later apologized saying:

I answered that question completely wrong. Without a doubt I wholeheartedly support programs at Microsoft and in the industry that bring more women into technology and close the pay gap. I believe men and women should get equal pay for equal work. And when it comes to career advice on getting a raise when you think it's deserved, Maria's [the interviewer's] advice was the right advice. If you think you deserve a raise, you should just ask.

Interestingly, shortly after these statements by Nadella, Amit Chowdhry, summarizing this situation in a Forbes article (www.forbes.com/sites/amitchowdhry/2014/10/10/microsoft-ceo-satya-nadella-apologizes-for-comments-on-womens-pay), noted: "Glassdoor, a website that contains information about jobs and salaries based on submissions by anonymous employees, showed that men at Microsoft make more than women in similar positions."

- Foster personal and professional resilience. Exercise the power that you have to define yourself, feel secure, become knowledge-able, remain visible, and stay flexible (Alfred, 2001). This may be particularly important for those coping with challenging family and life situations, work stressors, and feelings of injustice (see Chapter 7).
- Seek out developmental opportunities and take advantage of them (Thomas, 2005). Be willing to stretch, to take on the challenging tasks. Recognize "learning how to be an effective leader is like learning any complex skill: It rarely comes naturally and usually take a lot of practice" (Ibarra et al., 2013, p. 66). At the same time, choose well to minimize the risk of a glass cliff situation.
- Build mentoring and networking relationships (Cocchiara et al., 2006; Thomas, 2005). Search widely if you must to find mentors similar to you, but include dominant group members as well to broaden your access to power and possibilities. Use mentoring and networking programs in your organization.

## Summary

As we noted at the beginning of this chapter, career development for members of under-represented groups takes on multiple dimensions. Some concerns span across differences. Yet each group and the individuals that make it up also experience some unique challenges that we could not address in detail with the pages that we could devote to the topic here. Seek out that information. Recognize, too, that while we focused on non-dominant groups in this chapter to highlight their particular concerns, diversity means everyone. Each person, whether a member of the traditional majority or an under-represented group, makes up the diverse workforce. Together, we are the diversity in our organizations.

## References

Abele, A., Volmer, J., & Spurk, D. (2012). Career stagnation: Underlying dilemmas and solutions in contemporary work environments. In N. P. Reilly, M. J. Sirgy, & C. A. Gorman (Eds.), *Work and quality of life: Ethical practices in organizations* (pp. 107–132). New York: Springer.

Alfred, M. V. (2001). Expanding theories of career development: Adding the voices of African American women in the white academy. *Adult Education Quarterly 51*(2), 108–127.

Allport, G. W. (1979). *The nature of prejudice*. Reading, MA: Addison-Wesley.

Baruch, Y. & Bozionelos, N. (2011). Career issues. In S. Zedeck (Ed.), *APA handbook of industrial and organizational psychology* (pp. 67–113). Washington, DC: American Psychological Association.

Bell, E. L. J. E. & Nkomo, S. M. (2001). *Our separate ways: Black and white women and the struggle for professional identity*. Boston, MA: Harvard Business School.

Bell, M. P. (2012). *Diversity in organizations*. Mason, OH: South-Western, Cengage Learning.

Blustein, D. L., Coutinho, M. T. N., Murphy, K. A., Backus, F., & Catraio, C. (2011). Self and social class in career theory and practice. In P. Hartung & L. Subich (Eds.), *Developing self in work and career: Concepts, cases and contexts* (pp. 213–229). Washington, DC: American Psychological Association.

Bristol, T. L. & Tisdell, E. J. (2010). Leveraging diversity through career development: Social and cultural capital among African-American managers. *International Journal of Human Resources Development and Management 10*(3), 224–238.

Bullock, H. E. (2004). Class diversity in the workplace. In M. Stockdale & F. Crosby (Eds.). *The psychology and management of workplace diversity* (pp. 224–242). Oxford: Blackwell.

Caleo, S. & Heilman, M. E. (2013). Gender stereotypes and their implications for women's career progress. In S. Vinnicombe, R. J. Burke, S. Blake-Beard, & L. L. Moore (Eds.), *Handbook of research on promoting women's careers* (pp. 143–161). Cheltenham: Edward Elgar.

Chaudhuri, S. & Ghosh, R. (2012). Reverse mentoring: A social exchange tool for keeping the boomers engaged and millennials committed. *Human Resource Development Review, 11*(1), 55–76.

Cocchiara, F., Bell, M. P., & Berry, D. P. (2006). Latinas and black women: Key factors for a growing proportion of the US workforce. *Equal Opportunities International, 25*(4), 272–284.

Cokley, K., Dreher, G., & Stockdale, M. (2004). Toward the inclusiveness and career success of African Americans in the workplace. In M. Stockdale & F. Crosby (Eds.), *The psychology and management of workplace diversity* (pp. 168–190). Oxford: Blackwell.

Combs, G. M. (2003). The duality of race and gender for managerial African American women: Implications of informal social networks and career advancement. *Human Resource Development Quarterly, 2*(4), 385–405.

Cook, A. & Glass, C. (2014). Above the glass ceiling: When are women and racial/ethnic minorities promoted to CEO? *Strategic Management Journal, 35,* 1080–1089.

Cox, T., Jr. (1993). *Cultural diversity in organizations: Theory, research & practice.* San Francisco, CA: Berrett-Koehler.

Cox, T., Jr. (2001). *Creating the multicultural organization.* San Francisco, CA: Jossey-Bass.

Crawshaw, J. (2006). Justice source and justice content: Evaluating the fairness of organizational career management practices. *Human Resource Management Journal, 16*(1), 98–120.

Crawshaw, J. & Brodbeck, F. (2011). Justice and trust as antecedents of careerist orientation. *Personnel Review, 40*(1), 106–125.

Duffy, R. D. & Dik, B. J. (2009). Beyond the self: External influences in the career development process. *The Career Development Quarterly, 58,* 29–43.

Fernando, W. D. A. & Cohen, L. (2014). Respectable femininity and career agency: Exploring paradoxical imperatives. *Gender, Work and Organization, 21*(2), 149–164.

Fouad, N., Singh, R., Fitzpatrick, M., & Liu, J. (2012). Stemming the tide: Why women leave engineering. (Research Report Women in Engineering.) Retrieved from website: http://studyofwork.com/files/2011/03/NSF_Women-Full-Report-0314.pdf.

Gedro, J. (2009). LBGT career development. *Advances in Developing Human Resources, 11*(1), 54–66.

Giscombe, K. & Mattis, M. C. (2002). Leveling the playing field for women of color in corporate management: Is the business case enough? *Journal of Business Ethics, 37*(1), 103–119.

Heppner, M. J. & Fu, C. (2011). The gendered context of vocational self-construction. In P. Hartung & L. Subich (Eds.). *Developing self in work and career: Concepts, cases and contexts* (pp. 177–192). Washington, DC: American Psychological Association.

Hite, L. M. (2004). Black and white women managers: Access to opportunity. *Human Resource Development Quarterly, 15*(2), 131–146.

Holvino, H., Ferdman, B., & Merrill-Sands, D. (2004). Creating and sustaining diversity and inclusion in organizations: Strategies and approaches. In M. Stockdale & F. Crosby (Eds.), *The psychology and management of workplace diversity* (pp. 245–276). Oxford: Blackwell.

Ibarra, H., Ely, R., & Kolb, D. (2013, September). Women rising: The unseen barriers. *Harvard Business Review,* 61–66.

Kao, K., Rogers, A., Spitzmueller, C., Lin, M., & Lin, C. (2014). Who should serve as my mentor? The effects of mentor's gender and supervisory status on resilience in mentoring relationships. *Journal of Vocational Behavior, 85,* 191–203.

148    *Barriers and Diverse Populations*

Kaplan, D. M. (2014). Career anchors and paths: The case of gay, lesbian, and bisexual workers. *Human Resource Management Review, 24,* 119–130.

Kulik, C. T., Bainbridge, H. T. J., & Cregan, C. (2008). Known by the company we keep: Stigma-by-association effects in the workplace. *Academy of Management Review, 33*(1), 216–230.

Kulkarni, M. (2012). Social networks and career advancement of people with disabilities. *Human Resource Development Quarterly, 11*(2), 138–155.

Leslie, S., Cimpian, A., Meyer, M., & Freeland, E. (2015, January). Expectations of brilliance underlie gender distributions across academic disciplines. *Science, 347*(6219), 262–265.

Mohr, J. J. & Fassinger, R. E. (2013). Work, career, and sexual orientation. In C. Patterson & A. D'Augelli (Eds.), *Handbook of psychology and sexual orientation* (pp. 151–164). Oxford: Oxford University Press.

Mor Barak, M. E. (2014). *Managing diversity: Toward a globally inclusive workplace* (3rd edn.). Thousand Oaks, CA: Sage.

Murrell, A. J., Blake-Beard, S., Porter, M., Jr., & Perkins-Williamson, A. (2008). Interorganizational mentoring: Breaking the concrete ceiling sometimes requires support for the outside. *Human Resource Management, 47*(2), 275–294.

Naraine, M. D. & Lindsay, P. H. (2011). Social inclusion of employees who are blind or low vision. *Disability & Society, 26*(4), 389–403.

Ng, T. W. H. & Feldman, D. C. (2012). Aging and participation in career development activities. In J. W. Hedge & W. C. Boreman (Eds.), *The Oxford handbook of work and aging* (pp. 137–150). Oxford: Oxford University Press.

Niles, S. G. & Harris-Bowlsbey, J. (2013). *Career development interventions in the 21st century* (4th edn.). Boston, MA: Pearson.

Nugent, J. S., Dinolfo, S., & Giscombe, K. (2013). Advancing women: A focus on strategic initiatives. In S. Vinnicombe, R. J. Burke, S. Blake-Beard, & L. L. Moore (Eds.), *Handbook of research on promoting women's careers* (pp. 391–405). Cheltenham: Edward Elgar.

O'Neil, D. A., Hopkins, M. M., & Bilimoria, D. (2013). Sprinters, marathoners and relay runners: Profiles of women's career development over time. In S. Vinnicombe, R. J. Burke, S. Blake-Beard, & L. L. Moore (Eds.). *Handbook of research on promoting women's careers* (pp. 87–105). Cheltenham: Edward Elgar.

O'Neil, D. A., Hopkins, M. M., & Sullivan, S. E. (2011). Do women's networks help advance women's careers? *Career Development International, 16*(7), 733–754.

Peters, K., Ryan, M., & Haslam, S. A. (2013). Women's occupational motivation: The impact of being a woman in a man's world. In S. Vinnicombe, R. J. Burke, S. Blake-Beard, & L. L. Moore (Eds.), *Handbook of research on promoting women's careers* (pp. 162–177). Cheltenham: Edward Elgar.

Peters, K., Ryan, M., Haslam, S. A., & Fernandes, H. (2012). To belong or not to belong: Evidence that women's occupational disidentification is promoted by lack of fit with masculine occupational prototypes. *Journal of Personnel Psychology, 11*(3), 148–158.

Ragins, B. R. (1996). Jumping the hurdles: Barriers to mentoring for women in organizations. *Leadership & Organization Journal, 17*(3), 37–41.

Ragins, B. R. (2007). Diversity and workplace mentoring relationships: A review and positive social capital approach. In T. D. Allen & L. T. Eby (Eds.), *The Blackwell handbook of mentoring: A multiple perspectives approach* (pp. 281–300). Malden, MA: Blackwell.

Rocco, T. S., Bowman, L., & Bryant, L. O. (2014). Disability, health and wellness programs and the role of HRD. In N. Chalofsky, T. Rocco, & M. L. Morris (Eds.), *Handbook of human resource development* (pp. 299–313). Hoboken, NJ: Wiley.

Ryan, M. K. & Haslam, S. A. (2005). The glass cliff: Evidence that women are over-represented in precarious leadership positions. *British Journal of Management, 16*, 81–90.

Ryan, M. K. & Haslam, S. A. (2007). The glass cliff: Exploring the dynamics surrounding the appointment of women to precarious leadership positions. *The Academy of Management Review, 32*(2), 549–572.

Sagrestano, L. M. (2004). Health implications of workplace diversity. In M. Stockdale & F. Crosby (Eds.), *The psychology and management of workplace diversity* (pp. 122–144). Oxford: Blackwell.

Shore, L. M., Randel, A. E., Chung, B. G., Dean, M. A., Ehrhart, K. H., & Singh, G. (2011). Inclusion and diversity in work groups: A review and model for future research. *Journal of Management, 37*(4), 1262–1289.

Stone, D. L. & Stone-Romero, E. F. (2004). The influence of culture on role-taking in culturally diverse organizations. In M. Stockdale & F. Crosby (Eds.), *The psychology and management of workplace diversity* (pp.78–99). Oxford: Blackwell.

Thomas, K. M. (2005). *Diversity dynamics in the workplace.* Toronto, Canada: Thomson Wadsworth.

Tlaiss, H. & Kauser, S. (2010). Perceived organizational barriers to women's career advancement in Lebanon. *Gender in Management: An International Journal, 25*(6), 462–496.

van Veldhoven, M. & Dorenbosch, L. (2008). Age, proactivity and career development. *Career Development International, 13*(2), 112–131.

Villanueva-Flores, M., Valle-Cabrera, R., & Bornay-Barrachina, M. (2014). Career development and individuals with physical disabilities. *Career Development International, 19*(2), 222–243.

Voelpel, W., Sauer, A., & Biemann, T. (2012). Careeer planning for mid- and late-career workers. In J. W. Hedge & W. C. Boreman (Eds.), *The Oxford handbook of work and aging* (pp. 503–519). Oxford: Oxford University Press.

Wang, M., Olson, D. A., & Shultz, K. S. (2013). *Mid and late career issues: An integrative perspective.* New York: Routledge Taylor & Francis.

Wilson-Kovacs, D., Ryan, M. K., Haslam, S. A., & Rabinovich, A. (2008). Just because you can get a wheelchair in the building doesn't necessarily mean that you can still participate: Barriers to the career advancement of disabled professionals. *Disability & Society, 23*(7), 705–717.

Wooten, K. C. & Cobb, A. T. (1999). Career development and organizational justice: Practice and research implications. *Human Resource Development Quarterly, 10*(2), 173–179.

# 7 Career Challenges

Smooth seas do not make skillful sailors.

African proverb

Most individuals will experience challenges as they navigate their careers. These challenges will vary from person to person, and the outcomes of working through them will vary as well. We prefer the term "challenges" rather than "barriers" or "obstacles" because of the negative connotations that are usually attached to the latter terms. The issues we will discuss in this chapter are not necessarily perceived as negative career influences and potentially can result in positive outcomes. We will focus on four major challenges, recognizing that many more exist—but these four are salient to most individuals and are well documented in the literature. They are: job stress, career plateaus, work–life issues, and inadequate employment.

## Job Stress

Job stress can have a significant impact on an individual's performance in the workplace and one's career satisfaction and success (Baruch, 2006). The current career environment, characterized by turbulent economic conditions, increasing use of technology, and the increasing need to balance work and home, suggests that most workers will experience stress from time to time. The Stress in America 2013 survey found that 42 percent of adults reported an increased level of stress over the past five years and, although 61 percent felt managing stress is very important, only 35 percent felt they were managing it well (APA, 2013). A survey conducted in 2010–2011 in Slovenia found that 62 percent of the respondents found their work to be "stressful or highly stressful" and, while a survey in Belgium indicated employees were generally positive about their work, 30 percent still reported that job stress was an issue (EuroFound, 2014).

Selye (1974) defined stress simply as "the nonspecific response of the body to any demand made upon it" (p. 27). Since his seminal work on stress appeared, various definitions have been offered, but central to many of these explanations is the notion that stress is a condition that occurs when an individual is confronted with an opportunity, constraint, and/or demand, is uncertain of the outcome, and perceives the outcome as being important (Greenhaus, Callanan, & Godshalk, 2010; Schuler, 1980). Usually we associate negative consequences with job stress, and managers and HRD professionals clearly need to know how to attend to the detrimental effects of stress. Yet increasingly scholars are recognizing that there are positive forms of stress as well (Hargrove, Nelson, & Cooper, 2013). The concept "eustress," which is considered a positive response to stress, was introduced by Hans Selye in the 1970s (Selye, 1974). More recently, researchers have proposed two forms of self-reported work stressors: challenge-related stressors and hindrance-related stressors (Cavanaugh, Boswell, Roehling, & Boudreau, 2000). Challenge-related stressors are those "associated with challenging job demands" such as heavy workloads, responsibility, and broad job scope (Cavanaugh et al., 2000, p. 66). Hindrance-related stressors are those "constraints that interfere with or hinder an individual's ability to achieve valued goals" (p. 67). Examples of hindrance-related stressors might include excessive bureaucracy, organizational politics, and job security concerns. Whereas hindrance stressors are related to turnover intentions, job searches, and disengagement, challenge stressors are positively related to job satisfaction and organizational commitment (Cavanaugh et al., 2000; Podsakoff, LePine, & LePine, 2007). Demanding work that stretches employees' capabilities, a reasonable and realistic work pace, enough complexity in the job to keep it interesting and extend workers' capabilities, and assigning the appropriate level of responsibility are ways to infuse challenge stressors that may have positive results (Hargrove et al., 2013).

An employee's reaction to stressors is referred to as strain (Beehr, 1995; Hurrell, Nelson, & Simmons, 1998). Three major types of strain have been identified: physiological, psychological, and behavioral (Beehr, 1995; Schuler, 1980). Physiological strain includes responses such as hypertension, ulcers, compromised immune systems, and headaches (Hurrell et al., 1998; Schuler, 1980). Psychological strain involves those affective and cognitive responses that we often associate with stress (e.g., withdrawal, irritability, anxiety, and depression). Behavioral reactions might include changes in appearance, increase use of alcohol and tobacco, and absenteeism, to name a few (Schuler, 1980). All three types of strain have the potential to affect individual careers and to impact organizations. According to Gilbreath and Montesino (2006):

> Absenteeism and turnover are likely to increase as employees flee a negative work environment. Grievances, complaints and lawsuits are likely to increase as overly stressed employees seek redress. And health insurance premiums and workers' compensation rates increase as organizations' experience ratings (e.g., injury rates) begin to reflect the effects the workplace is having on employees.
> (p. 564)

Just as there are numerous reactions to job stress, there are many potential sources of stress as well. Some of the most common sources include the following:

- Role characteristics: stress often results due to role overload or underload (too much or not enough work), role ambiguity (job expectations are unclear), and role conflict (competing demands or expectations). Nurses, for example, consistently report that a heavy workload is a significant source of stress (McVicar, 2003).
- Organizational characteristics: there are a number of organizational factors such as compensation (e.g., pay inequities), inadequate resources, constant change, and poor communication that can result in increased levels of stress.
- Interpersonal relationships: incivility, competition among individuals and groups, perceptions of bias, and discrimination are examples of social interactions that may cause increase levels of stress in the workplace.
- Supervisors: individuals who experience abusive supervision often report increased levels of psychological distress (Tepper, 2000). Conversely, positive supervisor behaviors can significantly impact the psychological well-being of employees (Gilbreath & Benson, 2004).
- Technology: while technology often facilitates work, it can result in increased strain and stress (Day, Paquet, Scott, & Hambley, 2012). Increasingly, researchers are examining the relationship between job stress and information and communication technology (ICT), such as social media and email (Brown, Duck, & Jimmieson, 2014; Bucher, Fieseler, & Suphan, 2013). Common demands associated with ICT include information overload, hassles such as computer crashes, increased expectations regarding availability, increased workload,

lack of control over ICT, constant need to update and learn new ICT, potential for miscommunication, and concerns regarding the use of ICT to monitor employees' performance (Day et al., 2012).

- Job control: the amount of latitude an individual has in determining how and when the work gets done can impact stress levels. Perceived job control can result in individuals believing the stress is manageable and yield more constructive coping behaviors (Spector, 2002). Because high job control is linked to many positive outcomes (e.g., engaged employees, motivated employees), it is reasonable to assume that control over one's job may be associated with perceptions of career success (Eatough & Spector, 2014).

In many cases there are multiple variables interacting together that will potentially lead to stress. For example, Karasek's (1979) Job Demand–Control Model (JD–CM) proposes that having a high degree of job control will buffer the impact of high job demands, whereas high demands and a low degree of control will result in more employee strain. Yet, other individual and contextual factors may influence this interaction between job demands and job control. For example, Tucker, Jimmieson & Oei (2013) found that, when work groups perceived the group as being competent (e.g., collective efficacy), job control did serve as a buffer of high job demands. But high levels of job control did not serve as a buffer if the group perceived collective efficacy as being low; rather, it "appeared to act as a stress-exacerbator" (p. 15). The authors concluded that organizations need to consider both individual and contextual factors when designing stress interventions.

There are different ways to approach the management and prevention of occupational stress. Cooper and Cartwright (1997) identified three major types of interventions:

- Primary prevention involves taking actions to change or eliminate potential sources of stress in the workplace. Changing the workload, work schedule, task design, and/or social environment are all examples of primary intervention strategies.
- Secondary prevention is focused on assisting individuals in coping with and managing stress. Rather than concentrating on the sources of stress, secondary prevention will address the consequences of stress. Developing self-awareness, providing stress management training, and relieving the symptoms of stress (e.g., relaxation techniques, physical activity) are examples of secondary intervention strategies.
- Tertiary prevention is concerned with the rehabilitation and treatment of individuals who have experienced serious health problems

resulting from stress. Oftentimes organizations rely on employee assistance programs (EAPs) to help employees needing this type of assistance.

Another way to classify interventions concentrates on the focus of the intervention. DeFrank and Cooper (1987) categorized them as targeting:

- The individual. Like many secondary prevention strategies, these interventions help employees understand, manage, and cope with stress.
- The organization. These interventions include policies and practices that prevent or reduce employee stress. Biron, Cooper, & Gibbs (2012) identify these as "macro level" initiatives (p. 939).
- The individual/organization. The interventions address concerns related to the interconnection between employees and their work. For example, periodically assessing person–environment fit and role issues (e.g., ambiguity, conflict) would be considered interventions that might help with the stress occurring at this level (Giga, Cooper, & Faragher, 2003).

Most organizations tend to address stress-related problems by relying on secondary prevention or individual-level interventions (Beehr, 1995; Cooper & Cartwright, 1997). Giga et al. (2003) wrote that "This implies that stress in the workplace is still considered to be an issue that should be controlled by individual employees and that situations that get out of control are a direct consequence of human incompetence or weakness" (p. 288). While these interventions are helpful to individual employees, they are less likely to address the sources of the stress, and consequently the workplace will remain stressful.

There are numerous specific interventions that can help in the prevention and/or management of occupational stress (see Table 7.1 for specific examples). Additionally, positive approaches, such as appreciative inquiry and work policies promoting fun, are being encouraged as ways to promote employee well-being and healthy organizations (Biron et al., 2012). But before implementing interventions, organizations, with employee input, need to determine what stress-related issues must be addressed. Assessments such as employee attitude surveys, ergonomic analyses, turnover and absenteeism data, compensation claims, and stress audits will help determine what interventions appear most appropriate and will provide baseline measures for evaluation of implemented interventions (Giga et al., 2003; Gilbreath &

*Table 7.1* Stress Interventions

| Organizational (Primary Prevention) | Individual (Secondary Prevention) |
|---|---|
| Job redesign | Stress management training |
| Flexible work schedules and arrangements | Relaxation techniques |
| Pace-of-work alterations | Cognitive-behavioral therapy (CBT)* |
| Selection practices (e.g., determine P–E fit, realistic job preview) | Time management training |
| Fair, consistently applied workplace policies and reward systems | Wellness programs |
| Job and career training and development | Fitness programs |
| Supervisor training (e.g., to recognize signs of employee stress and their role in assisting workers) | Employee assistance programs (EAPs) |
| Participative management approaches | |
| Effective communication practices | |
| Cohesive teams | |
| Clear roles, expectations, and goals | |
| A psychosocial safety environment | |

Note: *Cognitive-behavioral therapy is an intervention often used to treat anxiety disorders. It involves challenging and altering thought processes to accept unpleasant experiences (Giga, et al., 2003).

Sources: Biron et al. (2012); Cooper & Cartwright (1997); Giga et al. (2003); Quick et al. (2014).

Montesino, 2006; Quick, Bennett, & Hargrove, 2014). Additionally, taking an integrated approach regarding interventions is important as well. A combination of both individual- and organization-level initiatives is necessary to create healthy work organizations (Biron et al., 2012; Cooper & Cartwright, 1997; Quick et al., 2014).

### *Burnout*

We would be remiss in leaving the topic of job stress without briefly discussing job burnout. The prevalence of burnout is difficult to ascertain; however, a study done with Swedish workers found that nearly a fifth (17.9 percent) of the respondents were categorized as experiencing a high level of burnout (Lindblom, Linton, Fedeli, & Bryngelsson, 2006). Much of the early work on burnout focused on individuals employed in education, human services, and health care; yet it is now widely acknowledged that burnout can occur in many occupations.

Job burnout has been defined as "a psychological syndrome in response to chronic interpersonal stressors on the job" (Maslach, Schaufeli, & Leiter, 2001, p. 399). There are three major dimensions of burnout: exhaustion, depersonalization (or cynicism), and inefficacy (or reduced personal accomplishment), although exhaustion is widely considered the most "obvious manifestation of this complex syndrome" (Maslach et al., 2001, p. 402). Both individual (e.g., personality characteristics) and organizational/environmental (e.g., workload, control, reward structure) factors have been found to correlate with burnout (Halbesleben & Buckley, 2004; Maslach et al., 2001). Specifically, Maslach et al. proposed that burnout occurs when there is a lack of fit between an employee and one or more dimensions of worklife. These major domains include: workload, control, reward, community, fairness, and values. Interventions targeting both individuals and organizations are recommended to help manage and prevent burnout, which may help cultivate engagement with work (Maslach et al., 2001).

Most researchers and practitioners focus on job burnout, rather than career burnout. However Pines (2000), employing a psychoanalytic–existential approach, has argued that individuals choose careers with the hope that they will engage in something that is significant and meaningful. Career burnout occurs when individuals no longer believe that what they are doing is meaningful; hence career choice plays a significant role in understanding burnout. A study done on medical students appears to support Pines's argument. Pagnin et al. (2013) found that medical students who indicated that they were motivated to become doctors because of an experience with an illness or death were more likely to experience emotional exhaustion. The authors provided an explanation for why this might happen, suggesting that this motivation may conflict with the focus on cognitive knowledge that so often dominates medical school training. This conflict may result in students feeling that what they are learning will not lead to making "a difference in the world" (p. 391). This literature points to the importance of career counseling and providing information regarding burnout in programs that prepare individuals for specific careers.

**Career Plateauing**

Career plateauing has been conceptualized as hierarchical plateauing, which occurs when it is unlikely that an individual will experience vertical movement in an organization (Allen, Poteet, & Russell, 1998; Feldman & Weitz, 1988). Career plateauing can also occur in terms of job content, meaning that the work one does is no longer perceived as challenging (Bardwick, 1988). According to Chao (1990, p. 182), career plateauing should be conceptualized as an "individual's perception of his or her career future" rather than using job tenure or age to define plateaus.

Career plateaus have been associated with several negative outcomes. Research has found that individuals who perceive themselves as plateaued are likely to report lower job and career satisfaction, lower organizational commitment and identification, and higher intentions to turnover than those who do not consider themselves plateaued (Allen et al., 1998; Chao, 1990; Lee, 2003). Additionally, plateaued employees have also been found to experience greater stress and more depression than the general population (McCleese, Eby, Scharlau, & Hoffman, 2007). These potential negative consequences suggest that organizations should be knowledgeable regarding why employees may plateau and what can be done to help those who have plateaued or are at risk of plateauing.

Let's first explore some of the reasons why people plateau in their careers. Feldman and Weitz (1988) identified six major sources of career plateaus. They are:

- Individual skills and abilities—insufficient knowledge, skills, and abilities (KSAs) can impede one's career progress.
- Individual needs and values—some individuals may value other aspects of life more than a career.
- Lack of intrinsic motivation—employees may perceive that their jobs lack challenge or that the work they do is meaningless.
- Lack of extrinsic rewards—no or small pay raises, perceptions of unfairness in the distribution of rewards, and other extrinsic incentives may result in dissatisfaction and poor performance.
- Stress and burnout—may lead to inadequate performance and negative attitudes regarding one's job.
- Slow organizational growth—the prevalence of organizations downsizing and flattening their structures can result in fewer career opportunities.

The turbulent economic environment, and increased use of technology to accomplish work, have potentially exacerbated the number of individuals feeling plateaued in their careers. And increasingly, some are considering "work as marginal"—choosing to focus on balance and viewing their jobs simply as means to other ends, secondary in importance to other aspects of their lives (Guest & Sturges, 2007).

There are, however, many individuals who would prefer to not feel plateaued in their careers. A variety of coping strategies and organizational strategies may be helpful in assisting these workers. Let's first consider what individuals can do:

- Discuss feelings of being plateaued with a supervisor, colleagues, or family members. McCleese et al. (2007) found that, although individuals reported using a variety of coping strategies when experiencing a plateau, discussing the problem and withdrawing on the job were the most frequently cited. While job withdrawal may have significant negative implications in terms of job performance, discussing the issue with those who may be able to assist can be a positive first step in alleviating perceptions of being plateaued.
- Engage in career development activities such as training, career planning, and career exploration. Allen, Russell, Poteet, & Dobbins (1999) found that those individuals who established a career plan, which included investigating various career paths and opportunities, were more likely to perceive that they had mobility and therefore perceptions of being plateaued were minimized.
- Seek out new opportunities like serving on a special project, taking on a different task/assignment or mentoring a less experienced employee (Rotondo & Perrewe, 2000). The impact of mentoring others has been studied and found to potentially "alleviate the negative effects associated with job content plateauing" (Lentz & Allen, 2009, p. 379).

Organizations also need to play a role in assisting those feeling plateaued. Some noteworthy interventions include:

- Careful examination of jobs to determine if re-designing them might alleviate perceptions of being plateaued. Expanding job responsibilities and working on projects as a team are two examples of how organizations might alter jobs to help employees feel challenged and engaged (Rotondo & Perrewe, 2000).
- Provide developmental activities such as training and career counseling to assist those who may be plateaued due to lack of skills. Opportunities to mentor others may be particularly helpful for those who feel job content plateaued and can lead to a variety of positive outcomes including job satisfaction, organizational commitment, and fewer turnover intentions (Lentz & Allen, 2009, p. 379).
- Develop alternative career paths focused on functional or technical competencies rather than hierarchical movement. This may

involve redesigning compensation systems to reward those who develop these competencies and demonstrate strong performance (Feldman & Weitz, 1988).

- Create a supportive culture that fosters learning, respect, and encouragement. Armstrong-Strassen (2008) found that older employees were less likely to report feelings of job content plateauing if they perceived organizational support and respect from the organization, their supervisor, and colleagues. Supervisors in particular play an important role in helping employees who may be feeling plateaued (Allen et al., 1999; McCleese et al., 2007). Often employees will seek them out to discuss their concerns, so managers need to be skilled in how to handle these conversations and provide meaningful assistance. HRD can help educate and train supervisors regarding ways to pro-actively deal with plateaued employees. One important message for managers to receive is that career plateauing is not necessarily related to age and job tenure, so they should not necessarily assume that their older or more experienced employees will be experiencing plateaus or that younger employees do not (Chao, 1990; Lee, 2003).

Like most of these career challenges, it is important to be aware that plateauing may be more widespread in particular types of organizations and/or in certain professions. Also, rather than looking at career plateauing as a dichotomous construct, it should be conceptualized on a continuum (Chao, 1990). Some individuals may perceive that their career is very stagnated, while others may feel slightly plateaued. These differences are likely to influence a host of important outcomes like job satisfaction, turnover intention, and organizational commitment. In addition, understanding that there is a broad range of "plateauness" is likely to influence what interventions are employed to assist the plateaued individual.

There may be little that managers and HRD practitioners can do to assist those experiencing hierarchical plateauing, given the push towards flattening organizational structures and the demise of "labor-intensive economies" (Lee, 2003, p. 539). However, much can be done to prevent job content plateauing. Bardwick (1986) wrote:

> content plateauing need never occur. No one ever knows everything; no one has ever done everything. There are no limits to change and challenge except those created by personal fear or organizational laziness. Content plateauing is preventable and, if it has occurred, is remediable.
>
> (p. 67)

Most of the recommendations listed above will address content plateauing rather than hierarchical plateauing.

## Work–Life Issues[1]

Consider these statistics:

- In 2013, approximately 70 percent of all US mothers with children under 18 were employed; 93 percent of all fathers with children under 18 were employed (Catalyst, 2012a).
- Labor force participation for mothers in Canada increased from 39 percent in 1976 to 73 percent in 2009 (Catalyst, 2012a).
- Women, on average, spend approximately 2.3 hours more per day doing unpaid work (e.g., caring, cleaning, and cooking) than men do in OECD (Organisation for Economic Co-operation and Development) nations. This discrepancy is even more pronounced in some countries (e.g., Mexico and Turkey), where women spend approximately 4.3 hours per day more than men on unpaid work (OECD, 2013).
- Men's levels of work–life conflict have increased from 34 percent in 1977 to 49 percent in 2008 (Catalyst, 2012b).
- A study conducted by Catalyst in India found that 90 percent of the women responded that the workplace does not meet their work–life needs (Catalyst, 2012b).
- Surveys on millennials indicate that a large majority (88 percent) want employment that fosters "work–life integration" (Asghar, 2014).

As these figures suggest, a significant career challenge for many individuals is negotiating the multitude of roles we undertake as adults. For the past four decades this has become a more important issue as women's participation in the workforce has steadily increased. Scholars and practitioners alike recognize the need to determine how to assist employees handling the intersection between work and family. As a result, a lot of research has been generated and many organizational initiatives have been developed; and much of this work has produced a number of constructs and approaches. Let's first discuss some of the most common frameworks used to understand this intersection:

- *Work–life conflict*: this construct is closely linked to job stress and occurs when one role (e.g., employee) conflicts with another (e.g., parent, spouse, or partner). Powell, Francesco, & Ling (2009) defined this conflict as "negative interdependencies between work and family roles" (p. 602). It is a bi-directional construct, where work may cause interference with family (w-to-f conflict) or family interferes with work (f-to-w conflict). A number of negative outcomes are associated with work–life conflict such as job dissatisfaction, intention to turn-over, poor job/family performance, family dissatisfaction, and health problems (Eby, Casper, Lockwood, Bordeaux, & Brinley, 2005; Frone, 2003). A meta-analysis of the literature found that work–life conflict was the predominant paradigm used to explore the intersection between work and family (Eby et al., 2005).

- *Work–life balance*: for many, this concept suggests an absence of work–life conflict (McMillan, Morris, & Atchley, 2011). And, while this concept is frequently used, there appears to be less agreement as to what work–life balance really means. Grzywacz and Carlson (2007) defined it as "accomplishment of role-related expectations that are negotiated and shared between an individual and his or her role-related partners in the work and family domains" (p. 458). This definition suggests that balance is a social construct (Grzywacz & Carlson, 2007), involving intention and action on the part of the agent. Another definition is "the extent to which an individual is equally engaged in—and equally satisfied with—his or her work role and family role" (Greenhaus, Collins, & Shaw, 2003, p. 513). These authors conceptualized balance as involving three components: time balance (meaning an equal amount of time for work and family roles), involvement balance (meaning an equal level of psychological involvement in these roles), and satisfaction balance (which suggests an equal level of satisfaction in both work and family roles). While these three components may be useful in analyzing one's specific work–life situation, the notion of "equal level" has been criticized as being overly prescriptive or, as Friedman (2014) indicated, it becomes a "zero-sum game." We prefer the more subjective approach advocated by Kossek, Valcour, & Lirio (2014) that "the picture of work–life balance looks different from one person to another, as well as at different points in a person's career and life" (p. 301).

- *Work–life enrichment*: many scholars and practitioners recognize that the intersection between work life and family life can have positive effects. According to Greenhaus and Powell (2006), work–life enrichment is "the extent to which experiences in one role improve the quality of life in the other role" (p. 73). Similar to work–life conflict, enrichment is conceived as being bi-directional. In other words, work can improve family life (work–family enrichment) and family experiences can enrich one's work (family–work enrichment). Many parents, for example, discuss how raising children helps them in their work environment (e.g., developing more patience with co-workers or clients, demonstrating a sense of humor). Likewise, in previous jobs as corporate trainers, employees would often tell us that the skills they learned in a training program on conflict management were being used at home to handle issues arising with a spouse, partner, or a teenage son or daughter.

- *Work–life harmony*: as a way to integrate work–life conflict and work–life enrichment, McMillan et al. (2011) proposed that "harmony" be used to describe the desired interaction between work and life. According to Morris and McMillan (2014), work–life harmony is:

> a state-like indicator of well-being influenced by adaptive strategies used to intentionally create a synchronized and complementary arrangement of work and life (e.g., personal, friend, spouse, parent, child) roles, relationships, and resources that are aligned and positively reinforce an integrated narrative of work and life that is productive, satisfying, and fulfilling in both domains.
>
> (p. 231)

This idea of harmony is not new. For example, it has been a focal point of Stewart Friedman's work on leadership and work–life integration for quite some time. One of the goals of his Total Leadership method, which identifies four domains in life—work, self, community, and home—is to produce harmony in these four domains (Friedman, 2014). Much of his work concentrates on helping individuals move towards this harmony as a way to improve performance. While much of Friedman's work focuses on the individual, McMillan et al. (2011) believed that harmony can be considered at both the individual and the organizational level. They argue that work–life harmony can be evaluated at the individual level (assessing conflicts experienced and enrichments gained) and at the organizational level (assessing the health of departments to determine what interventions might be needed to achieve harmony).

### Impact on Careers

Responsibilities in other life domains will have an impact on individuals' careers. For example, women are more likely to experience disruptions in their careers due to family obligations (Eby et al., 2005) and work–family conflict has been found to have a negative impact on the career satisfaction of women and on older male employees (Martins, Eddleston, & Veiga, 2002). Family responsibilities also have been found to nega-tively affect career success, which may be due to a number of factors. For example, family obligations may result in more career interruptions which then might impact success (Eby et al., 2005). Family roles may influence the amount of time and energy one can devote to work (work centrality) which will then affect both objective and subjective career success (Mayrhofer, Meyer, & Schiffinger, 2007). Increasingly work–life issues appear to influence career choice, with millennials in particular, who often have voiced strong expectations regarding the need for balance or harmony regarding work and other aspects of their lives (McDonald & Hite, 2008; Ng, Schweitzer, & Lyons, 2010).

From the enrichment perspective, non-work roles (e.g., parent, friend, volunteer) can make significant contributions to individuals' careers. A study done with women managers found that non-work roles provided them with psychological resources (e.g., confidence, esteem, satisfaction) and managerial skills that helped their work performance (Ruderman, Ohlott, Panzer, & King, 2002). Developing non-work roles can add value to one's work roles as this study clearly points out. These non-work roles can result in strong socio-emotional support which may also help individuals deal with work–family conflict and other job stressors (Martins et al., 2002) as well.

### Work–Life Initiatives

A recent article in our local paper titled "Work–life balance is big business" pointed out that "work–life balance is not a problem just for women or a concern that is going to be solved—but rather an ongoing challenge" (Goodman, 2014, p. 8B). With this now considered a multi-billion dollar industry, organizations have come to the realization that helping employ-ees negotiate work and non-work roles is important since it affects their bottom line. As a result, various initiatives have been developed to meet both employees' and organizations' needs. There are various ways to categorize and describe these interventions. Many organizations focus on what Kossek, Lewis, & Hammer (2009) refered to as *structural work–life support*, which includes a variety of initiatives such as:

- Human resources (HR) practices/policies and job redesign as ways to enhance workers' choices regarding "when, where, and for how long they engage in work-related tasks" (Hill et al., 2008, p.149);
- HR policies regarding absenteeism, vacations, and sick leave;
- child care and elder care benefits.

Table 7.2 provides a more comprehensive listing of these types of work–life initiatives.

However, these initiatives will only be effective if there is *cultural work–life support*. This support, defined as "informal workplace social and relational support" (Kossek et al., 2009, p. 4), needs to be present at the work group level (e.g., supervisors and co-workers) as well as the organizational level (e.g., resources allocated, values demonstrated). The importance of cultural work–life support should not be underestimated. Allen (2001) found that individuals who perceived that their organization was "family supportive" reported less work–life conflict, more job satisfaction, less turnover intention, and more organizational commitment than those who perceived their organization as not "family supportive." Cultural work–life support is important since it has a tremendous impact on whether employees will utilize the work–life initiatives provided (Allen, 2001; Kossek et al., 2009; Veiga, Baldridge, & Eddleston, 2004). Employees may believe that using a work–life benefit can result in unfair burdens placed on their co-workers, or that their supervisor or co-workers will develop unfavorable attitudes toward them, or that their careers will be jeopardized (Veiga et al., 2004). These concerns can be alleviated if the organization and work group demonstrate support for work–life integration. Particularly important in this discussion is the employee's supervisor (Allen, 2001; Kossek &

*Table 7.2* Organizational Work–Life Initiatives

*Work–Life Benefits*

- Flexible work arrangements (FWAs):
  - Compressed work week
  - Flexible hours
  - Telecommuting
  - Part-time work
  - Job sharing
  - Reduced hours
- On-site elder/child care
- Financial assistance for elder/child care
- Information/referral systems for elder/child care
- Employee assistance programs (e.g., family/individual counseling, financial assistance)
- Paid leaves and sabbaticals
- Phased-in work schedule after a leave
- Phased-in retirement
- Services at the work site (e.g., dry cleaners, fitness center)

Source: Sullivan & Mainiero (2007).

Ruderman, 2012; Morris, 2012; Purcell, Lewis, Smithson, & Caton, 2008; Swody & Powell, 2007; Veiga et al., 2004). Purcell et al., drawing conclusions based on a study of work–life practices in seven European countries, found that parents emphasized the importance of line managers in the implementation of these practices. Supportive supervisors play a key role, since they often are the ones that can most readily inform employees of these benefits, support participation in initiatives when needed, grant requests for participation, and encourage and support co-worker acceptance.

Other factors, beyond supervisors and managers, can contribute to an unsupportive work–life culture. Inconsistency and lack of clarity in HR policies and practices and poor communication about the availability, accessibility, affordability, and benefits of work–life initiatives can negatively impact both employees and organizations (Morris, 2012). HRD can play a significant role in developing cultural work–life support by:

- training supervisors so they have the skills and knowledge to assist employees with their work–life issues;
- conducting audits and/or assessments regarding usage of work–life benefits, obstacles individuals are encountering in accessing and using benefits, and employee satisfaction with work–life initiatives;
- assisting in organizational efforts to clearly communicate with employees regarding work–life issues and initiatives (e.g., educational programs);
- creating, developing, and promoting networks and mentor programs to provide socio-emotional support for individuals experiencing work–life conflict;
- advocating for redesigned work that promotes realistic workloads and deadlines (Kossek et al., 2014; Martins et al., 2002; Morris, 2012).

Another important issue that needs to be addressed is the impact that usage of work–life benefits can have on an individual's career. To date, only a few studies have examined this issue, and the results are mixed. A qualitative study of female part-time managers in the UK found that participants perceived their careers had stalled since beginning part-time status (Tomlinson & Durbin, 2010). However, other research has indicated that flexible work arrangements (e.g., reduced loads) help individuals sustain their careers by allowing them to stay in the workforce and help satisfy specific goals (e.g., balance) depending on their specific life/career circumstances

(Hall, Lee, Kossek, & Heras, 2012; Shapiro, Ingols, O'Neill, & Blake-Beard, 2009). A longitudinal study conducted by Konrad and Yang (2012) debunked the notion that using work–life benefits is a "career-limiting move," finding that benefit usage enhanced employee promotability—primarily due to the lessening of strain which led to improved performance. Leslie, Manchester, Park, & Mehng (2012) found that the usage of flexible work practices (FWP) had consequences in terms of career success—depending on managers' attributions of that usage. It (usage) had a positive impact on career success when managers attributed use to a "desire to improve productivity." However, if managers attributed usage to a "desire for personal life accommodations," it had the potential to constrain career success (p. 1425). In general, the research suggests work–life benefit usage is not necessarily a barrier to career development. Both individuals and managers need to take a long-term perspective regarding this issue. Employees need to recognize that using work–life benefits can make them more productive and, hence, more valuable to their employers. Managers need to realize that any inconveniences that might arise from employees using these benefits (and effective organizations will have mechanisms in place to prevent this) are likely to be short term, and the organization will benefit by retaining productive and satisfied employees.

Work–life initiatives can have a positive impact on organizational outcomes. Morris (2008) identified five:

- improved productivity;
- reductions in turnover and increases in retention;
- improved job satisfaction, morale, loyalty, commitment, motivation, organizational citizen behavior, volunteerism, and engagement;
- enhanced corporate image, customer satisfaction and loyalty, ethical behavior, and ability to attract investors;
- retaining women and re-engaging older employees (pp. 101–103).

Many of these outcomes were supported by a follow-up study conducted by Morris, Heames, & McMillan (2011) which looked at HR executives' perceptions of the strategic impact of work–life initiatives. However, they also found that most organizations surveyed had not developed metrics to assess the strategic impact of work–life initiatives. Clearly this is needed to ensure strong return on investment, to help with future decisions made on work–life issues, and to assist in recruiting talent.

The literature on work–life issues is vast, indicating that the intersection between work and non-work is complex. A number of contextual factors need to be considered beyond the organization. Family structure (e.g., dual-earner, single-earner, parental status), for example, will impact the amount of work–life conflict experienced, career decisions, life enrichment, and a host of other work–life issues. Socio-economics and status are important contextual factors as well. Individuals struggling to make ends meet by working two or three jobs may struggle to understand or relate to the notion of work–life enrichment or harmony.

Governmental policies can play an important role in facilitating work–life or cause greater inequities in supporting employees' needs. Munn (2013) pointed out that many employees in the US with low wages cannot realistically use unpaid FMLA (Family and Medical Leave Act) time. Many developed nations (e.g., the EU and Australia) provide work–life support through various policies and programs, yet, even in countries with these policies, individuals still may struggle to gain access to the benefits they are entitled to and need (Purcell et al., 2008). Kossek et al. (2009) speculated that, perhaps because of the lack of governmental support, the US focuses more on organizational based work–life initiatives than other countries. However, increasingly, governments throughout the world are recognizing the need to develop policies and provide assistance that support work–life issues (Munn & Lee, 2015).

Beyond governmental policies, the national culture needs to be considered as well. Lewis, Gambles, & Rapoport (2007) argued for "an international perspective" on work–life balance that questions the "Anglo-centric taken-for-granted assumptions embedded in the WLB discourses" (p. 362). Powell et al. (2009) emphasized the importance of culture-sensitive theories and practices regarding work–life issues for multinational corporations so that they will have a better understanding of what initiatives are needed, likely to be used, and likely to be effective in various parts of the world.

## Inadequate Employment

Economic unrest around the world has prevailed for about a decade, resulting in devastating consequences for many workers. Involuntary job loss and underemployment became pervasive during the Great Recession and these concerns remain important for many individuals. Even though many economies have recovered or are recovering, feelings of insecurity about jobs persist (Boswell, Olson-Buchanan, &

Harris, 2014). We recognize that the term "inadequate employment" is broad and potentially could cover a number of employment arrangements. We will focus on involuntary job loss and underemployment—both of which present challenges to employees and to organizations. It is important to recognize that these two types of inadequate employment overlap considerably in terms of their effect on individuals and organizations. However we will begin our discussion by focusing on involuntary job loss.

Job loss has a profound effect on many employees. It can result in loss of self-esteem and well-being and it is considered one of the most stressful life events (Gowan, 2014; Zikic & Klehe, 2006). Sometimes the reaction to experiencing job loss is such that people may display post-traumatic stress disorder (PTSD) symptoms "such as ruminating on or re-experiencing the layoff event, as well as anxiety or agitation that was triggered by job loss" (McKee-Ryan, Virick, Prussia, Harvey, & Lilly, 2009, p. 575). There are many factors associated with job loss that will produce stress such as lack of financial security, feelings of isolation due to the loss of opportunities to interact with others and be a member of a group, and feelings of inadequacy, which often results in pressures to develop new skills (Blustein, Kozan, & Connors-Kellgren, 2013). However, in some instances job loss can result in career growth (Gowan, 2014). For example, in a qualitative study conducted with unemployed and underemployed participants, Blustein et al. found that some individuals felt that their unemployment was a positive event in that it provided an opportunity to pursue another career.

There are a variety of factors that can influence employees' job loss experience. How the organization handled the lay-off or termination can impact employees' responses to job loss. Providing advance notice of the lay-off, offering outplacement services, and extending severance packages can influence employees' perceptions of fairness and help minimize the stress (McKee-Ryan et al., 2009). Individuals with strong social support networks often weather job loss better than those without strong support from family, friends, and colleagues (Blustein et al., 2013; Gowan, 2014). Additionally, individuals will react differently to job loss based on individual characteristics such as hardiness, resiliency, and employability. In Chapter 2, employability was presented as an important career construct consisting of three dimensions: adaptability, career identity, and human and social capital. Fugate, Kinicki, & Ashforth (2004) proposed that employable individuals will be less likely to be psychologically harmed by job loss, more likely to involve themselves in job searches, and apt to gain high quality re-employment. Support for these contentions was found in a study conducted with unemployed Australians. The authors concluded that employability plays a significant role "in relation to self-esteem, job search, and re-employment" (McArdle, Waters, Briscoe, & Hall, 2007, p. 262).

There are a variety of career interventions that can help those individuals who have suffered a job loss. Career and mental health counseling can help displaced workers come to grips with their distress, assist them in developing coping skills, and begin the process of sorting out next steps in their career journey (Blustein et al., 2013). Zikic & Klehe (2006) found that career exploration and planning had a significant impact on re-employment quality, suggesting a need for outplacement services that can help individuals gain the knowledge and skills to effectively engage in these activities. Outplacement programs that assist displaced employees in developing resiliency and employability are needed as well (Gowan, 2012). At the community and national level, interventions and policies to help the unemployed and to reduce unemployment are needed (Blustein et al., 2013). Gowan (2014) argued that, to shape governmental programs and public policy, new information is needed "about how to guide the unemployed into the right jobs programs and how to assist them in equipping themselves mentally and skill-wise to respond to inevitable career transitions" (p. 267).

### Underemployment

This phenomenon often occurs when individuals are re-employed after losing their jobs. However, underemployment can occur to anyone, at any time, for a variety of reasons. Underemployment is "when workers are employed in jobs which are substandard relative to their goals and expectations" (Maynard & Feldman, 2011, p. 1). There are several ways in which one might come to the conclusion that he/she is underemployed. Some of these are relatively objective job characteristics, and others are more subjective interpretations of one's job experiences (Feldman, Leana, & Bolino, 2002; McKee-Ryan & Harvey, 2011). Specifically, underemployment can mean that:

- employees are underpaid or at a lower hierarchical status than other similar workers (in terms of knowledge, skills, and abilities);
- employees are involuntarily working fewer hours than desired;
- employees are working a schedule, shift, or hours not congruent with their preference;
- employees are overeducated for the position they currently occupy;
- employees are working in a job outside the field in which they were educated or trained;

- employees' skills or experiences are underutilized in their current job;
- employees perceive that they are overqualified for the job they are doing; or
- employees perceive that their jobs are lacking and should be better (also known as "relative deprivation").

(Feldman et al., 2002; McKee-Ryan & Harvey, 2011)

There are a number of factors that lead to underemployment. Economic factors, such as the recent recession, often lead to greater underemployment. Other factors such as the type of jobs, employee characteristics and traits, work preferences, and career history may impact underemployment (McKee-Ryan & Harvey, 2011). There are also certain groups of individuals who are more likely to be underemployed. These include: youth, older workers, women, ethnic minorities and immigrants, and contingent employees (Maynard & Feldman, 2011).

There are several negative career outcomes of underemployment. For example, Nabi (2003) found that underemployed graduates reported lower career satisfaction, less opportunity to use skills, and lower extrinsic career success (e.g., earnings) than did fully employed graduates. Feldman et al. (2002) found that the inability to use one's skills resulted in negative reactions among underemployed executives—more so than salary cuts or demotions. It may be difficult to leave the ranks of the underemployed; there is evidence to suggest that individuals leaving jobs due to being overskilled do not necessarily improve their lot (Erdogan & Bauer, 2011). All of this points to a less than positive career trajectory for the underemployed.

There are, however, some interventions that might help the underemployed. Some of this needs to begin early on—providing information to teens and young adults regarding the importance of early job choices and career planning. On an individual level, workers may find it useful to develop a good relationship with their managers and demonstrate a willingness to take on new tasks and behave in prosocial ways (Erdogan & Bauer, 2011). This may lead to job enrichment and/or enlargement and the potential to move to a more desirable position (Nabi, 2003). HR needs to be vigilant in examining and analyzing their organization's employment trends and how these may lead to employees perceiving that they are underemployed. Managers and HR need to know their employees so that they can determine if an employee is underemployed by choice or because he/she needed a job. They also need to know what type of underemployment this employee is experiencing—does she feel she is overqualified for the job? Underutilized in terms of skills? Knowing this information can help managers and HR determine what they might be able to do to improve the situation (e.g., focus on restructuring the job, training/skill enhancement, changing work schedules).

## Additional Considerations

There are potentially many career challenges that individuals may face throughout their lifespans. We have chosen to focus on four that are frequently encountered and that can significantly affect careers. While we discuss them as distinct challenges, it is important to recognize that usually they will overlap and result in multiple challenges to assess and manage. For example, work–life issues, career plateauing, and inadequate employment are all likely to result in job stress. This suggests that both individual strategies and organizational interventions should be developed that can help employees handle multiple challenges.

How organizations and individuals respond to these four challenges is highly dependent on the culture of the organization and individual characteristics. When the organizational culture promotes open communication, creates a sense of caring for and among its employees, and supports employee learning and development, individuals are likely to respond positively to these challenges, resulting in happier and more productive employees. Throughout this chapter specific recommendations have been provided as to how organizations can assist individuals in handling job stress, career plateauing, work–life issues, and inadequate employment. Organizations that care about their employees and the development of their careers have adopted many of these recommendations and continually assess their effectiveness.

At the individual level, characteristics such as hardiness, high self-esteem, and a proactive personality have been found to impact how employees react to work–life challenges and unemployment (Frone, 2003; McArdle et al., 2007). But perhaps the most important individual characteristic needed to effectively respond to these challenges is resiliency. This concept was briefly introduced in Chapter 3 as an important individual characteristic influencing career development. Much of the early research on resiliency was done in clinical and developmental psychology; a focus on resilience at work has developed in the past 15–20 years (Caza & Milton, 2012; Youssef & Luthans, 2007). Resiliency is the ability to "bounce back" or "rebound" from adversity (Luthans, 2002). It is considered a state-like construct that is malleable (Luthans, Vogelgesang, & Lester, 2006; Luthans, Avey, Avolio, & Peterson, 2010). Therefore, it can be learned. As Youssef and Luthans (2007) explained, resiliency "allows for not only reactive recovery but also proactive learning and growth through conquering challenges" (p. 778).

There are a number of ways to develop one's resilience. There are, for example, several self-help books that offer information and self-guided activities to develop resiliency. Social support, such as networking and mentoring, can be helpful as well. A recent study found that mentoring—particularly psychosocial (e.g., providing emotional support), being mentored by one's supervisor, and cross-gender career mentoring relationships—resulted in higher protégé resilience (Kao, Rogers, Spitzmueller, Lin, & Lin, 2014). The authors reasoned that the functions that mentors serve (e.g., career advice, psychosocial support) and the positive outcomes that often occur from these relationships (e.g., increased salaries and promotions) would suggest that protégés' resiliency would be higher than non-mentored individuals.

Resilience training programs are yet another way to develop this capacity in individuals. This training takes various forms; it may involve developing a stronger awareness of the resources (e.g., talents, skills, and networks) one has available, as well as determining how these resources can be leveraged to accomplish goals and overcome obstacles (Luthans et al., 2010). Seligman (2011) described a training program for the US Army that begins with assessing soldiers' "psychological fitness," and then provides training modules that develop four types of fitness (emotional, family, social, and spiritual) and a module on "post-traumatic growth." This program also includes "Master Resilience Training" or MRT, which assists drill sergeants and other managers to learn about resiliency and their role in helping the soldiers they lead to develop this capacity. While the training will differ based on the needs of the individuals, there is evidence that these programs can help increase employees' resiliency (Bardoel, Pettit, De Cieri, & McMillan, 2014; Luthans et al., 2010).

Many of the organizational initiatives that will help employees and organizations handle the four challenges presented in this chapter can help build resilience. A variety of HR practices can enhance resiliency, including employee assistance programs, work–life initiatives, occupational health and safety systems, diversity management, social support networks, employee development programs (e.g., resilience training), policies and benefits, and crisis and risk management processes (Bardoel et al., 2014). As Luthans et al. (2006) wrote, "perhaps the biggest contribution to the resiliency process may be efficacy" (p. 34). So support systems, programs, and policies that enhance self-efficacy may be extremely helpful in developing resilience as well.

## Conclusion

The African proverb cited at the beginning of this chapter nicely sums up our intent. Most careers will experience rough seas periodically. But the hope is that individuals will emerge from these bumpy patches with a greater sense of what they want from their careers and plans to move forward to accomplish their goals. For some, these challenges are exciting and embraced. Others will struggle for a variety of reasons—perhaps the nature of the challenge, individual characteristics or traits, or unsupportive bosses or organizations will impede their progress. HR functions can help by advocating for, implementing, and assessing initiatives designed to minimize these challenges. On an individual level they can help employees develop or enhance their resilience and they can assist managers in developing the necessary skills they need to provide support and guidance to their direct reports.

## Note

1    Individuals often use the term "work–family" rather than "work–life" and, granted, much of the literature has focused on work and family rather than other aspects of life (e.g., community involvement, religion). We prefer the term work–life, given its broader focus and implications.

## References

Allen, T. D. (2001). Family-supportive work environments: The role of organizational perceptions. *Journal of Vocational Behavior, 58*, 414–435.

Allen, T. D., Poteet, M. L., & Russell, J. E. A. (1998). Attitudes of managers who are more or less career plateaued. *The Career Development Quarterly, 47*, 159–172.

Allen, T. D., Russell, J. E. A., Poteet, M. L., & Dobbins, G. H. (1999). Learning and development factors related to perceptions of job content and hierarchical plateauing. *Journal of Organizational Behavior, 20*, 1113–1137.

American Psychological Association (APA). (2013). *Stress in America 2013 highlights*. Retrieved from www.apa.org/news/press/releases/stress/2013/highlights.aspx.

Armstrong-Strassen, M. (2008). Factors associated with job content plateauing among older workers. *Career Development International, 13*, 594–613.

Asghar, R. (2014). *What millennials want in the workplace (and why you should start giving it to them)*. Retrieved from www.forbes.com/sites/robasghar/2014/01/13/what-millennials-want-in-the-workplace-and-why-you-should-start-giving-it-to-them.

Bardoel, E. A., Pettit, T. M., De Cieri, H., & McMillan, L. (2014). Employee resilience: An emerging challenge for HRM. *Asia Pacific Journal of Human Resources, 52,* 279–297.

Bardwick, J. M. (1988). *The plateauing trap: How to avoid it in your career ... and your life.* New York: AMACOM.

Baruch, Y. (2006). Career development in organizations and beyond: Balancing traditional and contemporary viewpoints. *Human Resource Management Review, 16,* 125–138.

Beehr, T. A. (1995). *Psychological stress in the workplace.* London: Routledge.

Biron, C., Cooper, C. L., & Gibbs, P. (2012). Stress interventions versus positive interventions: Apples or oranges? In K. S. Cameron & G. M. Spreitzer (Eds.), *The Oxford handbook of positive organizational scholarship* (pp. 938–950). Oxford: Oxford University Press.

Blustein, D. L., Kozan, S., & Connors-Kellgren, A. (2013). Unemployment and underemployment: A narrative analysis. *Journal of Vocational Behavior, 82,* 256–265.

Boswell, W. R., Olson-Buchanan, J. B., & Harris, T. B. (2014). I cannot afford to have a life: Employee adaptation to feelings of job insecurity. *Personnel Psychology, 67,* 877–915.

Brown, R., Duck, J., & Jimmieson, N. (2014). E-mail in the workplace: The role of stress appraisals and normative response pressure in the relationship between e-mail stressors and employee strain. *International Journal of Stress Management, 21*(4), 325–347.

Bucher, E., Fieseler, C., & Suphan, A. (2013). The stress potential of social media in the workplace. *Information, Communication & Society, 16*(10), 1639–1667.

Catalyst (2012a). *Catalyst quick take: Working parents.* Retrieved from www.catalyst.org/knowledge/working-parents.

Catalyst (2012b). *Catalyst quick take: Work–life: Prevalence, utilization, and benefits.* Retrieved from www.catalyst.org/knowledge/work–life-prevalence-utilization.

Cavanaugh, M. A., Boswell, W. R., Roehling, M. V., & Boudreau, J. W. (2000). An empirical examination of self-reported work stress among US managers. *Journal of Applied Psychology, 85,* 65–74.

Caza, B. B. & Milton, L. P. (2012). Resilience at work: Building capability in the face of adversity. In K. S. Cameron & G. M. Spreitzer (Eds.), *The Oxford handbook of positive scholarship* (pp. 895–908). Oxford: Oxford University Press.

Chao, G. T. (1990). Exploration of the conceptualization and measurement of career plateau: A comparative analysis. *Journal of Management, 16,* 181–193.

Cooper, C. L. & Cartwright, S. (1997). An intervention strategy for workplace stress. *Journal of Psychosomatic Research, 43*(1), 7–16.

Day, A., Paquet, S., Scott, N., & Hambley, L. (2012). Perceived information and communication technology (ICT) demands on employee outcomes:

The moderating effect of organizational ICT support. *Journal of Occupational Health Psychology, 17*(4), 473–491.

DeFrank, R. S. & Cooper, C. L. (1987). Worksite stress management interventions: Their effectiveness and conceptualization. *Journal of Managerial Psychology, 2*(1), 4–10.

Eatough, E. M. & Spector, P. E. (2014). The role of workplace control in positive health and wellbeing. In P. Y. Chen & C. L. Cooper (Eds.), *Work and wellbeing: Wellbeing: A complete reference guide, Vol. III* (pp. 91–109). Oxford: John Wiley & Sons.

Eby, L. T., Casper, W. J., Lockwood, A., Bordeaux, C., & Brinley, A. (2005). Work and family research in IO/OB: Content analysis and review of the literature (1980–2002). *Journal of Vocational Behavior, 66*, 124–187.

Erdogan, B. & Bauer, T. N. (2011). The impact of underemployment on turnover and career trajectories. In D. C. Maynard & D. C. Feldman (Eds.), *Underemployment: Psychological, economic, and social challenges* (pp. 215–232). New York: Springer.

Eurofound (2014). *Stress and burnout prevalent in the workplace.* Retrieved from www.eurofound.europa.eu/observatories/eurwork/articles/other-quality-of-life/stress-and-burnout-prevalent-in-the-workplace.

Feldman, D. C., Leana, C. R., & Bolino, M. C. (2002). Underemployment and relative deprivation among re-employed executives. *Journal of Occupational and Organizational Psychology, 75*, 453–471.

Feldman, D. C. & Weitz, B. A. (1988). Career plateaus reconsidered. *Journal of Management, 14*, 69–80.

Friedman, S. D. (2014). *Total leadership: Be a better leader, have a richer life.* Boston, MA: Harvard Business Review Press.

Frone, M. R. (2003). Work–family balance. In J. C. Quick & L. E. Tetrick (Eds.), *Handbook of occupational health psychology* (pp. 143–162). Washington, DC: American Psychological Association.

Fugate, M., Kinicki, A. J., & Ashforth, B. E. (2004). Employability: A psycho-social construct, its dimensions, and applications. *Journal of Vocational Behavior, 65*, 14–38.

Giga, S. I., Cooper, C. L., & Faragher, B. (2003). The development of a framework for a comprehensive approach to stress management interventions at work. *International Journal of Stress Management, 10*(4), 280–296.

Gilbreath, B. & Benson, P. G. (2004). The contribution of supervisor behavior to employee psychological well-being. *Work & Stress, 18*(3), 255–266.

Gilbreath, B. & Montesino, M. U. (2006). Expanding the HRD role: Improving employee well-being and organizational performance. *Human Resource Development International, 9*, 563–571.

Goodman, C. K. (2014, September 2). Work–life balance is big business. *The Journal-Gazette*, 8B.

Gowan, M. A. (2012). Employability, well-being and job satisfaction following a job loss. *Journal of Managerial Psychology, 27*, 780–798.

Gowan, M. A. (2014). Moving from job loss to career management: The past, present, and future of involuntary job loss research. *Human Resource Management Review, 24,* 258–270.

Greenhaus, J. H., Callanan, G. A., & Godshalk, V. M. (2010). *Career Management* (4th ed.). Los Angeles, CA: Sage.

Greenhaus, J. H., Collins, K. M., & Shaw, J. D. (2003). The relation between work–family balance and quality of life. *Journal of Vocational Behavior, 63,* 510–531.

Greenhaus, J. H. & Powell, G. N. (2006). When work and family are allies: A theory of work–family enrichment. *Academy of Management Review, 31,* 72–92.

Grzywacz, J. G. & Carlson, D. S. (2007). Conceptualizing work–family balance: Implications for practice and research. *Advances in Developing Human Resources, 9,* 455–471.

Guest, D. E. & Sturges, J. (2007). Living to work—working to live: Conceptualizations of careers among contemporary workers. In H. Gunz & M. Peiperl (Eds.), *Handbook of career studies* (pp. 310–326). Los Angeles, CA: Sage Publications.

Halbesleben, J. R. B. & Buckley, M. R. (2004). Burnout in organizational life. *Journal of Management, 30,* 859–879.

Hall, D. T., Lee, M. D., Kossek, E. E., & Heras, M. L. (2012). Pursuing career success while sustaining personal and family well-being: A study of reduced-load professionals over time. *Journal of Social Issues, 68,* 742–766.

Hargrove, M. B., Nelson, D. L., & Cooper, C. L. (2013). Generating eustress by challenging employees: Helping people savor their work. *Organizational Dynamics, 42,* 61–69.

Hill, E. J., Grzywacz, J. G., Allen, S., Blanchard, V. L., Matz-Costa, C., Shulkin, S., & Pitt-Catsouphes, M. (2008). Defining and conceptualizing workplace flexibility. *Community, Work & Family, 11,* 149–163.

Hurrell, J. J., Jr., Nelson, D. L., & Simmons, B. L. (1998). Measuring job stressors and strains: Where we have been, where we are, and where we need to go. *Journal of Occupational Health Psychology, 3*(4), 368–389.

Kao, K., Rogers, A., Spitzmueller, C., Lin, M., & Lin, C. (2014). Who should serve as my mentor? The effects of mentor's gender and supervisory status on resilience in mentoring relationships. *Journal of Vocational Behavior, 85,* 191–203.

Karasek, R. A., Jr. (1979). Job demands, job discussion latitude, and mental strain: Implications for job redesign. *Administrative Science Quarterly, 24,* 285–308.

Konrad, A. M. & Yang, Y. (2012). Is using work–life interface benefits a career-limiting move? An examination of women, men, lone parents, and parents with partners. *Journal of Organizational Behavior, 33,* 1095–1119.

Kossek, E. E., Lewis, S., & Hammer, L. B. (2009). Work–life initiatives and organizational change: Overcoming mixed messages to move from the margin to the mainstream. *Human Relations, 63,* 3–19.

Kossek, E. E. & Ruderman, M. N. (2012). Work–family flexibility and the employment relationship. In L. M. Shore, J. A-M. Coyle-Shapiro, & L. E. Tetrick (Eds.), *The employee–organization relationship: Applications for the 21st century* (pp. 223–253). New York: Routledge.

Kossek, E. E., Valcour, M., & Lirio, P. (2014). The sustainable workforce: Organizational strategies for promoting work–life balance and wellbeing. In P. Y. Chen & C. L. Cooper (Eds.), *Work and wellbeing: Wellbeing: A complete reference guide, Vol. III* (pp. 295–318). West Sussex: John Wiley & Sons.

Lee, P. C. B. (2003). Going beyond career plateau: Using professional plateau to account for work outcomes. *Journal of Management Development, 22*, 538–551.

Lentz, E. & Allen, T. D. (2009). The role of mentoring others in the career plateauing phenomenon. *Group & Organization Management, 34*, 358–384.

Leslie, L. M., Manchester, C. F., Park, T., & Mehng, S. A. (2012). Flexible work practices: A source of career premiums or penalties? *Academy of Management Journal, 55*, 1407–1428.

Lewis, S., Gambles, R., & Rapoport, R. (2007). The constraints of a 'work–life balance' approach: An international perspective. *International Journal of Human Resource Management, 18*, 360–373.

Lindblom, K. M., Linton, S. J., Fedeli, C., & Bryngelsson, I. (2006). Burnout in the working population: Relations to psychosocial work factors. *International Journal of Behavioral Medicine, 13*, 51–59.

Luthans, F. (2002). The need for and meaning of positive organizational behavior. *Journal of Organizational Behavior, 23*, 695–706.

Luthans, F., Avey, J. B., Avolio, B. J., & Peterson, S. J. (2010). The development and resulting performance impact of positive psychology capital. *Human Resource Development Quarterly, 21*, 41–68.

Luthans, F., Vogelgesang, G. R., & Lester, P. B. (2006). Developing the psychological capital of resiliency. *Human Resource Development Review, 5*, 25–44.

Martins, L. I., Eddleston, K. A., & Veiga, J. F. (2002). Moderators of the relationship between work–family conflict and career satisfaction. *Academy of Management Journal, 45*, 399–409.

Maslach, C., Schaufeli, W. B., & Leiter, M. P. (2001). Job burnout. *Annual Review of Psychology, 52*, 397–422.

Maynard, D. C. & Feldman, D. C. (2011). Introduction. In D. C. Maynard & D. C. Feldman (Eds.), *Underemployment: Psychological, economic, and social challenges* (pp. 1–9). New York: Springer.

Mayrhofer, W., Meyer, M., Schiffinger, M., & Schmidt, A. (2007). The influence of family responsibilities, career fields and gender on career success. *Journal of Managerial Psychology, 23*, 292–323.

McArdle, S., Waters, L., Briscoe, J. P., & Hall, D. T. (2007). Employability during unemployment: Adaptability, career identity and human and social capital. *Journal of Vocational Behavior, 71*, 247–264.

McCleese, C. S., Eby, L. T., Scharlau, E. A., & Hoffman, B. H. (2007). Hierarchical, job content, and double plateaus: A mixed-method study of stress, depression and coping responses. *Journal of Vocational Behavior, 71*, 282–299.

McDonald, K. S. & Hite, L. M. (2008). The next generation of career success: Implications for HRD. *Advances in Developing Human Resources, 10*, 86–103. doi: 10.1177/1523422307310116.

McKee-Ryan, F. M. & Harvey, J. (2011). "I have a job, but ...": A review of underemployment. *Journal of Management, 37*, 962–996.

McKee-Ryan, F. M., Virick, M., Prussia, G. E., Harvey, J., & Lilly, J. D. (2009). Life after the layoff: Getting a job worth keeping. *Journal of Organizational Behavior, 30*, 561–580.

McMillan, H. S., Morris, M. L., & Atchley, E. K. (2011). Constructs of the work/life interface: A synthesis of the literature and introduction of the concept of work/life harmony. *Human Resource Development Review, 10*, 6–25.

McVicar, A. (2003). Workplace stress in nursing: A literature review. *Journal of Advanced Nursing, 44*(6), 633–642.

Morris, M. L. (2008). Combating workplace stressors: Using work-life initiatives as an OD intervention. *Human Resource Development Quarterly, 19*, 95–105.

Morris, M. L. (2012). Unleashing human expertise through work/life initiatives. *Human Resource Development Quarterly, 23*, 427–439.

Morris, M. L., Heames, J. T., & McMillan, H. S. (2011). Human resource executives' perceptions and measurement of the strategic impact of work/life initiatives. *Human Resource Development Quarterly, 22*, 265–295.

Morris, M. L. & McMillan, H. S. (2014). Guiding HRD research in the work/life interface: The importance of work/life harmony in the development of interventions. In N. E. Chalofsky, T. S. Rocco, & M. L. Morris (Eds.), *Handbook of human resource development* (pp. 228–245). Hoboken, NJ: John Wiley & Sons, Inc.

Munn, S. L. (2013). Unveiling the work–life system: The influence of work–life balance on meaningful work. *Advances in Developing Human Resources, 15*, 401–417.

Munn, S. L. & Lee, H. (2015). An international perspective of the work–life system within HRD. In R. F. Poell, T. S. Rocco, & G. L. Roth (Eds.), *The Routledge companion to human resource development* (pp. 552–561). London: Routledge.

Nabi, G. R. (2003). Graduate employment and underemployment: Opportunity for skill use and career experiences amongst recent business graduates. *Education + Training, 45*, 371–382.

Ng, E. S. W., Schweitzer, L., & Lyons, S. T. (2010). New generation, great expectations: A field study of the millennial generation. *Journal of Business and Psychology, 25*, 281–292. doi: 10.1007/s10869-010-9159-4.

OECD (2013). *Work–life balance*. Retrieved from www.oecdbetterlifeindex.org/topics/work–life-balance.

Pagnin, D., De Queiroz, V., Filho, M. A. D. O., Gonzalez, N. V. A., Salgado, A. E. T., Oliveira, B. C., Lodi, C. S., & Melo, M. D. S. (2013). Burnout and career choice motivation in medical students. *Medical Teacher, 35*, 388–394.

Pines, A. M. (2000). Treating career burnout: A psychodynamic existential perspective. *JCLP/In Session: Psychotherapy in Practice, 56*, 633–642.

Podsakoff, N. P., LePine, J. A., & LePine, M. A. (2007). Differential challenge stressor-hindrance stressor relationships with job attitudes, turnover intentions, turnover, and withdrawal behavior: A meta-analysis. *Journal of Applied Psychology, 92*, 438–454.

Powell, G. N., Francesco, A. M. & Ling, Y. (2009). Toward culture-sensitive theories of the work–family interface. *Journal of Organizational Behavior, 30*, 597–616.

Purcell, C., Lewis, S., Smithson, J. & Caton, S. (2008). Work–life balance, best practices and healthy organisations: A European perspective. In R. J. Burke & C. L. Cooper (Eds.), *Building more effective organizations: HR management and performance in practice* (pp. 228–251). New York: Cambridge University Press.

Quick, J. C., Bennett, J., & Hargrove, M. B. (2014). Stress, health, and wellbeing in practice. In P. Y. Chen & C. L. Cooper (Eds.), *Work and wellbeing: Wellbeing: A complete reference guide, Vol. III* (pp. 175–203). Oxford: John Wiley & Sons.

Rotondo, D. M. & Perrewe, P. L. (2000). Coping with a career plateau: An empirical examination of what works and what doesn't. *Journal of Applied Social Psychology, 30*, 2622–2646.

Ruderman, M. N., Ohlott, P. J., Panzer, K., & King, S. N. (2002). Benefits of multiple roles for managerial women. *Academy of Management Journal, 45*, 369–386.

Schuler, R. S. (1980). Definition and conceptualization of stress in organizations. *Organizational Behavior and Human Performance, 25*, 184–215.

Seligman, M. E. P. (2011, April). Building resilience. *Harvard Business Review*, 100–106.

Selye, H. (1974) *Stress without distress.* Philadelphia: Lippincott Williams & Wilkins.

Shapiro, M., Ingols, C., O'Neill, R., & Blake-Beard, S. (2009). Making sense of women as career self-agents: Implications for human resource development. *Human Resource Development Quarterly, 20*, 477–501.

Spector, P. E. (2002). Employee control and occupational stress. *Current Directions in Psychological Science, 11*(4), 133–136.

Sullivan, S. E. & Mainiero, L. A. (2007). Benchmarking ideas for fostering family-friendly workplaces. *Organizational Dynamics, 36*, 45–62.

Swody, C. A. & Powell, G. N. (2007). Determinants of employee participation in organizations' family-friendly programs: A multi-level approach. *Journal of Business Psychology, 22*, 111–122.

Tepper, B. J. (2000). Consequences of abusive supervision. *Academy of Management Journal, 43*(2), 178–190.

Tomlinson, J. & Durbin, S. (2010). Female part-time managers: Work–life balance, aspirations and career mobility. *Equality, Diversity and Inclusion: An International Journal, 29,* 255–270.

Tucker, M. K., Jimmieson, N. L. & Oei, T. P. (2013). The relevance of shared experiences: A multi-level study of collective efficacy as a moderator of job control in the stressor–strain relationship. *Work & Stress, 27*(1), 1–21.

Veiga, J. F., Baldridge, D. C., & Eddleston, K. A. (2004). Toward understanding employee reluctance to participate in family-friendly programs. *Human Resource Management Review, 14,* 337–351.

Youssef, C. M. & Luthans, F. (2007). Positive organizational behavior in the workplace: The impact of hope, optimism, and resilience. *Journal of Management, 33,* 774–800.

Zikic, J. & Klehe, U. (2006). Job loss as a blessing in disguise: The role of career exploration and career planning in predicting reemployment quality. *Journal of Vocational Behavior, 69,* 391–409.

# 8 Ethical Considerations and Conclusions

> It is curious—curious that physical courage should be so common in the world, and moral courage so rare.
>
> Mark Twain

> There is no such thing as a minor lapse of integrity.
>
> Tom Peters

This book would not be complete without a discussion of ethical issues related to career development. However, since our focus has been on career development (CD) as it occurs primarily within organizations, the treatment of ethics is complicated. Practitioners need to be aware of potential issues that can arise working one-on-one with employees, but they also can play an important role in shaping the ethical climate of the organization. We will briefly discuss the former—relying on literature from career counseling, mentoring, and coaching that describe common dilemmas. Then we will explore the impact that the organizational climate can have on ethics in career development. The second half of this chapter will provide some concluding thoughts (themes) on career development that must be considered when helping individuals grow and develop their careers.

## Ethical Issues Facing Practitioners

According to Abele, Volmer, & Spurk (2012), unethical behavior is "the injury of employees' rights of balance, respect, responsibility, autonomy, participation, justice, and voice" (p. 108). Therefore, practitioners working with individuals to develop their careers should strive to respect these rights when providing guidance or designing and implementing initiatives or interventions, and in assessing the impact of these efforts. While this may appear to be fairly straightforward and simple to do, often it is not. Career development practitioners must begin by examining their own values, assumptions and biases. Niles and Harris-Bowlsbey (2013) wrote:

> value issues permeate the career development intervention process. Any intervention in the lifespace or lifestyle of people carries with it values implications.... The need for practitioners to clearly understand their own values represents an essential starting point for career service delivery and is an ethical issue within career services. Because value-free career interventions do not exist, career practitioners must be cognizant of how their personal values influence their work with clients
>
> (p. 470)

Beyond understanding oneself, practitioners need to be cognizant of the types of dilemmas they may encounter. This can help them identify potential problems early on and proactively work to resolve them. Several bodies of literature have addressed ethical issues as they pertain to certain initiatives designed to help individual employees develop their careers. Specifically the career counseling, coaching, and mentoring literature identifies potential dilemmas that practitioners may face. The most common include:

- Confidentiality: whether helping an individual deal with a career transition, career stagnation, work–life conflict or a number of other career-related issues, it is important that the human resource practitioner respect the confidential nature of the relationship established with the employee. Often this becomes a dilemma when someone else in the organization (e.g., the employee's supervisor) wants information regarding the employee's progress regarding the issue at hand. Clearly letting both parties (in this case the employee and the supervisor) know what you will divulge up front can alleviate this issue. Another recommendation is to encourage the employee to discuss his/her progress with the supervisor (Brennan & Wildflower, 2014). This is just one example of how confidentiality plays a role in career development.
- Conflicts of interest: there is always the potential for competing interests to occur between the employee or client and the career development practitioner or any person charged with helping the employee. This can occur, for example, when an employee with a strong performance record begins to inquire about career advancement opportunities and the supervisor, fearing she may lose a valued

employee, ignores or delays providing any information. The supervisor should disclose her interest in retaining this employee and then proceed to assist the individual in advancing his/her career.

- Competence: career development practitioners need to be aware of their competencies and what they should not take on due to lack of knowledge, skill, or training. For example, most HRD practitioners have not been trained to do career counseling and may best serve employees by contracting this service. There are many individuals who potentially can offer career services to individuals. HRD practitioners, career counselors, and coaches (e.g., management, executive, career, and life) are just a few of the types of professionals who may consider themselves experts in career development. The potential problem is that, with the exception of career counseling, there is no standard certification or training that individuals must undertake before practicing career development (Chung & Gfroerer, 2003; Krishna, 2014). Gottfredson (2005) characterized staffing in the career development field as "where unqualified or quasi-qualified practitioners are spreading like weeds in a corn field" (p. 311) and recommended that those who oversee career development services have both training and experience in industrial–organizational and vocational psychology. Most ethical standards or codes mention the importance of competence, including the Academy of Human Resource Development Standards on Ethics and Integrity (Russ-Eft, 2014). Some codes provide specifics as to what competence entails. For example, the American Counseling Association's (ACA) (2014) includes information regarding qualifications for being employed as a counselor, monitoring effectiveness, responsibilities for continuing education, handling impairment, etc. However, many codes of ethics simply emphasize the importance of knowing the boundaries of one's competence. In other words, they are primarily aspirational reminders and will not necessarily prevent incompetence.

- Power differentials: typically there is an unequal balance of power in most career development relationships. Whether it is a supervisor, mentor, coach, or counselor providing career development guidance, the relationship will typically be characterized as one of unequal power. This power differential can become even more problematic in cross-gender, cross-race, or cross-cultural relationships (McDonald & Hite, 2005; Toporek, Kwan, & Williams, 2012). Regarding cross-cultural relationships, Niles and Harris-Bowlsbey (2013) wrote that "a career practitioner adhering to European–American career intervention models steeped in individual action runs the risk of violating clients' values when those values reflect a collectivistic orientation" (p. 471). The ethical consequences of this imbalance are most apparent when the power is abused, resulting in a dysfunctional relationship. A dysfunctional relationship can occur due to a variety of issues such as sabotage, harassment, deceit, intentional exclusion (e.g., information, access), or imposing one's value system on a client (Eby & Allen, 2002; Niles & Harris-Bowlsbey, 2013).

To avoid and effectively resolve these potential dilemmas, individual practitioners need to become knowledgeable and skilled in career development theory and practice (Niles & Harris-Bowlsbey, 2013). Unfortunately there are too many individuals providing career services without career development training. There are degree programs as well as certification programs available that will provide the prerequisite knowledge and skills needed to practice career development. There are a number of codes of ethics that address career development issues and can provide guidance as well. For example, the ACA code of ethics offers principles that can be helpful to any career development practitioner— even those not providing career counseling. These principles are:

- autonomy, or fostering the right to control the direction of one's life;
- nonmaleficence, or avoiding actions that cause harm;
- beneficence, or working for the good of the individual and society by promoting mental health and well-being;
- justice, or treating individuals equitably and fostering fairness and equality;
- fidelity, or honoring commitments and keeping promises, including fulfilling one's responsibilities of trust in professional relationships; and
- veracity, or dealing truthfully with individuals with whom career development professionals come into contact (ACA, 2014, p. 3).

Other sources of codes of ethics are included in Table 8.1.

### Ethical Career Climate

As we have mentioned in other chapters, the organizational culture can have an important impact on how career development is implemented. It also can have a profound effect on whether it is implemented and managed in an ethical manner. Increasingly, the ethics involved in career development have become more pronounced, as Adams (2006) explained:

> As organizational changes accelerate, new situations with uncertain ethical overtones require action: downsizing, outsourcing,

*Table 8.1* Codes of Ethics Relevant to Career Development

| *Codes of Ethics* |
| --- |
| Academy of Human Resource Development (AHRD) Standards on Ethics and Integrity |
| Academy of Management (AOM) Code of Ethics |
| American Counseling Association (ACA) Code of Ethics |
| American Psychological Association (APA) Ethical Principles of Psychologists and Code of Conduct |
| British Columbia Career Development Association (BCCDA) Code of Ethics |
| Career Development Association of New Zealand (CDANZ) Code of Ethics and Professional Conduct for Career Practitioners |
| Career Industry Council of Australia, Inc., Professional Standards for Australian Career Development Practitioners |
| Career Professionals of Canada (CPC) Standards and Ethics |
| Global Career Development Facilitator (GCDF) Code of Ethics |
| Indian Career Education and Development Council (ICEDC) Code of Ethics |
| International Association of Educational and Vocational Guidance (IAEVG) Ethical Standards |
| National Board for Certified Counselors (NBCC) Code of Ethics |
| National Career Development Association (NCDA) Code of Ethics |
| Society of Human Resource Management (SHRM) Code of Ethical and Professional Standards in Human Resource Management |

> employability replacing career ladders, use of contingent workers, technological changes, and the increasingly global nature of competition. These changes impact careers at all organizational levels and present new challenges to those trying to balance their own career development and the needs of the organizations that employ them. The changing nature of workers' psychological contracts introduces new tensions between individual career considerations and obligations to employers.
>
> (p. 299)

There are a number of ways in which the corporate culture can perpetuate unethical practices affecting individuals' careers. We will focus on three: career success, career inequalities, and the changing career landscape.

### Organizational Culture and Career Success

The culture of an organization can influence individual career success. For example, a culture with a strong emphasis on objective indicators of success (e.g., pay, promotions) may result in an environment characterized by competition, workaholism, and impression management as individuals vie to get ahead. As Callanan (2003) explained:

> This narrow view of success leads to career goals and strategies that can be inconsistent with personal values and beliefs. Further, many highly successful managers and executives can experience feelings of personal failure, reflecting regret over having sacrificed family relationships and other affiliations in the ambitious pursuit of the objective form of career success.
>
> (p. 131)

A culture that treats its employees as disposable commodities or engages in other questionable activities may find workers conforming as a way to maintain employment. Those who choose not to remain silent or question authority may end up plateaued or looking for a job (Callanan, 2003). Another potential response to an inhospitable career culture is increased problematic behavior on the part of employees. Vardi and Kim (2007), in their framework of organizational misbehavior management (OMB), suggested that employees may respond with a number of misbehaviors including:

- intrapersonal (e.g., workaholism)
- interpersonal (e.g., violence, bullying, harassment)
- production (e.g., social loafing)
- property (e.g., theft, vandalism)
- political (e.g., favoritism).

In turn, these misbehaviors are likely to result in both financial and social costs and can negatively affect both individuals' careers and organizations.

### Organizational Culture and Career Inequalities

Van Buren (2003) categorized most workforces in industrialized societies as being "two-tiered." The top tier is a relatively small group of employees with skills that are in demand and enable them to "receive fair treatment from employers." The second tier is a large group of workers "whose skills are fungible and easily replaced" (p. 134). Unfortunately, organizations often ignore the career needs of this second tier of employees and often these are individuals from underrepresented and/or socially marginalized groups. In Chapter 6 we discuss how these inequalities manifest as differential treatment in terms of selection and evaluation, and accessibility and access to opportunities, and ultimately influence career success.

There is increasing recognition that the gap between the haves and the have-nots is widening. According to the OECD:

> The gap between rich and poor is at its highest level in most OECD countries in 30 years. Today the richest 10% of the population in the OECD area earn 9.5 times more than the poorest 10%. By contrast, in the 1980s the ratio stood at 7:1.
>
> (OECD, 2014, p. 1)

Organizations often through their culture, policies, and practices perpetuate and exacerbate this gap. While income is only one indicator of career success, it is important and has important implications for employees' lives beyond the workplace. Organizations have an ethical responsibility to consider these inequalities and act to minimize them.

### Organizational Culture and the Changing Career Landscape

Newer career approaches such as the boundaryless career are based on a transactional contract rather than a relational one (Callanan, 2003; Van Buren, 2003). Whereas a relational contract is typically long term, involving commitment and loyalty in exchange for job security, workers in a transactional contract are likely to have less stable jobs and lower levels of commitment to their employers.

Van Buren (2003) argued that particularly the boundaryless career pattern is fraught with fairness issues. For example, second-tiered employees who have replaceable skills are likely to suffer most since they will be in a weaker bargaining position than first-tiered employees. In most situations, the majority of risk is transferred to employees since employers can reduce costs under these arrangements, yet employees must absorb the costs associated with more frequent job transitions. He concluded that employers have an ethical obligation to ensure the employability of workers, which can be accomplished by investing in employees' skill development. He wrote:

> By ensuring the continued employability of individual workers, employers will be acting in ways that ensure individual and collective well-being. The ability of employers to structure as they see fit the terms of exchange agreements with employees must therefore be tempered by considerations of justice and benevolence. In the absence of justice and benevolence, it is likely that

employers will seek to shift responsibility for employee skill enhancement to employees—with deleterious effects on employers, employees, and society.

(p. 144)

### Recommendations

These cultural issues are not easily changed. As we have previously discussed, often these dilemmas have existed so long that they may be deeply ingrained in the organization. Developing awareness may be the first step in recognizing that an organizational culture is not conducive for ethical career development. Practitioners who have responsibilities for career development must begin by:

- examining how the organization views and promotes career success. Does it focus primarily on objective indicators of success (e.g., salary and promotions)? How are individuals rewarded and how might these reward structures foster misbehavior or unethical behavior?
- reviewing policies and practices regarding career development opportunities. Do under-represented and marginalized groups have access to career development activities that can lead to better career opportunities? Are they encouraged to engage in career development? A number of considerations to address inequalities are provided in Chapter 6.
- analyzing employment practices such as the retention of employees, employee engagement, and the use of contract and/or temporary workers. Are there trends to indicate that a transactional contract exists between employees and the organization? What is being done within the organization to ensure the employability of workers?

## Conclusions

Throughout this book a number of re-occurring themes about careers have been introduced that are important to reinforce. We believe that they serve as important reminders of how careers are evolving and, therefore, have valuable implications for all practitioners whose responsibilities include career development for individuals.

### Technology Impacts Careers

The ways in which technology has changed our lives and the pace in which these changes have occurred is often difficult to comprehend. Technological advances have resulted in jobs being created as well as being eliminated. Technology has changed how we work, when we work, and with whom we work. The skills we need to develop successful careers in a technology-driven age are different from the skills needed by our ancestors. Conceição and Thomas (2015) wrote: "Problem solving, knowledge management, development of creative solutions, information technology management and collaboration are all essential skills to keep up with the demands of a digital workplace" (p. 612).

Technology can assist individuals developing their careers and organizations implementing career development initiatives. Tracking systems for talent management, on-line training, virtual job fairs, and webcasts are just a few ways in which technology can assist in making career opportunities easily accessible to employees (Conceição & Thomas, 2015). However, Cascio (2007) pointed out that, "while technology frees people to work anytime, anywhere, it also shackles them as never before" (p. 553). Having the tools to stay connected with work at all times can result in work–life conflict and job stress. Organizations, through their managers and human resource (HR) practitioners, must assist employees in setting boundaries and creating a culture where "healthy work practices" are the norm (Kossek, Valcour, & Lirio, 2014).

### Leadership is Essential in Effective Career Development

Top management and supervisors are important influences in how career development is enacted in organizations. Leadership at the executive level is important in fostering a culture that promotes employees' career growth. Specifically, a culture that is inclusive, ethical, and learning oriented needs to be promoted if career development efforts are to be effective. A "positive career development culture" can result in more engaged and productive employees, equal opportunity for all employees, and forecasting and planning of future talent needs, including succession plans (Conger, 2002).

Employees' immediate supervisors may be the most important link in individual career development. Research clearly suggests that supervisors play a key role in promoting career development, providing access to career development, removing obstacles to career development, and serving as career developers. According to McGuire and Kissack (2015), line managers increasingly are taking on a number of roles often considered to be HR tasks, including:

- workforce planning, including scouting for talent
- coaching
- mentoring
- fostering a learning climate

- career planning
- operational training (pp. 525–527).

These roles add to managers' already heavy workloads, and many have received little or no training in how to effectively undertake these tasks (McGuire & Kissack, 2015; Renwick & MacNeil, 2002). Additional concerns may come from HR functions within the organization that may perceive supervisors as encroaching on their territory and making their work redundant (Renwick & MacNeil, 2002). These concerns point to the importance of developing a learning culture that embraces and supports employees, HR, and management's role in career development. HRD needs to partner with supervisors by providing training, resources, and encouragement to managers so that they can effectively do their part to help with career development efforts. Additionally, supervisors need to be rewarded for their contributions in developing employees' careers (McGuire & Kissack, 2015).

### Career Development Cannot Be a "One-Size-Fits-All" Endeavor

A multitude of contextual factors and individual differences must be considered when planning and implementing career development. In Chapter 3 various contextual factors—both external to the organization and internal—are described as influencing a career development strategy. Additional individual differences—including traits and skills, demographic characteristics, and employment status—need to be considered in planning for career development. Employment status alone might include a variety of employment arrangements (e.g., part time, full time, contingent, temporary) as well as types or categories of workers (e.g., blue collar, exempt, non-exempt, professional, managerial, clerical, skilled, semi-skilled). Organizations will vary in what they need and hope to accomplish through career development efforts, just as individual employees will differ in their career development needs and goals.

In the past we have advocated for organizations to be "agile and creative" in how they approach and implement career development initiatives (McDonald & Hite, 2014). Developing a "continuous learning climate" (Park & Rothwell, 2009, p. 401) and preparing managers to take on career development roles are two ways to begin developing a career development strategy to meet the needs of the organization and its employees. Managers, working in collaboration with HR, are in a position to better understand their direct reports' career needs and advocate for customized career development efforts. In addition, employees need to be socialized to take control of their careers, which should involve taking the initiative to seek out the support and opportunities that they need to achieve their specific career goals.

### The Boundaries Between Work and Other Aspects of Life Have Become Blurred

There are a number of reasons for the interdependencies between work and life outside of work. More diversity in the workplace (e.g., dual-earner partners, single parents, women's participation), technology, and flexible work arrangements are just three reasons why these boundaries are becoming blurred. In response to this phenomenon, scholars are suggesting new perspectives on careers. For example, Greenhaus and Kossek (2014) have proposed a work–home perspective that "explicitly recognizes the interdependencies between individuals' work and home domains" (p. 363) ("home" includes various non-work roles and settings). They argued that the work–home perspective is different from work–life conflict or work–life enrichment in that these interdependencies do not necessarily result in negative or positive outcomes. A work–home perspective would focus on individuals' priorities regarding these domains, "the permeability of the boundaries they construct around the domains …, and the way in which they define success in each domain" (Greenhaus & Kossek, 2014, p. 364).

Another new perspective that recognizes the intersection between work and other aspects of life is the sustainable career. According to Newman (2011), sustainability suggests "preserving and enhancing human capital" and "restoring and maintaining balance" (p. 138). She indicated there are three aspects of a sustainable career: opportunities for renewal, careers that are flexible and adaptable, and an integration "across life spheres and experiences that lead to wholeness, completeness, and meaning" (p. 138). Kossek, Valcour, & Lirio (2014) defined a sustainable career as one that offers enough security to handle economic needs, provides a fit between career and life values, affords "flexibility and capability of evolving to satisfy individuals' changing needs and interests," and offers renewal so that individuals can rejuvenate (p. 309). Both Newman (2011) and Kossek et al. (2014) offered a number of recommendations for organizations to promote sustainable careers such as leave control (e.g., sabbaticals, part-time work), reducing work intensification (e.g., job redesign, realistic deadlines), and social support at work (e.g., cross-training).

The work–home perspective and the sustainable career overlap considerably in their focus, Greenhaus and Kossek (2014) pointed to the sustainable career as a major influence in their conception of the work–home perspective. Both clearly address the blurring boundaries between work and life outside of work. However, to date little research has been done to determine what is needed to support a work–home perspective or a sustainable career (Greenhaus & Kossek, 2014). It may involve some radical changes in how organizations and societies organize work. One of our concerns is that these perspectives may help employees in professional, technical, and managerial positions, but organizations may choose not to consider supporting a work–home perspective or a sustainable career for those employees considered as "second-tiered" workers.

### A Social Justice Perspective is Needed in CD

Careers are important to us. Blustein (2008) eloquently described the meaning of work when he wrote: "work is a central aspect of life; indeed, the struggle to earn one's livelihood represents perhaps the most consistent and profound way in which individuals interface with their social, economic, and political contexts" (p. 237). Yet, while our work is important to us, Blustein and colleagues previously had noted that: "Indeed, the world of work ... represents life contexts in which the harsh reality of social inequities and injustices is perhaps most evident" (Blustein, McWhirter, & Perry, 2005, p. 142). We have attempted to describe this challenging reality, particularly in demonstrating the restricted access, inadequate inclusion, and the underutilization of under-represented populations in organizations (Fassinger, 2008).

The notion of social justice is not new for the discipline of vocational guidance and counseling. Pope, Briddick, & Wilson (2013) traced the roots of career counseling to the progressive social reform movement in the late 1890s and early 1900s. Frank Parsons, commonly considered the founder of the vocational guidance movement, had a strong commitment to social justice issues and was involved in various social justice organizations (Pope et al., 2013). However, for many practitioners (e.g., human resource development (HRD) and HRM practitioners), particularly those who work within for-profit organizations, social justice is rarely discussed and even less likely to be acted upon. Byrd (2014) wrote: "In the field of HRD, a paradigm shift toward social justice means not only taking an active stance against social oppression through research and practice, but assuming a moral responsibility in our professional communities; it means enacting moral agency" (p. 292).

A social justice perspective suggests that systems that perpetuate inequalities in career development and that disempower individuals need to be changed or demolished. Throughout this book we have discussed various ways in which organizations can create more inclusive cultures that promote equity in career development opportunities for all employees, that consider perceptions of fairness when making career development decisions, and that have policies and practices that help all employees handle challenges that they are likely to face periodically throughout their careers. HRD practitioners can serve as both advocates for a fair and just organization and as educators working to instill "critical consciousness" among the "powerful and privileged" (Blustein et al., 2005, p. 167).

Beyond organizational change, societal change is also important to achieve fairness and equality. Both Blustein (2008) and Fassinger (2008) advocated for public policies to address the needs of marginalized groups. Blustein indicated that, because work is so central to individuals' psychological well-being, public policies that help those recovering from a serious mental illness, policies that support occupational health psychology, and policies that address racism still need to be crafted and implemented.

## Summary

Career development practitioners must consider the ethical issues involved in helping individuals develop their careers. This chapter focused on some common ethical dilemmas that practitioners may face: confidentiality issues, questions of competence, potential conflicts of interests, and power differentials that often exist in career development relationships. The importance of an ethical career climate was highlighted as well. The organizational culture impacts this climate in a variety of ways. One is through the signals that are sent about what constitutes career success and how it is achieved. Additional ethical implications arise when an organization perpetuates career inequalities and when an organization embraces a transactional rather than relational employment arrangement for its employees.

We conclude this final chapter with five important themes that are suggested in current career literature. These themes attempt to describe today's career landscape and to inspire practitioners to consider their roles in shaping the future of careers. HR is well positioned to take the lead in creating the new era of career development. There is much work to be done!

## References

Abele, A. E., Volmer, J., & Spurk, D. (2012). Career stagnation: Underlying dilemmas and solutions in contemporary work environments. In N. P. Reilly,

M. J. Sirgy, & C. A. Gorman (Eds.), *Work and quality of life: Ethical practices in organizations* (pp. 107–132). New York: Springer.

Adams, J. S. (2006). Ethics and careers. In J. H. Greenhaus & G. A. Callanan (Eds.), *Encyclopedia of Career Development* (pp. 298–302). Thousand Oaks, CA: Sage Publications.

American Counseling Association (ACA) (2014). *Code of ethics*. Retrieved from www.counseling.org/knowledge-center/ethics.

Blustein, D. L. (2008). The role of work in psychological health and well-being. *American Psychologist, 63*, 228–240.

Blustein, D. L., McWhirter, E. H., & Perry, J. C. (2005). An emancipatory communitarian approach to vocational development theory, research, and practice. *The Counseling Psychologist, 33*, 141–179.

Brennan, D. & Wildflower, L. (2014). Ethics in coaching. In E. Cox, T. Bachkirova, & D. A. Clutterbuck (Eds.), *The complete handbook of coaching* (2nd edn.) (pp. 430–444). Los Angeles, CA: Sage Publications.

Byrd, M. Y. (2014). A social justice paradigm for HRD: Philosophical and theoretical foundations. In N. E. Chalofsky, T. S. Rocco, & M. L. Morris (Eds.), *Handbook of human resource development* (pp. 281–298). Hoboken, NJ: John Wiley & Sons, Inc.

Callanan, G. A. (2003). What price career success? *Career Development International, 8*, 126–133.

Cascio, W. F. (2007). Trends, paradoxes, and some directions for research in career studies. In H. Gunz & M. Peiperl. (Eds.), *Handbook of career studies* (pp. 549–557). Los Angeles, CA: Sage Publications.

Chung, Y. B. & Gfoerer, M. C. A. (2003). Career coaching: Practice, training, professional, and ethical issues. *The Career Development Quarterly, 52*, 141–152.

Conceição, S. C. O. & Thomas, K. J. (2015). Virtual HRD (VHRD). In R. F. Poell, T. S. Rocco, & G. L. Roth (Eds.), *The Routledge companion to human resource development* (pp. 606–615). London: Routledge.

Conger, S. (2002). Fostering a career development culture: Reflections on the roles of managers, employees and supervisors. *Career Development International, 7*, 371–375.

Eby, L. T. & Allen, T. D. (2002). Further investigation of protégés' negative mentoring experiences. *Group & Organization Management, 27*, 456–479.

Fassinger, R. E. (2008). Workplace diversity and public policy. *American Psychologist, 63*, 252–268.

Gottfredson, G. D. (2005). Career development in organizations. In W. B. Walsh & M. L. Savickas (Eds.), *Handbook of vocational psychology* (3rd edn.) (pp. 297–318). Mahwah, NJ: Lawrence Erlbaum Associates.

Greenhaus, J. H. & Kossek, E. E. (2014). A contemporary career: A work–home perspective. *Annual Review of Organizational Psychology, 1*, 361–388.

Kossek, E. E., Valcour, M., & Lirio, P. (2014). The sustainable workforce: Organizational strategies for promoting work–life balance and wellbeing. In P. Y. Chen & G. L. Cooper (Eds.), *Work and wellbeing: Wellbeing: A complete reference guide, volume III* (pp. 295–318). Chichester: John Wiley & Sons.

Krishna, V. (2014). Certification of HRD professionals. In N. E. Chalofsky, T. S. Rocco, & M. L. Morris (Eds.), *Handbook of human resource development* (pp. 661–672). Hoboken, NJ: John Wiley & Sons, Inc.

McDonald, K. S. & Hite, L. M. (2005). Ethical issues in mentoring: The role of HRD. *Advances in Developing Human Resources, 7,* 569–582.

McDonald, K. S. & Hite, L. M. (2014). Contemporary career literature and HRD. In N. E. Chalofsky, T. S. Rocco, & M. L. Morris (Eds.), *Handbook of human resource development* (pp. 353–368). Hoboken, NJ: John Wiley & Sons, Inc.

McGuire, D. & Kissack, H. C. (2015). Line managers and HRD. In R. F. Poell, T. S. Rocco, & G. L. Roth (Eds.), *The Routledge companion to human resource development* (pp. 521–530). London: Routledge.

Newman, K. L. (2011). Sustainable careers: Lifecycle engagement in work. *Organizational Dynamics, 40,* 136–143.

Niles, S. G. & Harris-Bowlsbey, J. (2013). *Career development interventions in the 21st century* (4th ed.). Boston, MA: Pearson.

OECD (2014, December). *Focus on inequality and growth.* Retrieved from www.oecd.org/social/Focus-Inequality-and-Growth-2014.pdf.

Park, Y. & Rothwell, W. J. (2009). The effects of organizational learning climate, career-enhancing strategy, and work orientation on the protean career. *Human Resource Development International, 12,* 387–405.

Pope, M., Briddick, W. C., & Wilson, F. (2013). The historical importance of social justice in the founding of the National Career Development Association. *The Career Development Quarterly, 61,* 368–373.

Renwick, D. & MacNeil, C. M. (2002). Line manager involvement in careers. *Career Development International, 7,* 407–414.

Russ-Eft, D. (2014). Morality and ethics in HRD. In N. E. Chalofsky, T. S. Rocco, & M. L. Morris (Eds.), *Handbook of human resource development* (pp. 510–525). Hoboken, NJ: John Wiley & Sons, Inc.

Toporek, R. L., Kwan, K. K., & Williams, R. A. (2012). Ethics and social justice in counseling psychology. In N. A. Fouad (Ed.), *APA handbook of counseling psychology: Vol. 2. Practice, interventions, and applications* (pp. 305–332). Washington, DC: The American Psychological Association.

Van Buren III, H. J. (2003). Boundaryless careers and employability obligations. *Business Ethics Quarterly, 13,* 131–149.

Vardi, Y. & Kim, S. H. (2007). Considering the darker side of careers: Toward a more balanced perspective. In H. Gunz & M. Peiperl (Eds.), *Handbook of career studies* (pp. 502–511). Los Angeles, CA: Sage Publications.

# Index

Lightning Source UK Ltd.
Milton Keynes UK
UKHW022157031219
354731UK00007B/100/P